IMAGES
of America

YUKON

On the Cover: Emma Sanger Bass sits on the far right in the buggy, and her daughter Wenona is out front holding a hat. Emma was married to George Bass of Bass Mercantile Company fame. The historic Bass Building still graces the southeast corner of Fifth and Main Streets, and the Bass grandsons own the building. (Courtesy Bass and Ramey families.)

IMAGES
of America

YUKON

Carol Mowdy Bond

ARCADIA
PUBLISHING

ISBN 978-1-4671-0765-5

Published by Arcadia Publishing
Charleston, South Carolina

Printed in the United States of America

Library of Congress Control Number: 2021942996

For all general information, please contact Arcadia Publishing:
Telephone 843-853-2070
Fax 843-853-0044
E-mail sales@arcadiapublishing.com
For customer service and orders:
Toll-Free 1-888-313-2665

Visit us on the Internet at www.arcadiapublishing.com

For my grandchildren, who know the inspiration,
reproof, and fascination of history.

Gloria in Deo plures.

Contents

ACKNOWLEDGMENTS

When I announced this project, individuals, entire families, and community groups scrambled to help. They scoured attics, scrapbooks, files, closets, and basements. Some raced all over town and made tons of phone calls, rounding up what I needed. And they spent many hours with me either in person or by telephone, email, or texting.

Thank you to all who gave photographs, memorabilia, or information—or all three—or advice, encouragement, ideas, inspiration, and more: Dana Mowdy Spencer, Yukon Czech Hall, Yukon Historical Society, Yukon Chamber of Commerce, Canadian County Cowboy Church-Yukon Round Up Club, Carnegie Library in El Reno, Oklahoma Digital Maps Collection at the Oklahoma State University Library, Kathryn Kroutil Wright family, Mike Schulte, Terry Martin, Pam Team Adamson, Donna Anderson Mills, Keith Ball, Milo Shedeck, Dee Cordry, Shirley Davis, the LaVerne and Victor Benda family, Betty Sackett and the Trch family archives, the Bass and Ramey families, Lydia Gholston, Genie Vinson, the Phil Carson family, John Kouba, Eve Plumb, the Yanda family, Jenna Roberson, Cherie Logan, and John Turner.

Thank you to my young grandsons who informed me they will each need their own copy of the book. And last but never least, thanks to my parents, JoAnn and Elzy Mowdy, who stopped the family car at every single historical marker and historical site across the nation throughout my entire childhood because I begged them to do so.

What an incredible treasure hunt!

INTRODUCTION

In the 21st century, Yukon sprawls across eastern Canadian County in central Oklahoma. Known as Oklahoma's Czech Capital, the city is brimming with a diverse mix of demographics. But Yukon initially emerged from the vast, wide-open prairies. Embedded in the Louisiana Territory, the area was alive with primitive energy and a very old soul. Native American groups roamed and lived in the area at different times, including the Cheyenne, Arapaho, Wichita, Caddo, Tawakoni, Waco, Hainai, Anadarko, Kichai, Choctaw, Creek, and Seminole. Today's Cheyenne and Arapaho Tribes still headquarter not far away in Concho.

Tall, native grasses and foliage painted the Great Plains' flat prairie lands, occasionally broken by rolling hills. In centuries past, up until at least 1870, North America's largest land mammals were masters of indigenous wildlife. The American bison or buffalo were primarily known to exist in two major herds. Living in today's Oklahoma, the ground shook when the massive Southern Herd roared through the area. As they grazed, buffalo rolled and wallowed in mud and dust, creating buffalo wallows, depressions that still remain in Yukon's ground. When the wallows filled with rainwaters, the children of future prairie settlers and early homesteaders used them as swimming pools.

From 1869 to 1887, the Chisholm Trail blazed north from Texas to the Kansas railheads. Cowboys, or drovers, drove thousands of longhorn cattle straight through the future Yukon. A 2,500-head herd could span one mile and be about 50 feet wide at certain points. Buckaroos looked for today's Mulvey Pond as a landmark, and as the last chance of clean, spring-fed water for their cattle.

The United States originally labeled a huge area as Indian Territory. In 1830, the government began forcibly removing native groups from their homelands across the nation, along their trails of tears, into this area. Last to become a state, Oklahoma was the remaining, controversial, and chaotic Indian Territory with relocated tribes interacting with indigenous plains tribes, outlaws, and would-be settlers.

In 1870, the future Oklahoma Territory, including Canadian County, was surveyed. In 1889, the federal government officially grabbed a bit more than the western half of Indian Territory and labeled it as Oklahoma Territory. Included in the territory were two million acres split into 160-acre tracts, also called quarter sections, that made up the so-called Unassigned Lands. At noon on April 22, 1889, thousands of settlers and cattlemen scrambled and fought for land in six of today's Oklahoma counties, including part of Canadian County and Yukon. By day's end, all the sections were claimed. As the territory's first of five land runs, it was a dangerous endeavor for anyone with the guts to take part. When the dust cleared, the future Yukon area was made of quarter sections on their way to becoming farms, and remained so for a while. Various ethnic groups were among the first homesteaders, including a few from Bohemia. To shop, get supplies, and pick up their mail, settlers went to nearby Frisco, the largest town in the county. In 1891, Canadian County was half the size it is now.

Civil War Union veterans could pre-file for quarters in the 1889 land run. As a result, a large group of veterans started the town of Veteran City, just west of future Yukon. When they learned the Frisco Railroad promised to go through their town, they renamed the settlement Frisco. With an established stage route, Frisco grew quickly and became a prominent hub of commercial and political activity.

But brothers Lewis Mortimer "L.M." Spencer and Augustus Newton "A.N." Spencer had other ideas. Of European ancestry by way of New England, they were born in Ohio in 1842 and 1850, respectively. They were two of seven close-knit, entrepreneurial, and visionary siblings, and much of the family relocated to Yukon. In fact, the Spencer family not only founded Yukon, but also managed its growth for a number of years. Others involved with the high-octane enterprise included Dan Hogan, Sam Hogan, George Hogan, J.M. "Doc" Farris, Joe Farris, D.S. McEwen, and H.K. Ricker.

L.M. Spencer and A.N. Spencer had heavily invested in Indian Territory railroads. With cattle in Texas, New Mexico, Kansas, Indian Territory, and other areas, A.N. drove his cattle up the Chisholm Trail numerous times. L.M. was herding cattle in three states and two territories. The brothers realized there were no major towns on the south side of the North Fork of the Canadian River, now known as the North Canadian River, from El Reno to Oklahoma City. By fall 1890, the two were actively planning their settlement. By 1890 or 1891, they purchased land from Minnie Taylor and Luther S. Morrison, who had acquired it in the 1889 land run. The quarter section ran from present-day Main Street to Ash Avenue, and from Piedmont Road/Highway 4 to about Seventh Street.

L.M. and A.N. kept buying land, and managed to reroute the railroad that was to go from Fort Reno to Frisco so that it would go through the gold mine of a town they envisioned. By April 1891, part of the Choctaw, Oklahoma & Gulf Railway that ran from El Reno to Oklahoma City included a depot in Yukon. A.N. was also building railroads in Indiana and Wyoming. One of their daughters claimed they named their new settlement after the Yukon gold rush in Canada.

The Spencer siblings continued expanding their land holdings and dove into real estate and all sorts of ambitious ventures. In fact, L.M. was dubbed the "Father of Yukon." So, businesses in Frisco navigated toward Yukon and El Reno and elsewhere. By February 1905, Frisco officially dissolved.

The Spencer story is a whirlwind tale. They moved so quickly that entrepreneurs gravitated to Yukon, getting in on the ground floor of an economy and culture that quickly matured.

But other elements loomed on the horizon. In 1867, Europe's multi-national Austro-Hungarian Empire emerged, with a population of over 51 million, at least 12 ethnic groups, and 15 languages. Religious, cultural, economic, post-war, and nationalistic tensions ensued, and large numbers headed to the United States searching for freedom and a better way of life. By the late 19th century, Bohemians heavily invested themselves in Yukon. Czechoslovakia was formed from the former lands of Bohemia, Moravia, and Slovakia. By the 1920s and 1930s, the rural but lively Yukon was reenergized due to an era of modern inventions.

It was in Yukon where Bob Funk purchased farms and headquartered his Express Ranches and agricultural endeavors. And it was in Yukon where Garth Brooks grew up and participated in football, baseball, and track and field before the world came to know the megastar. But unpacking the origins, we see the back-breaking work of sodbusters looking for a fresh shot at life and those with self-serving, ingenious ideas that also benefited the community as a whole. And the saga begins.

One

Water, Land, and a Railroad

The Civil War's aftermath left chaos and challenges. Families and groups were disrupted and displaced, the loss of life and property was staggering, and lawlessness exacerbated the problems. As well, populations east of the Mississippi River were growing. Many felt suffocated and longed for more room to live and create and breathe.

The Chisholm Trail, among numerous that cut through Indian Territory, allowed drovers to experience the Great Plains and the resources, water, and land. The area was enticing to some.

Parts of the American West and heartland were still seen, whether legally or illegally, as a frontier to be conquered. Though Native American nations were legally established in what would become Oklahoma, the US government made changes to treaties and agreements. Pioneers and settlers considered the land and resources as a chance for new beginnings.

The Land Run of 1889 was the first of five in Oklahoma Territory, which encompassed most of the western half of today's Oklahoma. The land runs, land lotteries, land allotments, and lands opened by sealed bids offered hope and opportunity. But simultaneously, the events sounded the death knell for the sovereignty of the native tribes.

At the same time, various European nations were in upheaval with a myriad of problems. Europeans learned about the available land, and many journeyed to the United States.

With Oklahoma as center stage, entrepreneurs with guts, determination, and dreams entered the future Yukon area. They wrangled and maneuvered, and in so doing, killed off the thriving town of Frisco, which sat to the west. What was initially a prairie carpeted by "89er" homesteads became treasures to seize. The tiny Yukon settlement grew over time with Spencer Avenue a central hub. By 1910, the avenue was renamed Main Street. There were doctors and dentists. And there were lawmen, including Pop Floyd, a fearless crime fighter from the 1920s through the 1950s.

This is an almost unbelievable story, as seen in the faces of those who came first and the enterprises they established, and as told by their written works and their descendants.

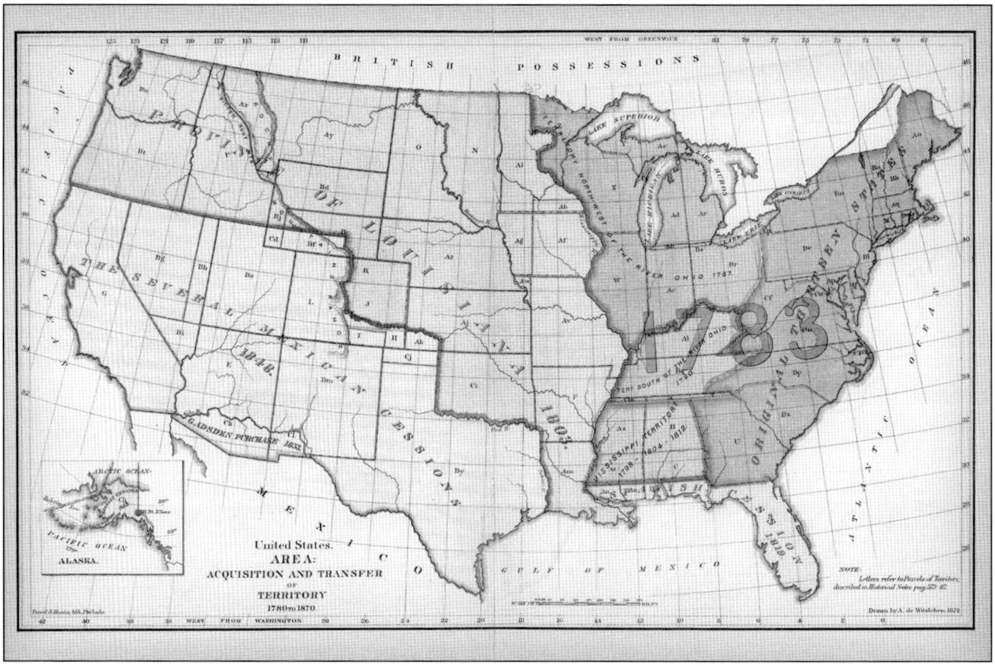

In 1803, France sold its North American lands west of the Mississippi River to the United States. All or parts of approximately 13 states, including Oklahoma, emerged from the Louisiana Purchase. The future Yukon was part of that area, and Oklahoma was the last of those states to gain statehood, in 1907. (Courtesy Oklahoma Digital Maps Collection, Oklahoma State University Library.)

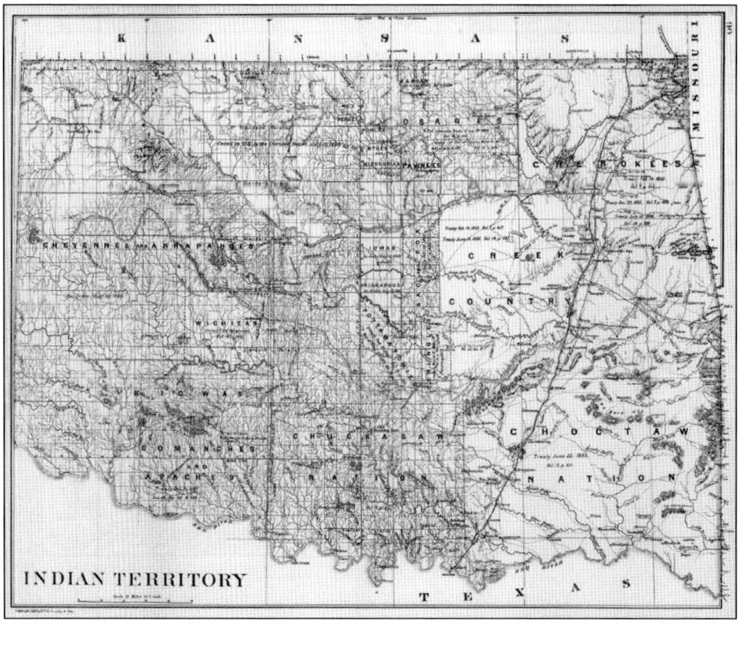

The United States forcibly moved Native American groups into Indian Territory, where plains tribes already lived. Then the United States reshuffled the areas where they allowed each tribe to live. This map shows the territory after much reshuffling of the tribes. (Courtesy Oklahoma Digital Maps Collection, Oklahoma State University Library.)

In 1889, the United States grabbed a bit more than the western half of Indian Territory, and labeled it as Oklahoma Territory. Included were two million acres that made up the so-called Unassigned Lands. In 1889, thousands of settlers and cattlemen raced for land in six of today's Oklahoma counties, including part of today's Canadian County where Yukon sits. (Courtesy Oklahoma Digital Maps Collection, Oklahoma State University Library.)

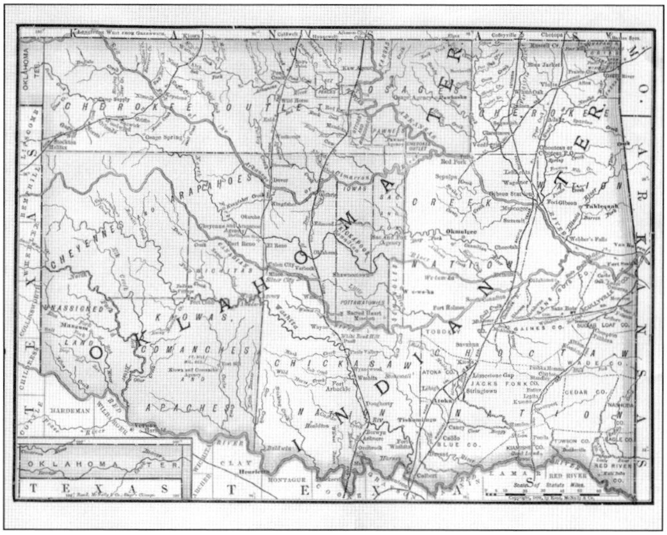

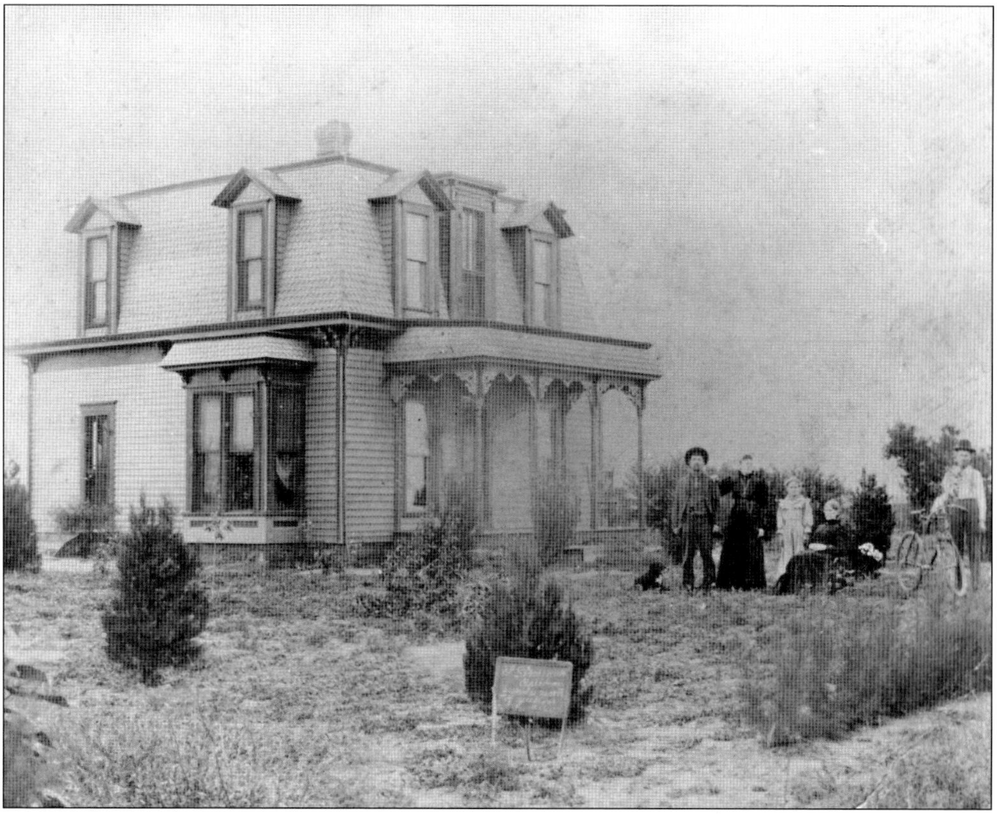

Isaac "Ike" Simmons and his wife, Belle Hamilton Simmons, stand at left. Their son Sewell is at far right. Ike nabbed this quarter section of land in the 1889 land run, building this home with the front door approximately where Surrey Hills Boulevard and Mustang Road intersect. Belle's parents and siblings filed adjoining claims. The group hailed from Alabama, Georgia, Missouri, and New York. The Hamilton family died early, and their land went to the Simmons family. (Courtesy Mike Schulte.)

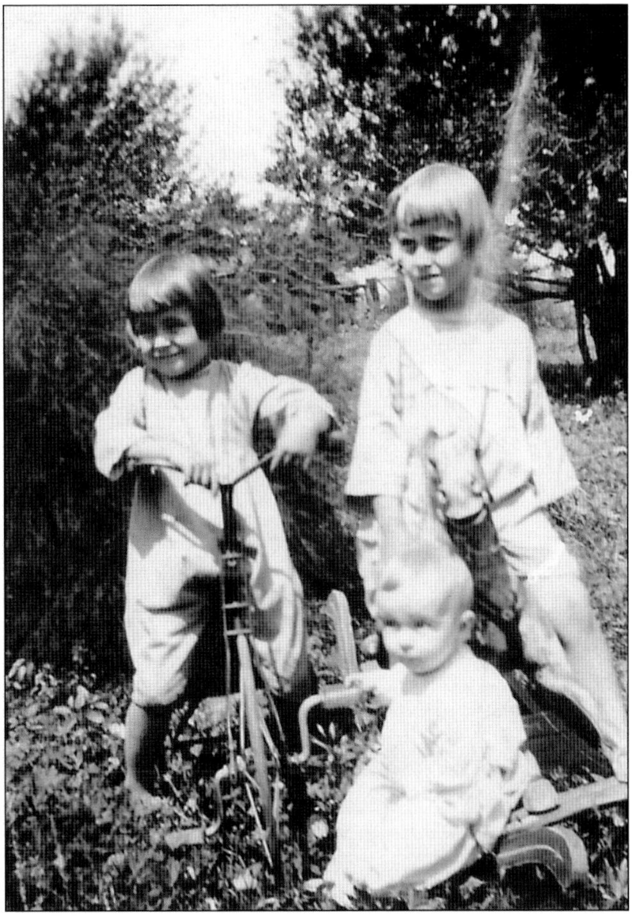

Shown are Essa and Sewell Simmons's children (clockwise from left) Eileen, June, and Jean Pauline around 1921. Sewell's father, Ike Simmons, had a barn/granary, cave, chicken house, well, and orchard trees and farmed his land. Around 1900, fencing arrived by railroad from St. Louis to surround the Frisco Cemetery graves of the Simmons and Hamilton families. Around the 1950s, the Surrey Hills Addition was born from the Simmons and Hamilton lands. (Courtesy Mike Schulte.)

Essa and Sewell Simmons built this 1930s home. They farmed six quarters of land, all the way to Highway 4. At some point, they sold this home, and until 1965, it served as the temporary clubhouse for the Surrey Hills Golf Club in Yukon's Surrey Hills Addition. (Courtesy Mike Schulte.)

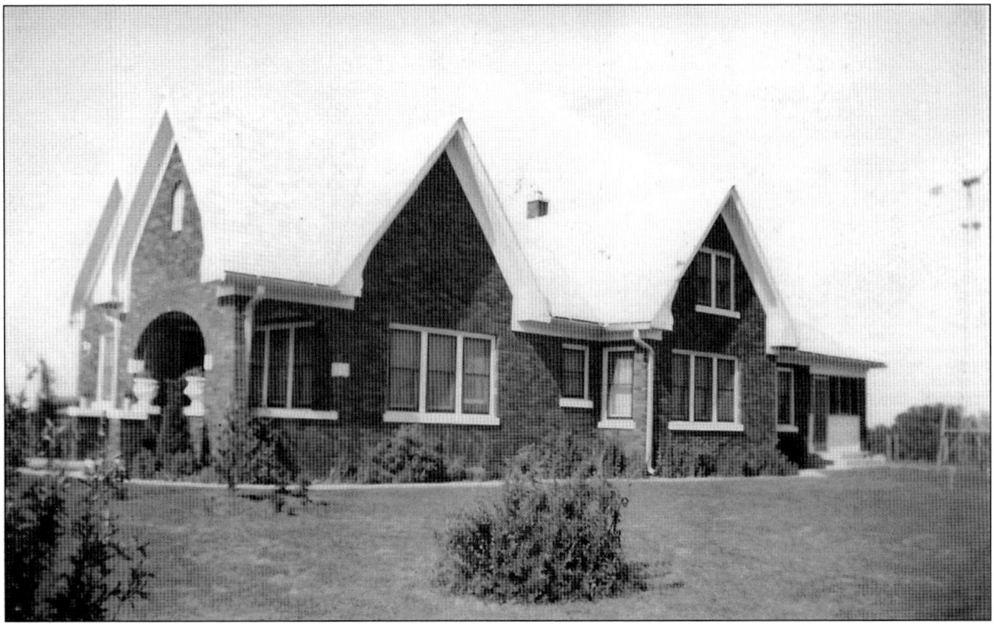

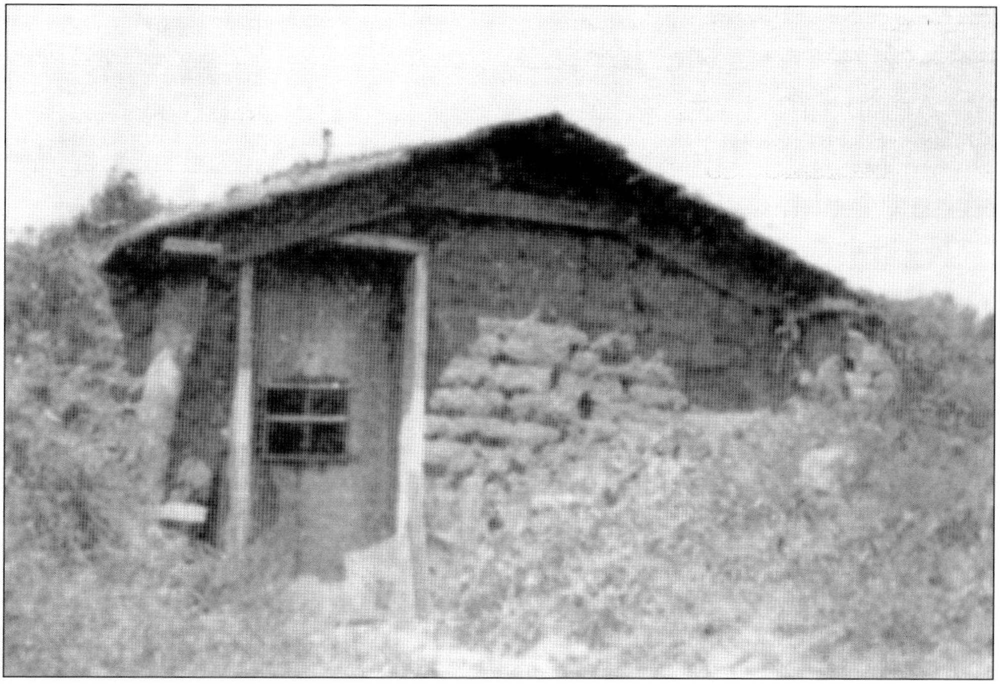

Both from Bohemia, Minnie and Paul Kouba arrived in 1890. Before building a house, they erected and lived in this sod dugout for about six months, mixing lime and cow manure for the floor. Friendly Native Americans sometimes camped nearby and asked them for food. Their descendants now farm cotton on 600 acres in Yukon and say the lime floor of the dugout was impossible to break apart. (Courtesy John Kouba.)

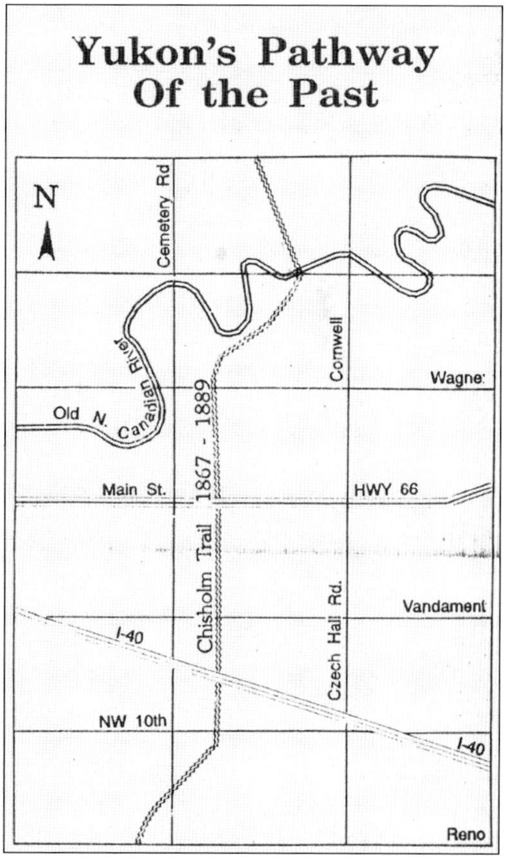

Of European ancestry, brothers Lewis and Augustus Spencer were born in Ohio in 1842 and 1850, respectively. They were two of seven close-knit, entrepreneurial, and visionary siblings, and parts of the family relocated to the future Yukon. With cattle in multiple states and Indian Territory, A.N. Spencer drove his herds up the Chisholm Trail numerous times. L.M. Spencer herded cattle in three states and two territories. (Courtesy Yukon Chamber of Commerce.)

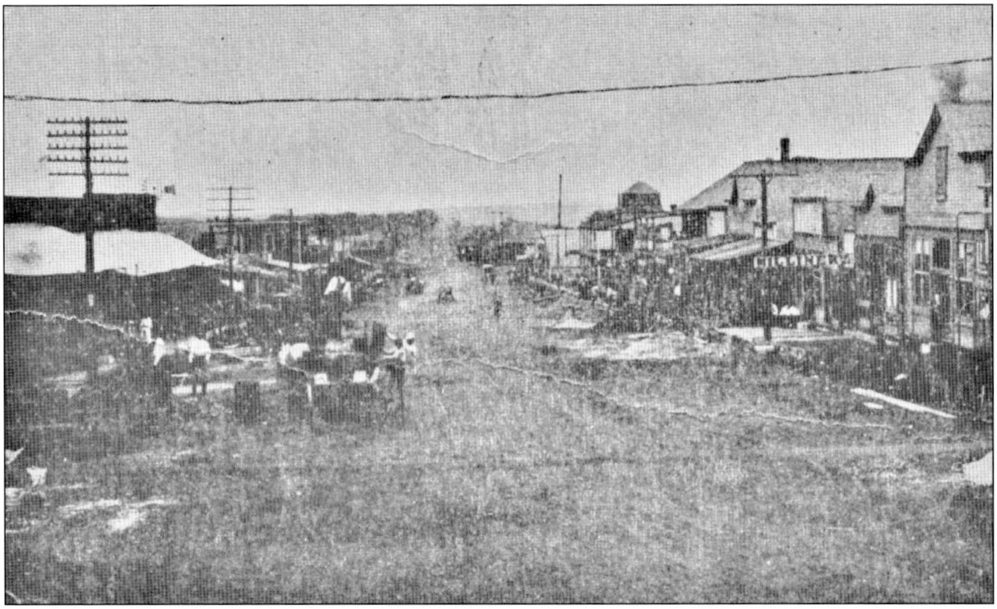

Between El Reno and Oklahoma City, L.M. and A.N. Spencer found no major towns on the south side of the North Fork of the Canadian River, now known as the North Canadian River. By fall 1890, the brothers were actively planning their town and buying homesteads from 89ers. Today's main thoroughfare, Main Street, was originally named Spencer Avenue. (Courtesy Yukon Historical Society.)

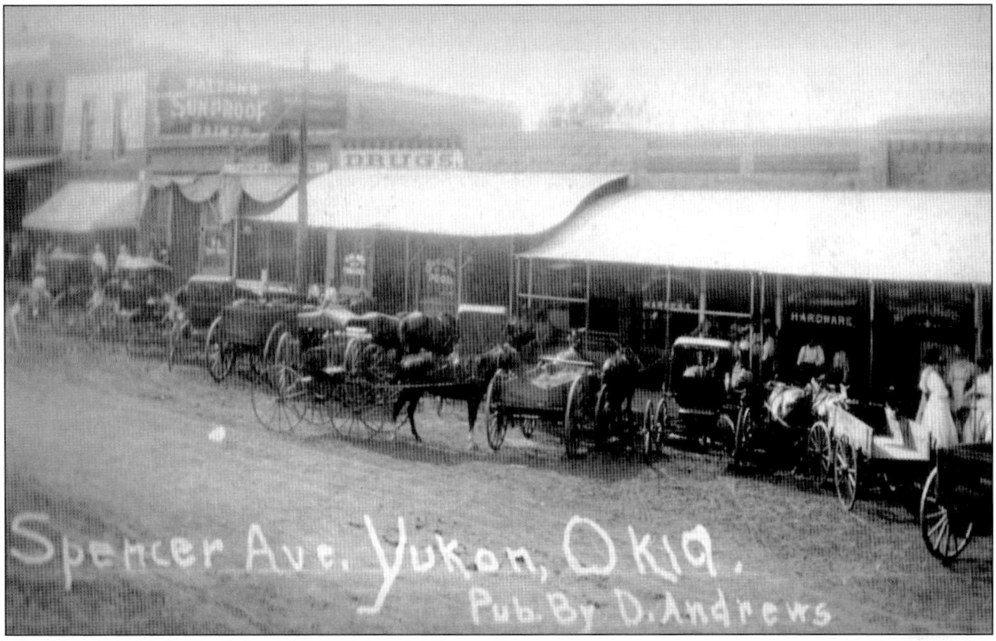

The Spencers, their siblings, and associates rapidly bought land and built businesses and houses. They named two streets Kalia and Inla. By February 1891, there were 15 businesses, 25 homes, and 81 residents. Spencer Avenue was renamed Main Street around 1910. This photograph shows 405 West Main Street with a hardware store. The window on the far right reads, "Mulvey Mercantile." The side of the tall building reads, "Patton's Sunproof Paints." (Courtesy Genie Vinson.)

Railroad magnates L.M. and A.N. Spencer heavily invested in Indian Territory railroads, including the Rock Island Railroad and the Choctaw, Oklahoma, & Gulf Railroad. They rerouted the railroad to go through Yukon instead of Frisco. Shown here around 1910 is the Ellison Hotel on the southwest corner of Fourth Street and Spencer Avenue. Signs read, "Ice Cold Coca-Cola Sold Here," "South Side Restaurant," and "E.B. Ellison Real Estate." (Courtesy Yukon Historical Society.)

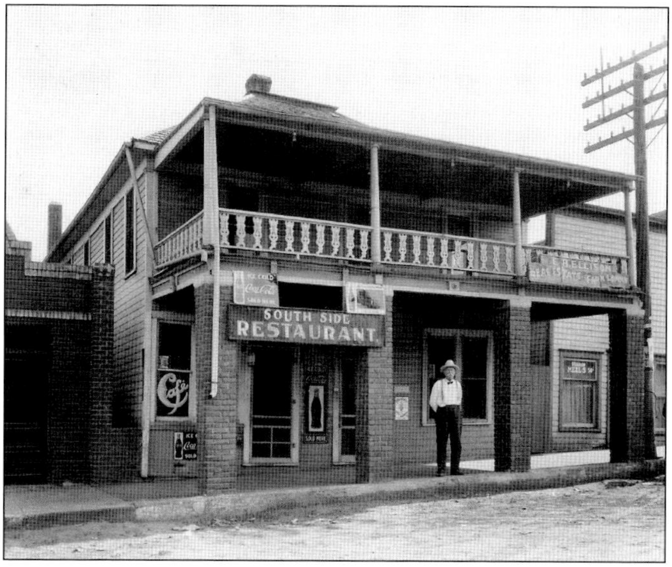

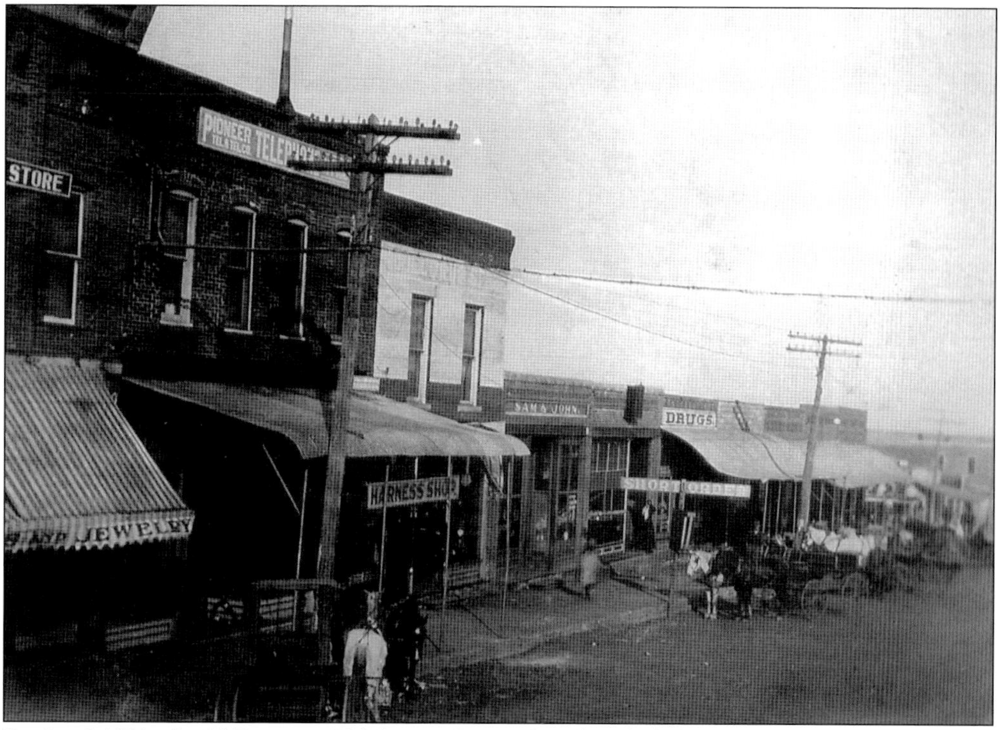

By April 1891, the El Reno to Oklahoma City railroad included a Yukon depot. The Spencer entourage dove into real estate and other ventures, naming their town after Canada's Yukon River gold rush. This 1905 photograph shows Spencer Avenue looking northeast from Fifth Street. Signs read, "Sam & John," "Harness Shop," "Jewelry," "Short Order," and "Pioneer Tel. and Tel. Co." Horses and buggies line the street. (Courtesy Phil Carson family.)

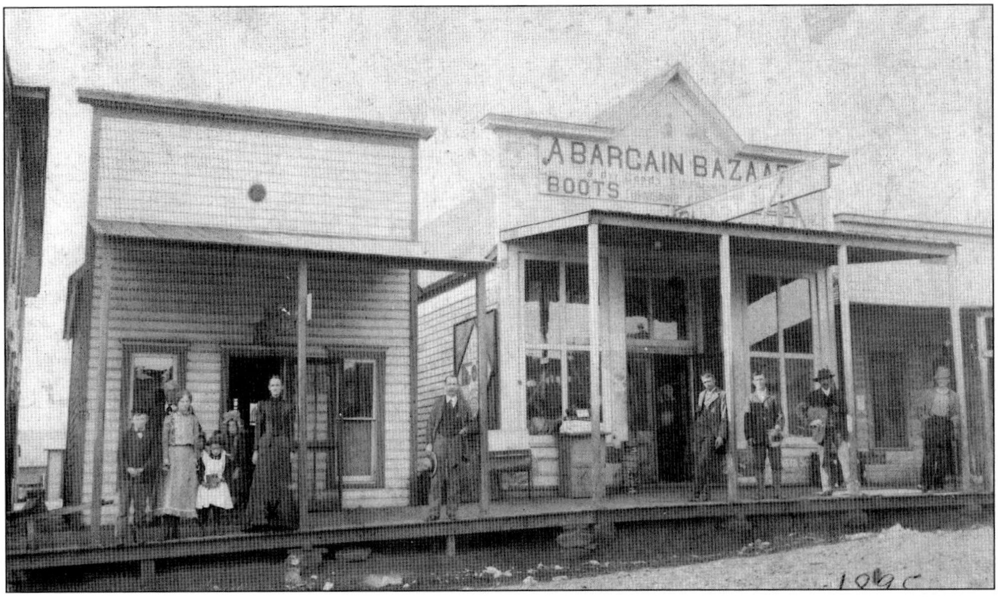

Yukon's post office was established on March 28, 1891. The railroad did not chug through town until April. Prior to that, the mail came by other means. The post office relocated several times. In 1893, it was in the one-story house shown on the left on Spencer Avenue's south side. Standing in front is postmistress Mary Volney Russel, who lived there with her family. (Courtesy Yukon Historical Society.)

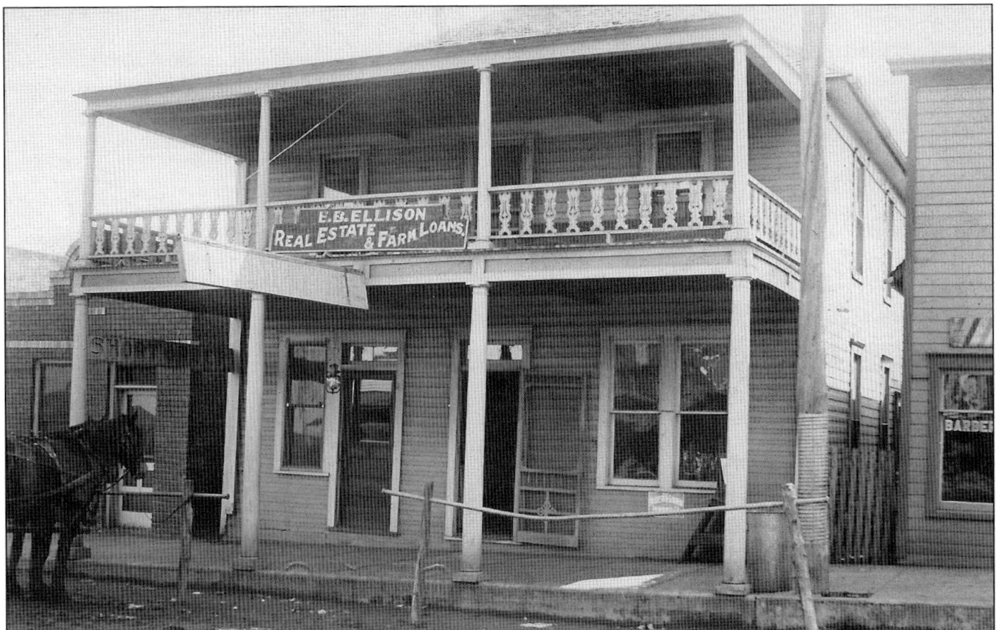

In 1892, George Brooking built a hotel at 424 West Main Street, which later had several owners. E.B. Ellison then owned the location as Ellison Hotel, shown here in 1910 with a horse out front. Signs read, "E.B. Ellison Real Estate & Farm Loans" and "Barber." In 1897, the Arkansas Valley Telephone Company began connecting Oklahoma locations. In 1902, its name changed to Pioneer Telephone Company. (Courtesy Yukon Historical Society.)

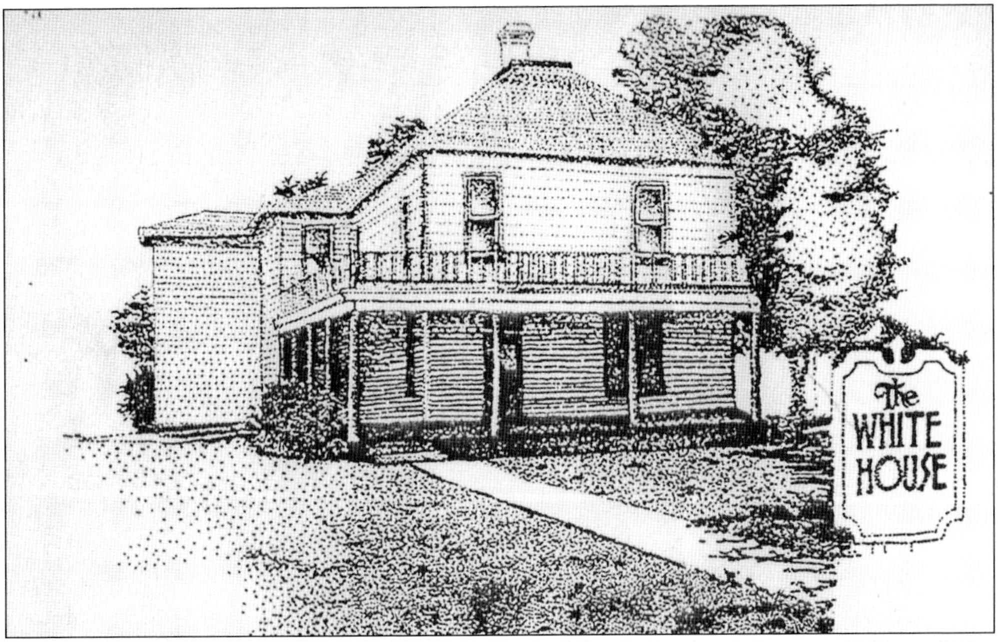

In 1891, L.M. Spencer, the "Father of Yukon," built Yukon's first brick home at Fifth and Elm Streets. Around 1892, A.N. Spencer built a two-story home on Poplar Avenue, shown in this drawing and known as the "White House." The family lived there until moving to Kansas in 1898. Both homes had modern comforts that others did not have. One or both had an indoor bathroom. (Courtesy Yukon Chamber of Commerce.)

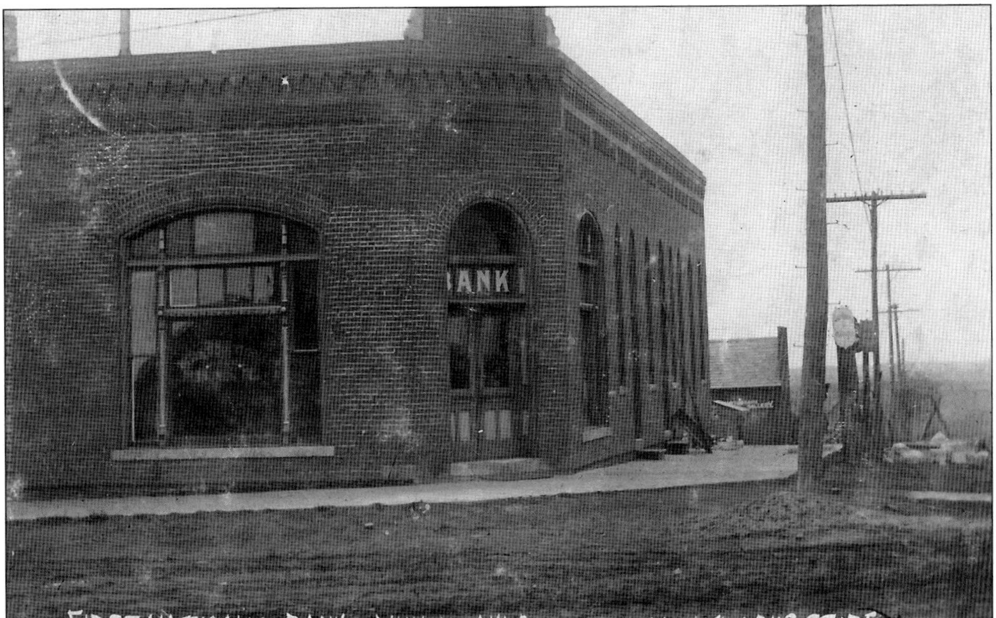

A.N. Spencer; his wife, Elizabeth; and H.K. Ricker established this private bank, the Bank of Oklahoma. In 1892, it became a state bank. On the northwest corner of Fifth Street and Spencer Avenue, the bank became the First National Bank, Canadian County's first bank, on May 5, 1902. (Courtesy Yukon Historical Society.)

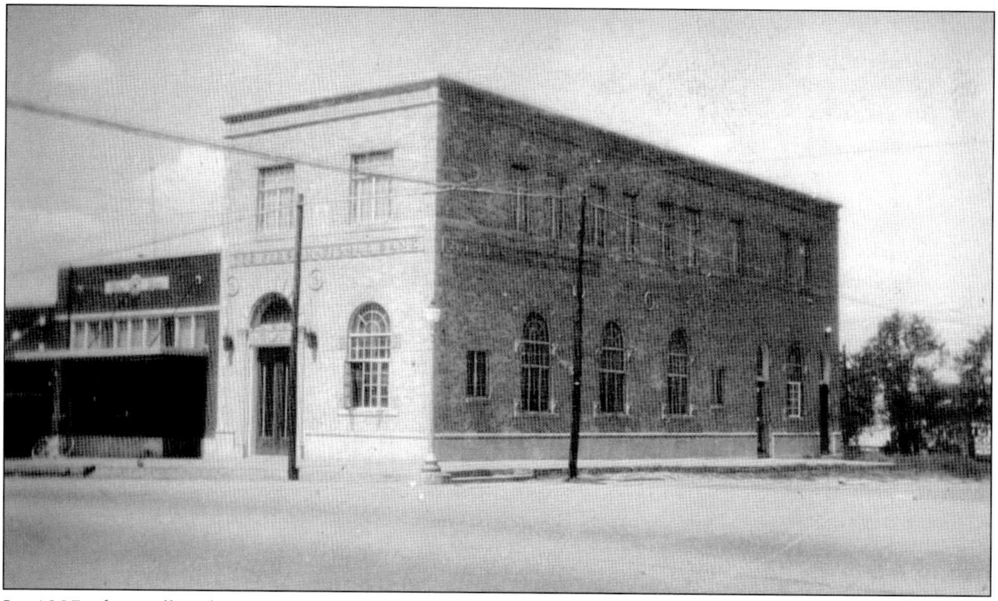

In 1927, the redbrick First National Bank evolved into today's two-story buff-colored building with the door relocated, on the northwest corner of Fifth and Main Streets, as seen here in 1935. The words "The First National Bank" are part of the building's masonry. The *Yukon Sun* building is on the left. (Courtesy Genie Vinson.)

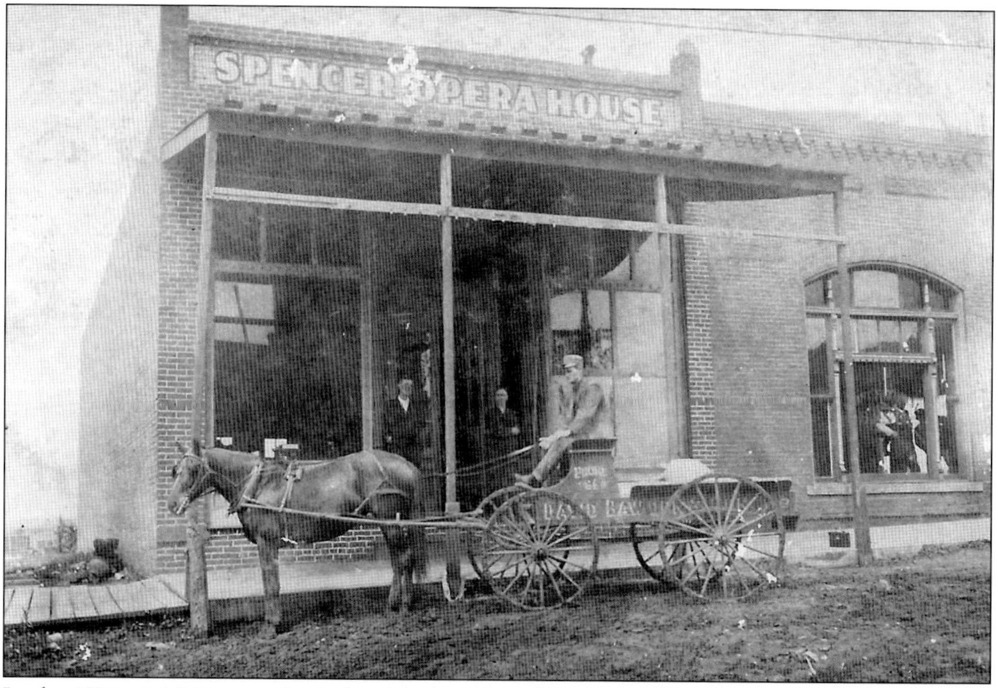

In the 1890s, L.M. Spencer built the Spencer Opera House at today's 505 Main Street. Traveling companies performed plays, musicals, wrestling matches, and other entertainment there. Spencer stood out front selling tickets and barking, "show tonight!" This 1908 photograph shows the First National Bank on the northwest corner of Fifth Street and Spencer Avenue to the right of the opera house. (Courtesy Yukon Historical Society.)

When the Spencers rerouted the railroad away from Frisco through Yukon, Frisco businesses relocated to Yukon, El Reno, and elsewhere. Entrepreneurs gravitated to Yukon, getting in on the fast-growing economy. In this undated photograph, M.R. Belisle (left) stands with Sam W. Major inside a Main Street haberdashery. (Courtesy Yukon Historical Society.)

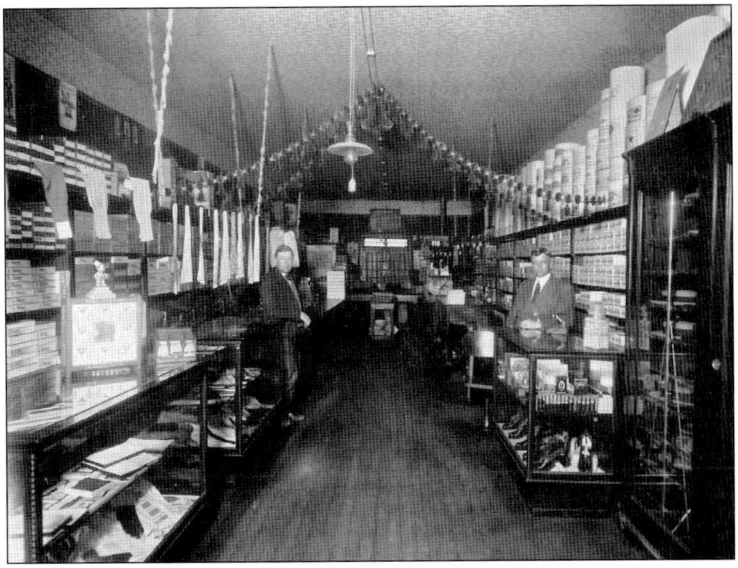

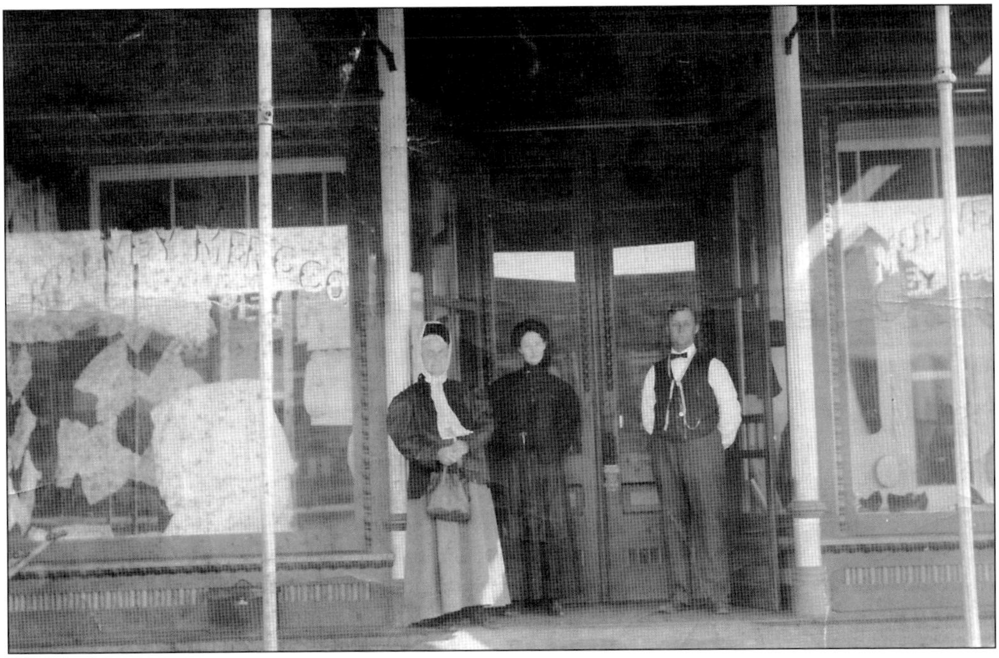

In 1893, Irish twins Odie and Mike Mulvey arrived in Yukon and bought stock in a small grocery store on the south side of Spencer Avenue. Their business remained there until 1904, when their new building was completed on the north side of Spencer Avenue, today's 425 West Main Street. The windows on this undated photograph read, "Mulvey Merc Co." The location is unknown. (Courtesy Mike Schulte.)

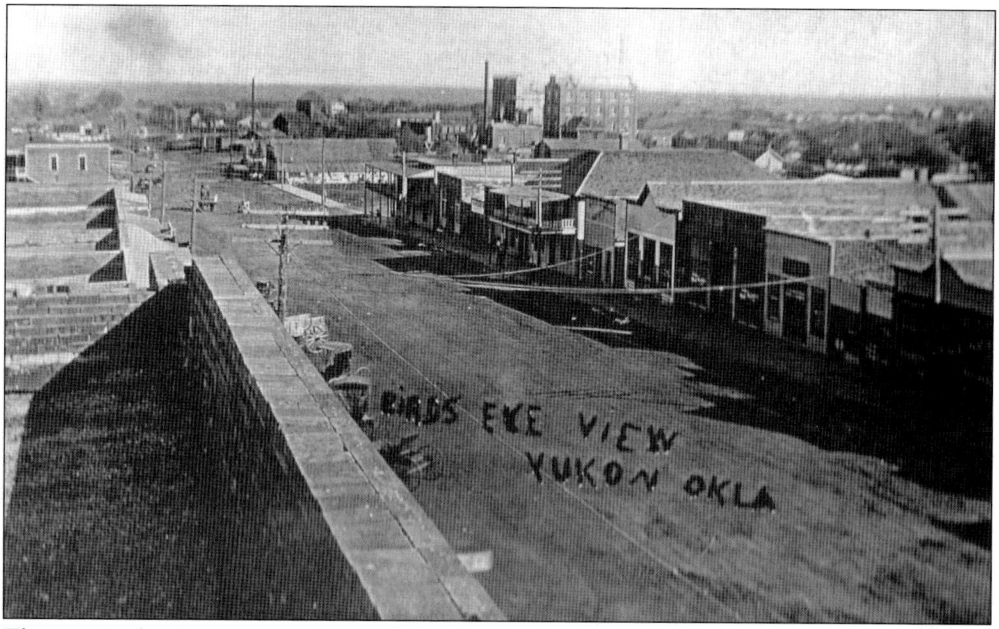

The new Mulvey's entryway tiles read, "Mulvey Mercantile Co," and are still in place in 2021. Smaller businesses on the street lost steam, and the Mulveys bought them through 1909. Eventually, half the buildings on the north side of Spencer Avenue, from Fourth to Fifth Streets, were part of Mulvey's. A photographer snapped this 1910 photograph from atop the new building at 425 Spencer Avenue looking east. (Courtesy Genie Vinson.)

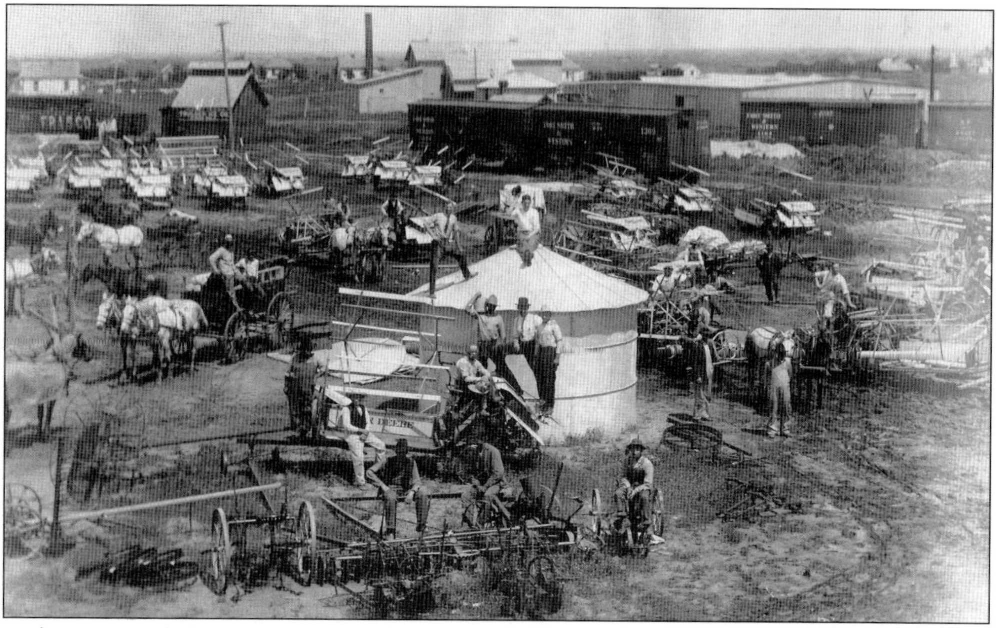

Mulvey's expanded at some point, building another Mulvey Mercantile. The location was the first brick building in Piedmont, at today's 100 Monroe Avenue Northwest. The building is still there in 2021. This undated Piedmont Mulvey's photograph shows a granary with men on top and all sorts of farm equipment. Railroad cars read, "Fort Smith & Western" and "Frisco." A sign reads, "Trulock Ice Co." (Courtesy Mike Schulte.)

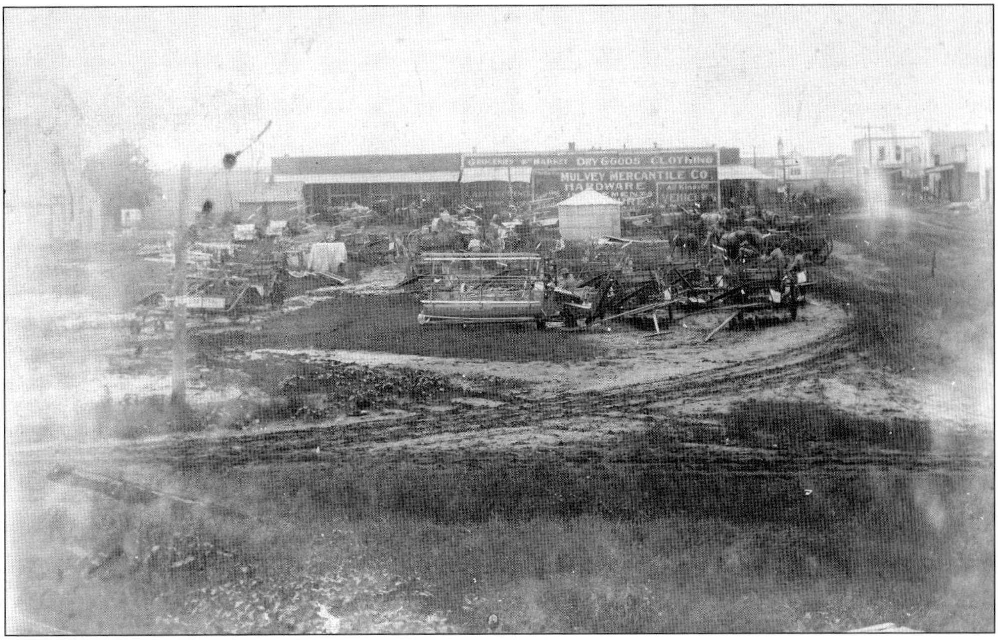

This photograph shows the Piedmont Mulvey's building, farm equipment, railroad tracks, people, and horses. The side of the building reads, "Mulvey Mercantile Co," "Groceries," "Meat Market," "Dry Goods," "Clothing," "Hardware," "All Kinds Of Vehicles," "Sporting Goods," and "Ladies & Gents." Piedmont's Monroe Avenue can be seen on the right of the Mulvey Building. (Courtesy Mike Schulte.)

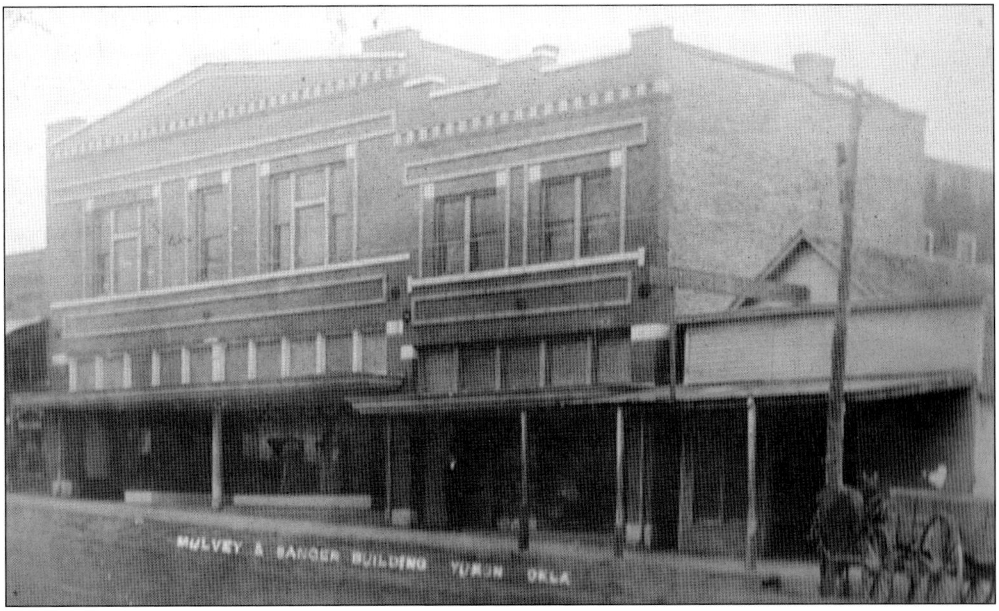

In 1903, grain binders hit the market. The Mulveys brought in 150 McCormick grain binders by train and sold them all. They threw a giant, free barbecue with music and dancing. All the farmers used their best horses to pull their grain binders in a parade hosted by the Mulveys. This 1910 photograph shows the side-by-side Mulvey and Sanger buildings, with Mulvey's on the left. (Courtesy Genie Vinson.)

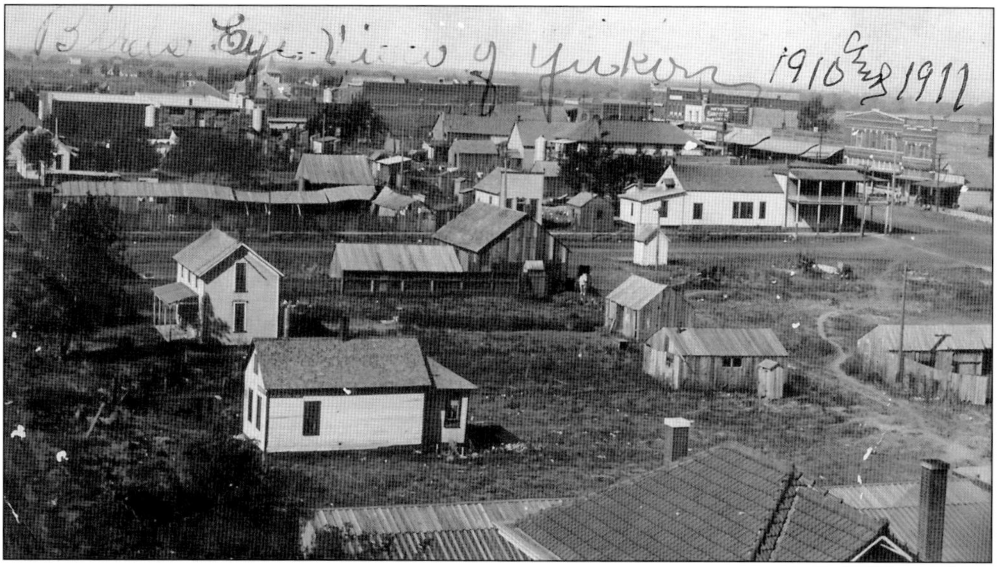

From 1910 to 1920, Mulvey Mercantile's business mushroomed, and the retailer became the largest in Yukon. Some claim the mercantile was the largest retailer in Oklahoma. In this c. 1910 photograph, Mulvey's can be seen at far right. Twins Odie and Mike Mulvey were 30 years old in 1890. (Courtesy Yukon Historical Society.)

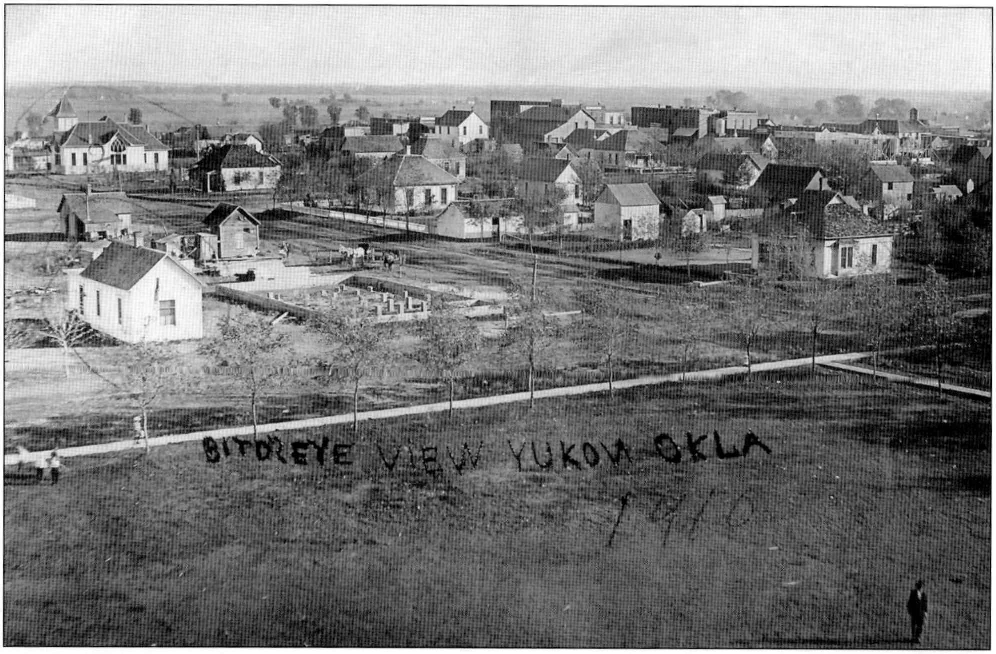

This c. 1910 photograph shows a growing Yukon. On the north side of today's Main Street, from Fourth to Fifth Streets, there were passageways between individual businesses. Owners have now closed them off. But it appears the Mulvey brothers created a lucrative emporium, or early mall. Odie Mulvey's wife, Fannie Elizabeth White Mulvey, was an area teacher. (Courtesy Yukon Historical Society.)

Mulvey's sold groceries and everything else imaginable, and offered repairs, a blacksmith, and embalming services. Possibly selling out in 1923, different parts of the business were purchased by different people, including the Wheatleys, Whelans, and others. This image from the 1912 Yukon High School yearbook shows Mike Mulvey when he was serving on the school board. (Courtesy Phil Carson family.)

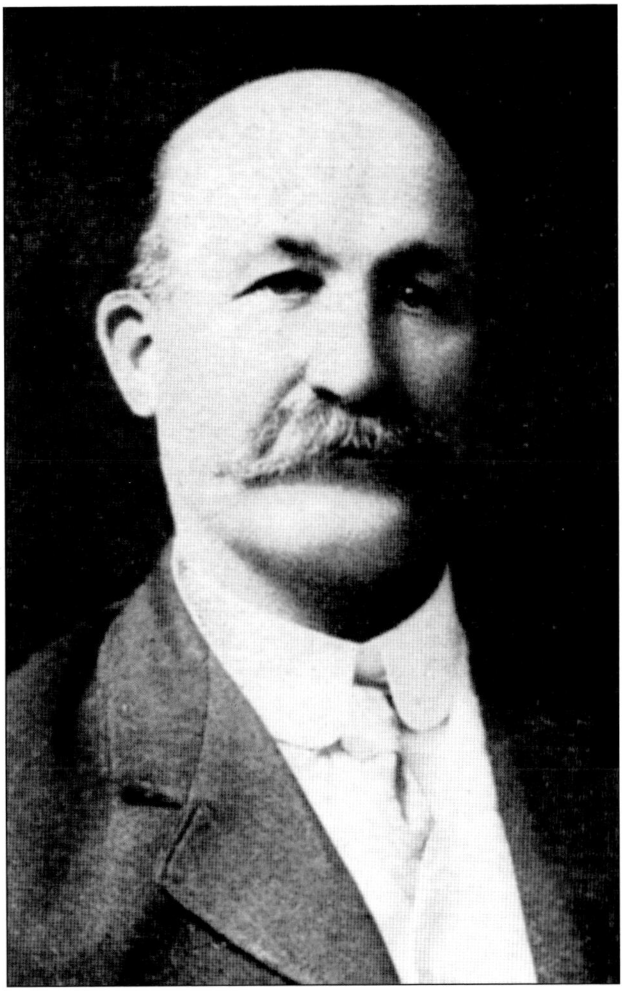

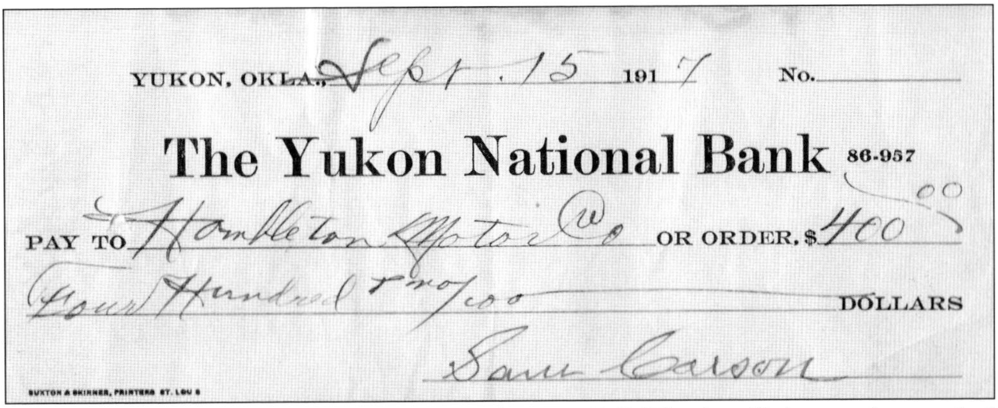

YUKON, OKLA., Sept. 15 1917 No.

The Yukon National Bank 86-957

PAY TO Hamilton Motor Co OR ORDER, $400.00

Four Hundred & no/100 DOLLARS

Sam Carson

BUXTON & SKINNER, PRINTERS ST. LOUIS

Of Irish ancestry, Kentuckian Sam Carson was born in 1862. The sheriff's favorite dog attacked 14-year-old Carson, who shot and killed the dog. Carson strapped on a six-shooter and fled Kentucky, fearing reprisal. He hunted with Buffalo Bill Cody, and married Sallie Armstrong in 1889. This 1917 check paid for Carson's first car from Yukon's first car dealership, Hamilton Motor Company. (Courtesy Phil Carson family.)

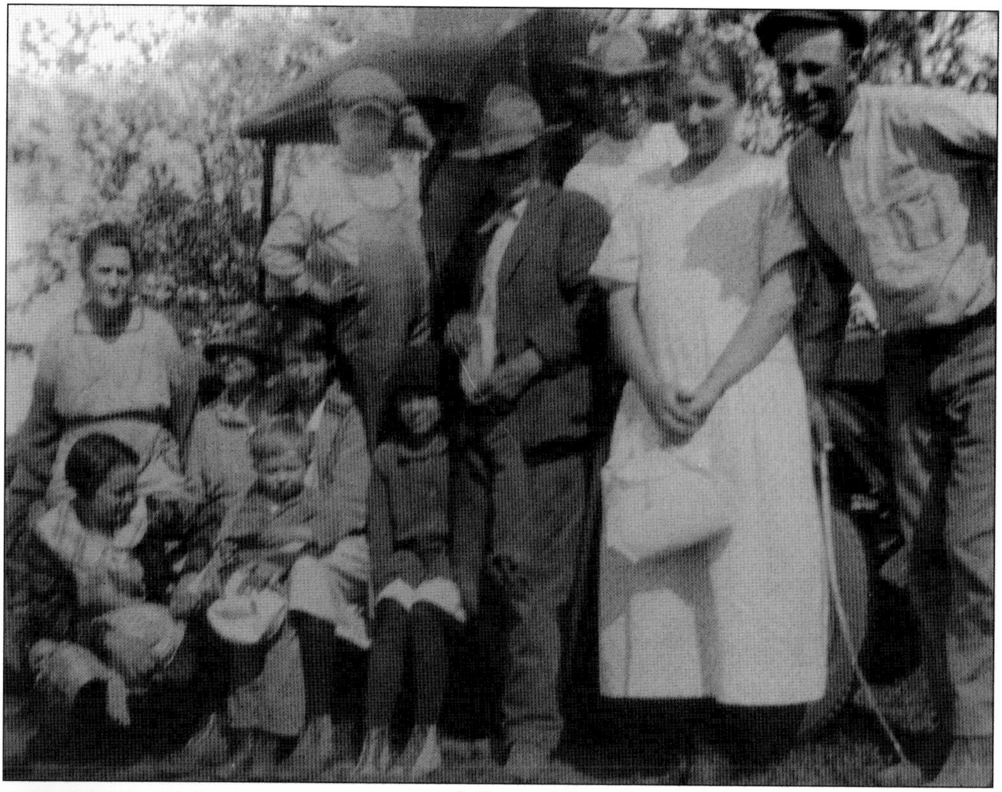

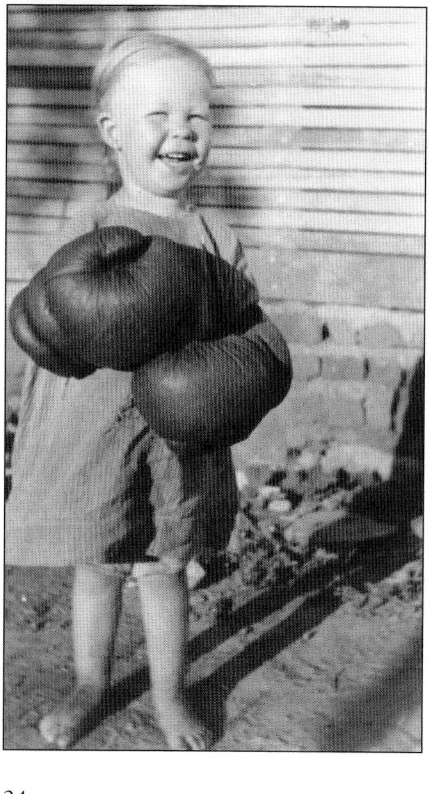

Sallie and Sam Carson left Nebraska, traveling three weeks in a covered wagon pulled by a team of Clydesdales, making their home in Yukon in 1894. Sallie and Sam pose in front of the family car with some of their grown children. In the back row are, from left to right, Sallie, Jim Carson, Sam, Glen Carson, and Nell and her husband, Doug Carson. (Courtesy Phil Carson family.)

Sam Carson was Yukon's first machinist. He built the family home and his machine-blacksmith shop in 1894, installing a 40-foot-tall windmill with a 16-foot blade to run his machines. Born in 1914 in the family home on Carson Corner, Jim Carson is shown enjoying his brother Bob's boxing gloves. Whenever the circus arrived, Bob always won when sparring with circus boxers. (Courtesy Phil Carson family.)

Sam Carson built his shop and home at Third and Elm Streets. He sold the land so the Yukon Mill office could be built there. He used horses to move the family house to 15 acres on the southwest corner of Main and Cornwell Streets, known since 1904 as Carson Corner. His grandson Phil holds an icicle in front of the Yukon Mill grain elevators. (Courtesy Phil Carson family.)

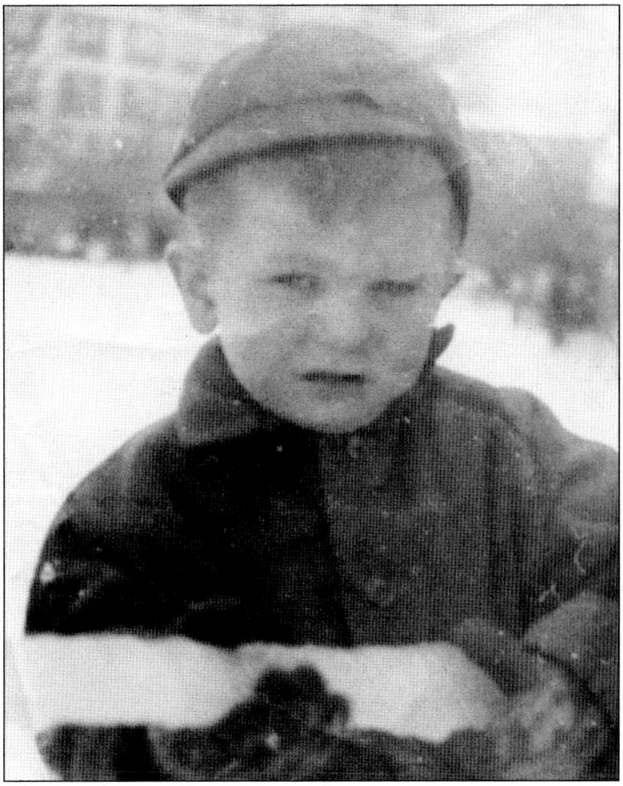

This hand-drawn map shows Carson Corner prior to 1939. Yukon men knocked on the Carson door one night. Opposing bigotry and vigilantism, Sam refused to hand over a non-Caucasian stranger who was staying in his home, and brandished a shotgun to clarify his point. (Courtesy Phil Carson family.)

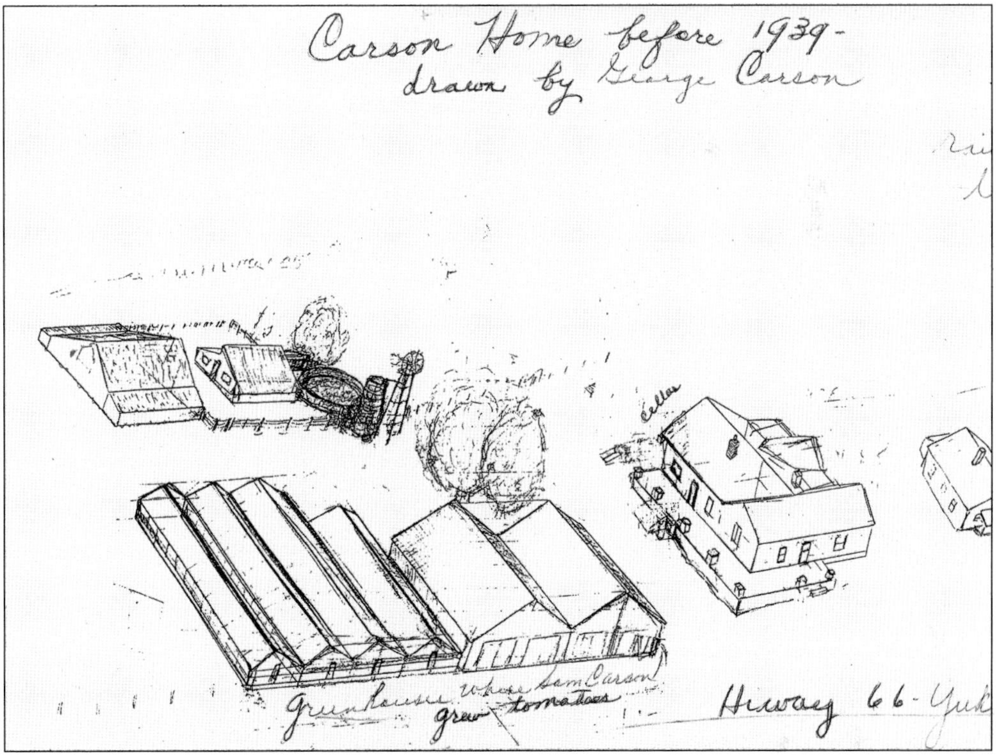

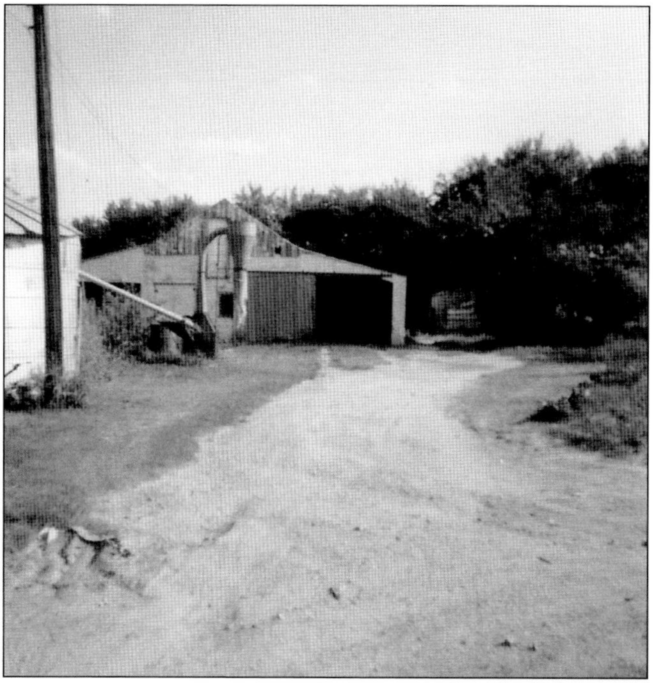

Sam Carson built this barn on Carson Corner. He maintained a fruit orchard, grew tomatoes in his greenhouses, had a cellar behind the family home, and maintained a rental house on the 15-acre property. (Courtesy Phil Carson family.)

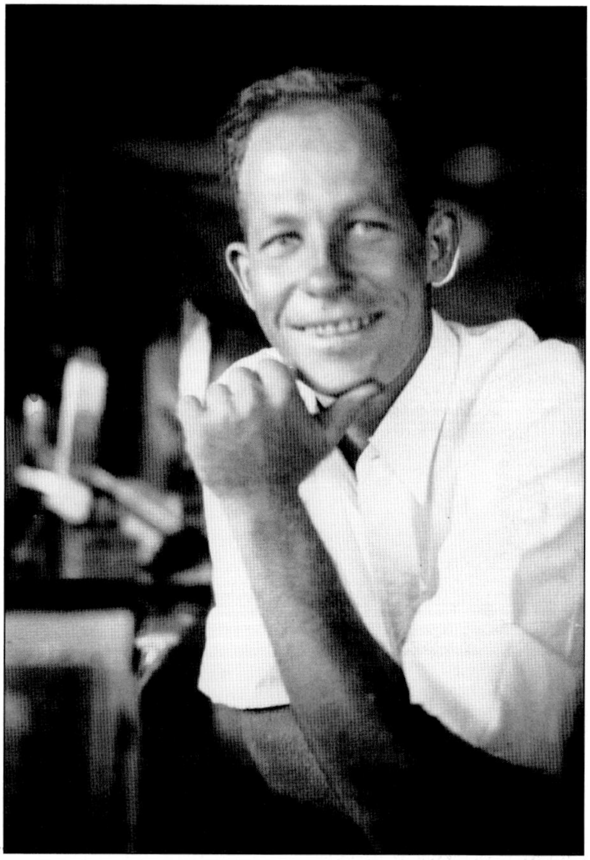

Jim Carson learned the Czech language from his neighbors. In first grade, he interpreted for Czechoslovakian children in school, who needed help with the English language. As an adult, he became an on-the-farm slaughter butcher. He helped build Dobry Mill, and also worked there. (Courtesy Phil Carson family.)

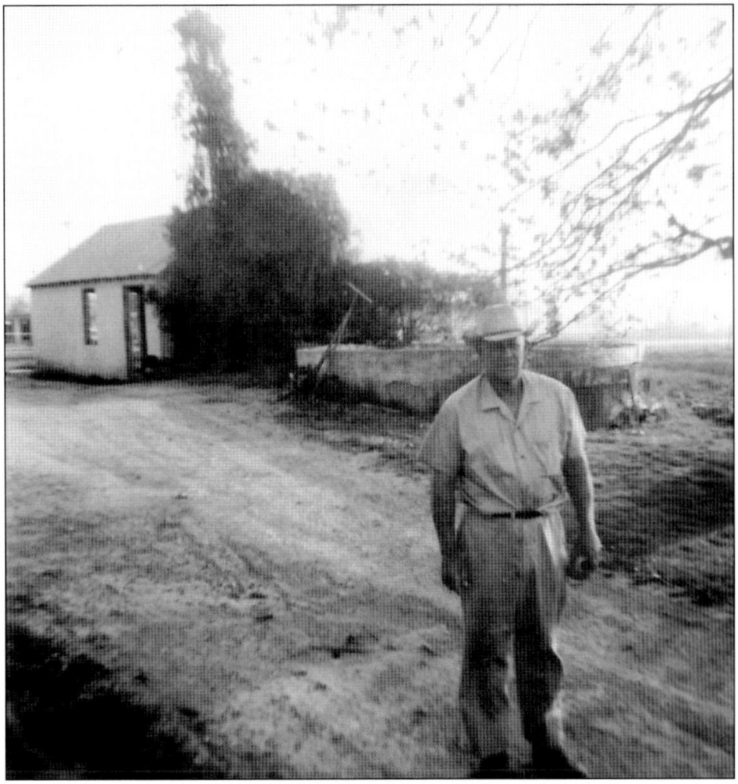

Standing behind Jim Carson is the windmill his father, Sam, built to pump water to the stock tank for his dairy cows. The creek on Carson Corner flows from Mulvey Pond. Sam siphoned water from the tank for his greenhouse and his crops. Jim's wife, Muriel, and their son Phil milked cows and delivered milk all over Yukon. (Courtesy Phil Carson family.)

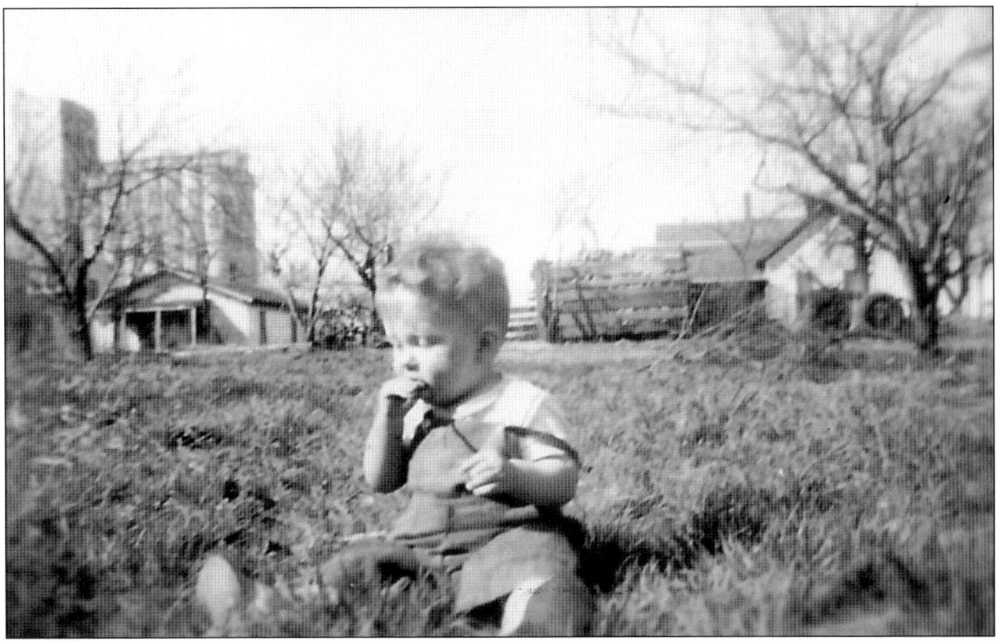

Toddler Phil Carson, son of Muriel and Jim Carson, sits in Carson Corner's cow pasture with the Dobry Mill in the background on the left. Dobry Mill was across the street from their family farm, which once belonged to Phil's grandparents Sallie and Sam Carson. Carson Corner now includes 10 West Main Street. (Courtesy Phil Carson family.)

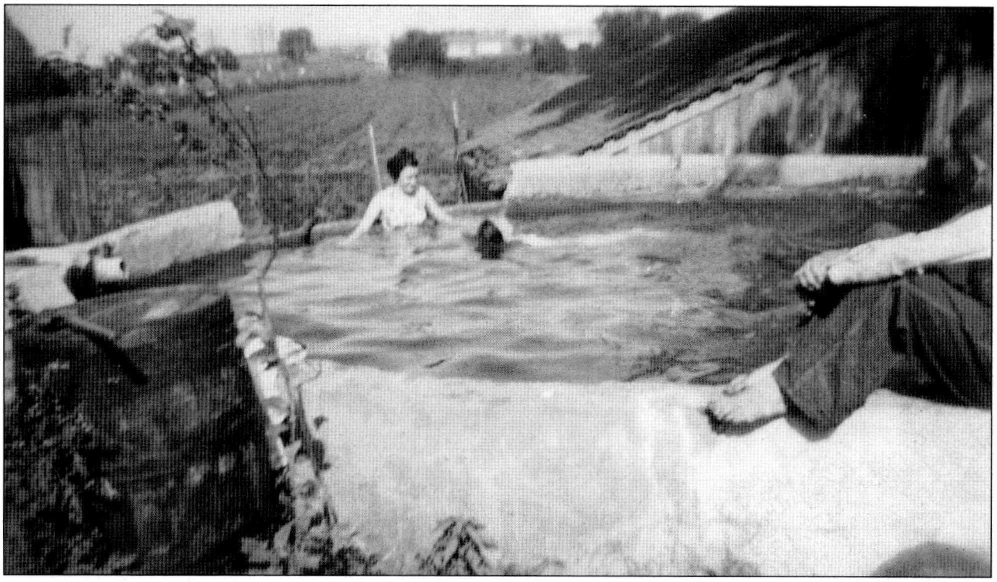

On the left, Muriel Carson swims in the farm stock tank. Local children came and swam with the family. Lamar Yount later created Yount's Grocery on Carson Corner. In 1959, Pat and Jim Snyder moved to Yukon, where Jim opened Snyder's IGA. He moved Snyder's from Town Plaza to today's 10 West Main Street location. The stock tank sat where Snyder's later stood. (Courtesy Phil Carson family.)

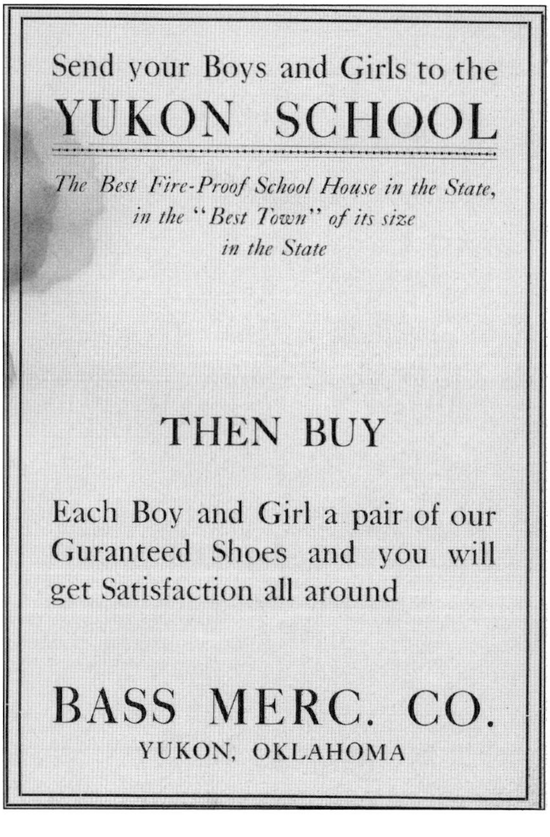

In 1895, brothers George and Harry Bass arrived from Ohio and purchased the Townley Confectionery, formerly J.W. Walker's Saloon, on the southeast corner of Fifth Street and Spencer Avenue. They established Bass Brothers Grocery and Dry Goods, which became Bass Mercantile Company. Harry moved to Oklahoma City in 1916, but George kept the business alive. This 1912 advertisement supports the Yukon public schools while promoting Bass store's shoes. (Courtesy Phil Carson family.)

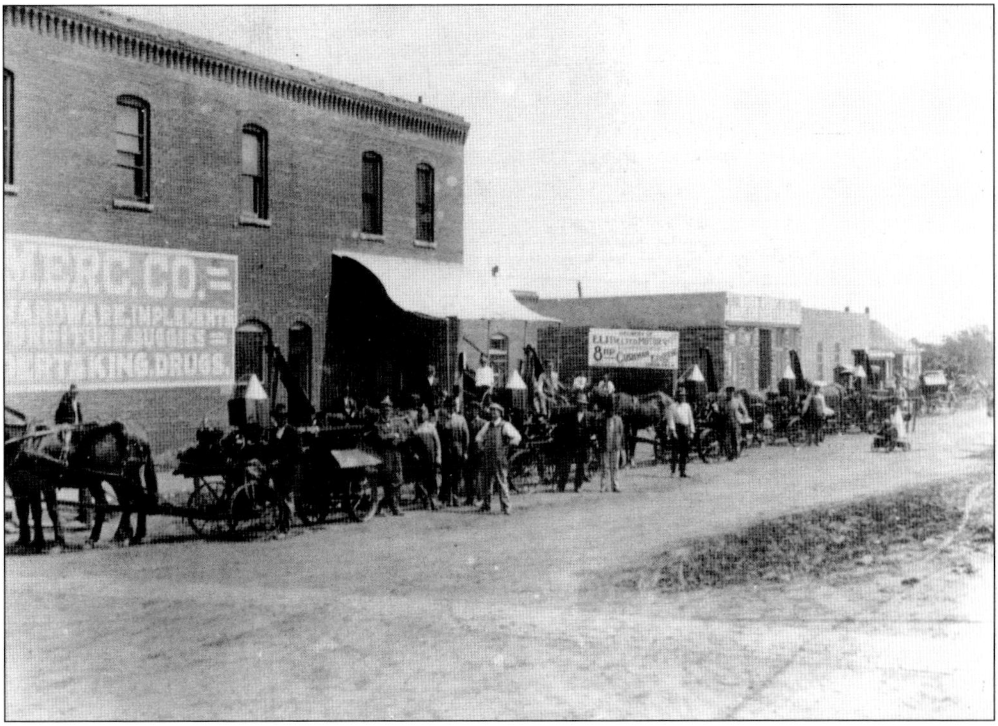

The west side of Bass Mercantile reads, "Hardware, Implements, Furniture, Buggies, Undertaking, Drugs." But the store sold everything imaginable. Steam farm machinery was sold on the streets beside the store in the early 1900s. The white sign near the middle reads, "Delivery of Eli Belted Motors, SHP Cushman Engine." Today's Bass Building still has its original wood floors, brick interior walls, and front door. (Courtesy Bass and Ramey families.)

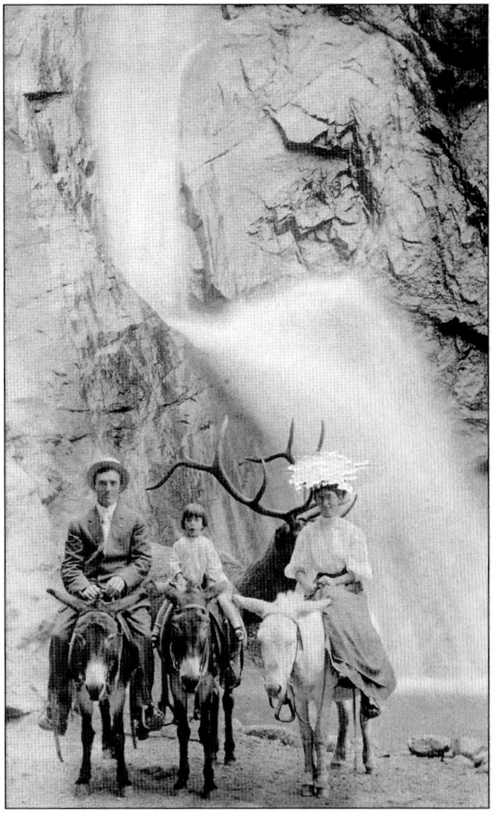

Shown riding burros at Seven Falls, Colorado, in 1908 are, from left to right, George Bass with his two-year-old daughter Wenona and his wife, Emma. When the Bass brothers started in business, they moved the existing white building into the street, and continued conducting business there while their new brick building was being built. The 1898 Bass Building remains at 456 and 458 West Main Street. (Courtesy Bass and Ramey families.)

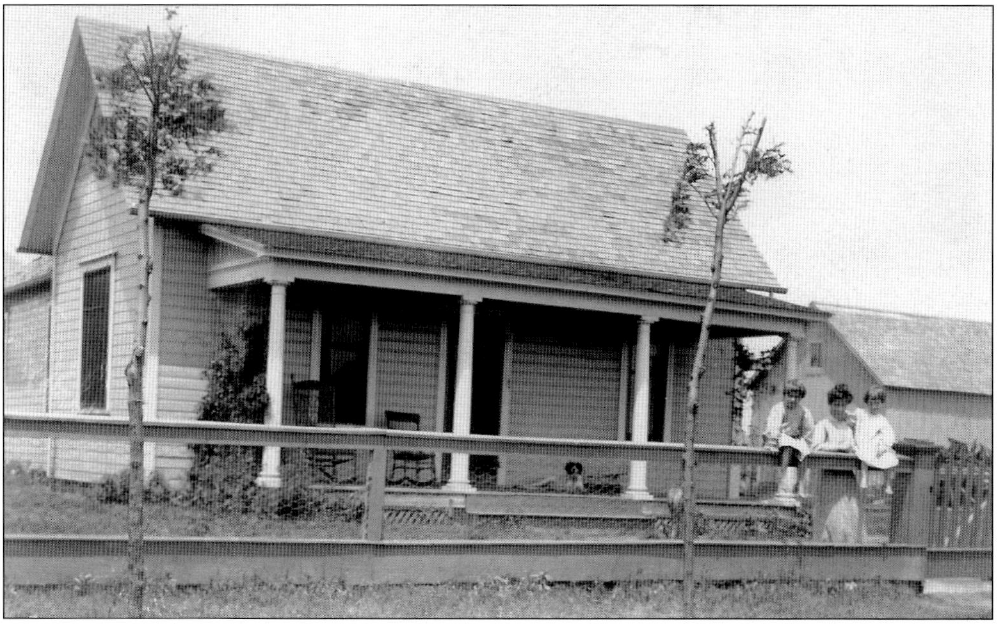

George Bass's wife, Emma, is shown with her daughter Wenona on the right in front of the family's early Yukon home. George and Emma had two other daughters, Eunice and Ruth. All three attended and graduated from Yukon schools, then studied at Oklahoma Agricultural and Mechanical College, now Oklahoma State University in Stillwater. (Courtesy Bass and Ramey families.)

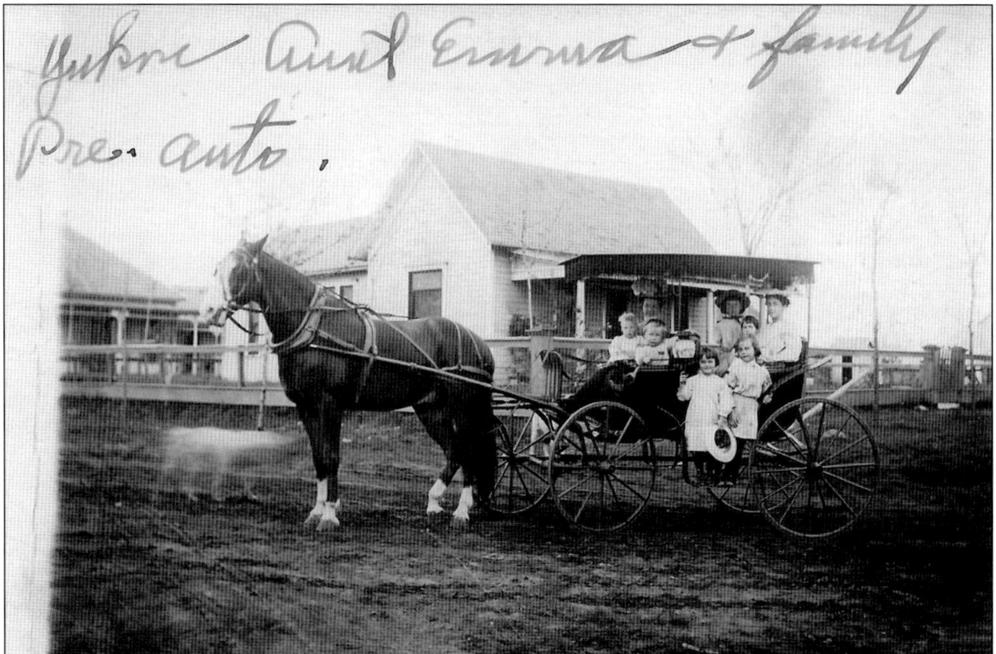

Emma Bass sits on the far right in the buggy, and her daughter Wenona is out front holding a hat. On the second floor of Bass Mercantile, a midwife had an office, as did a men's benevolence group, and John Turner embalmed bodies. One day, daughter Ruth Bass hid in a casket, and when the family walked in, she sat up and scared them. (Courtesy Bass and Ramey families.)

Emma Bass is seated with her daughters (from left to right) Eunice, Wenona, and Ruth. George Bass was one of Yukon's first volunteer firemen. Emma performed at Spencer's Opera House as a pianist. Today, their grandsons George Ramey and Fenton Ramey have their law offices in the Bass Building. (Courtesy Bass and Ramey families.)

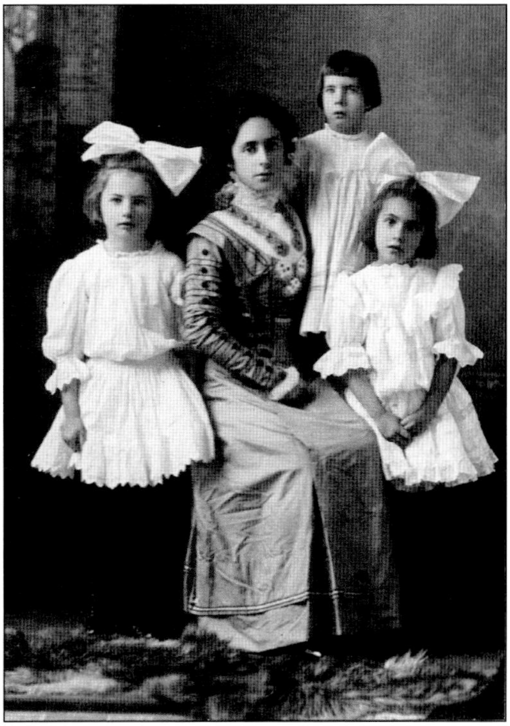

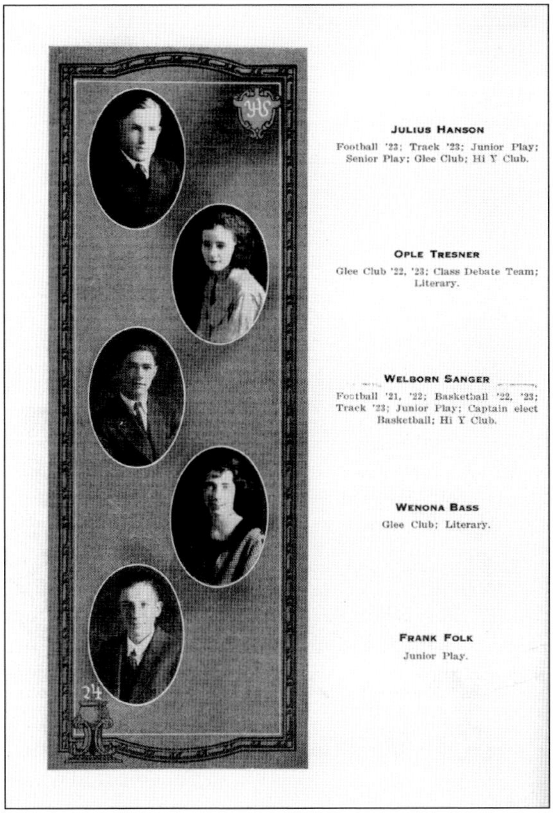

Julius Hanson
Football '23; Track '23; Junior Play; Senior Play; Glee Club; Hi Y Club.

Ople Tresner
Glee Club '22, '23; Class Debate Team; Literary.

Welborn Sanger
Football '21, '22; Basketball '22, '23; Track '23; Junior Play; Captain elect Basketball; Hi Y Club.

Wenona Bass
Glee Club; Literary.

Frank Folk
Junior Play.

Wenona Bass is seen here in a page from the 1923 Yukon High School yearbook, *The Javelin*. She worked in the family store by age 14 and never worked anywhere else. She attended socials in the Kroutil Mansion ballroom and Mulvey Mercantile's second floor, and married Hardin Ramey. Wenona turned Bass Mercantile into a department store and then a dress shop. Both of her sons, George and Fenton Ramey, are former judges. (Courtesy Phil Carson family.)

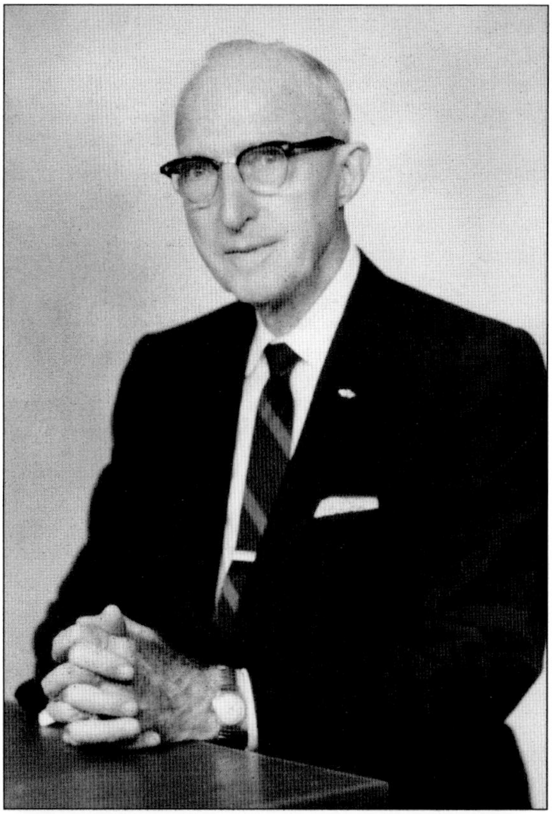

George Bass often loaded his wagon and went into the countryside to sell or barter. When people could not pay, he carried their accounts. He bought eggs and butter from local farmers to sell. His grandson George Ramey still wears the watch seen in this photograph. (Courtesy Bass and Ramey families.)

Shown in 1902, Warren Hooper Drug was on the north side of Spencer Avenue. Pharmacist Edward Dempsey Ellison stands second from right. The town grew relatively slowly. By 1899, there were four telephones, but the town lacked water and sewer systems and electricity and natural gas. Area residents formed groups in order to improve conditions. (Courtesy Yukon Historical Society.)

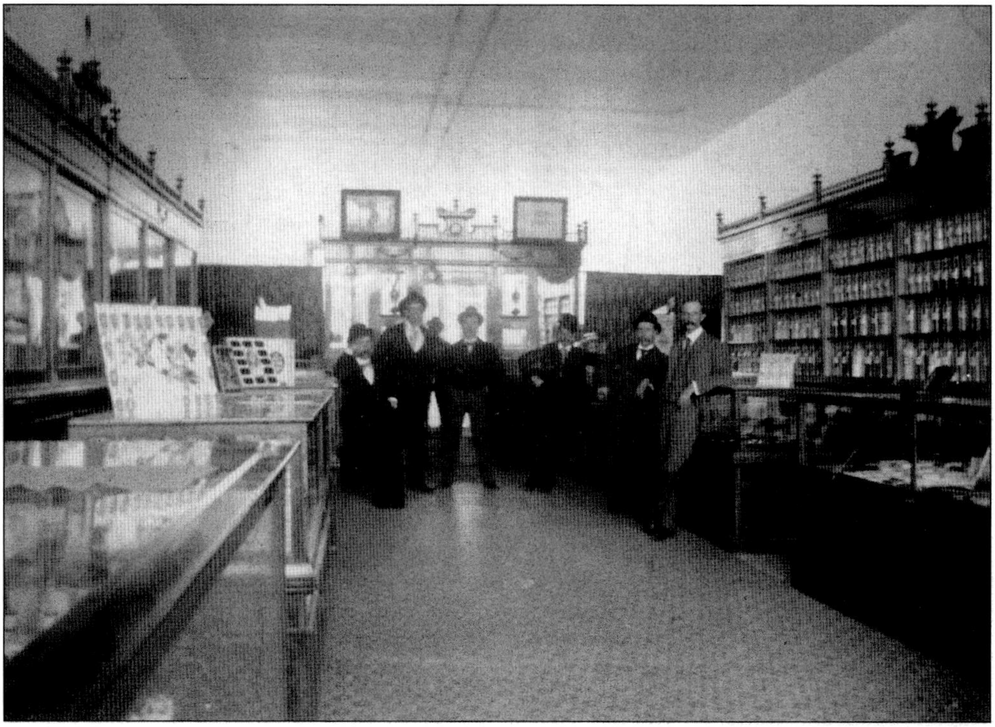

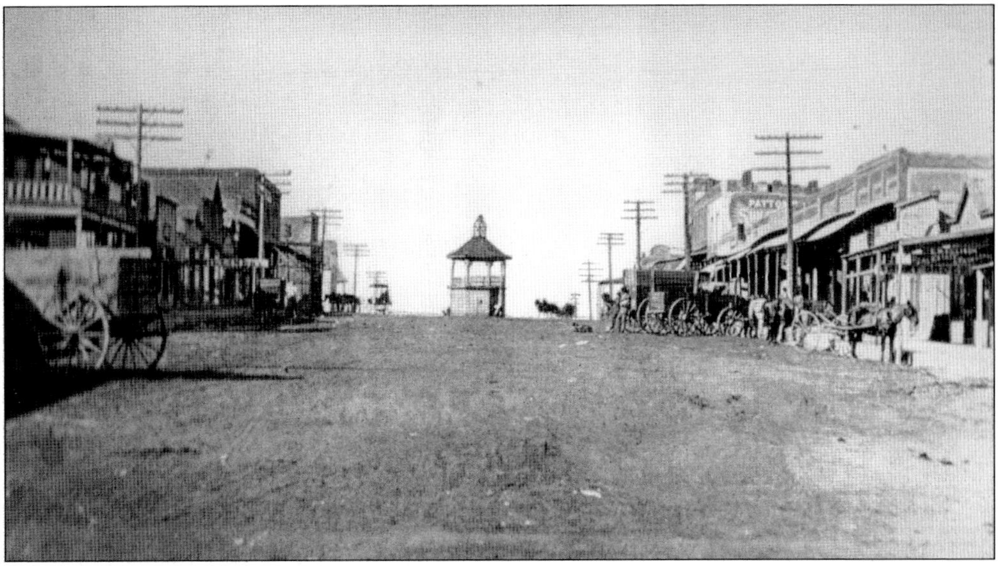

Looking west from Fourth Street around 1907, the bandstand is in the middle of Spencer Avenue. Likely erected prior to 1900, it was used for everything from speeches to music. Around 1911, a Civil War veterans' fife and drum corps performed. Pranksters sometimes coaxed cows onto the bandstand, which was a fairly high structure. A millinery sign is on the left. (Courtesy Genie Vinson.)

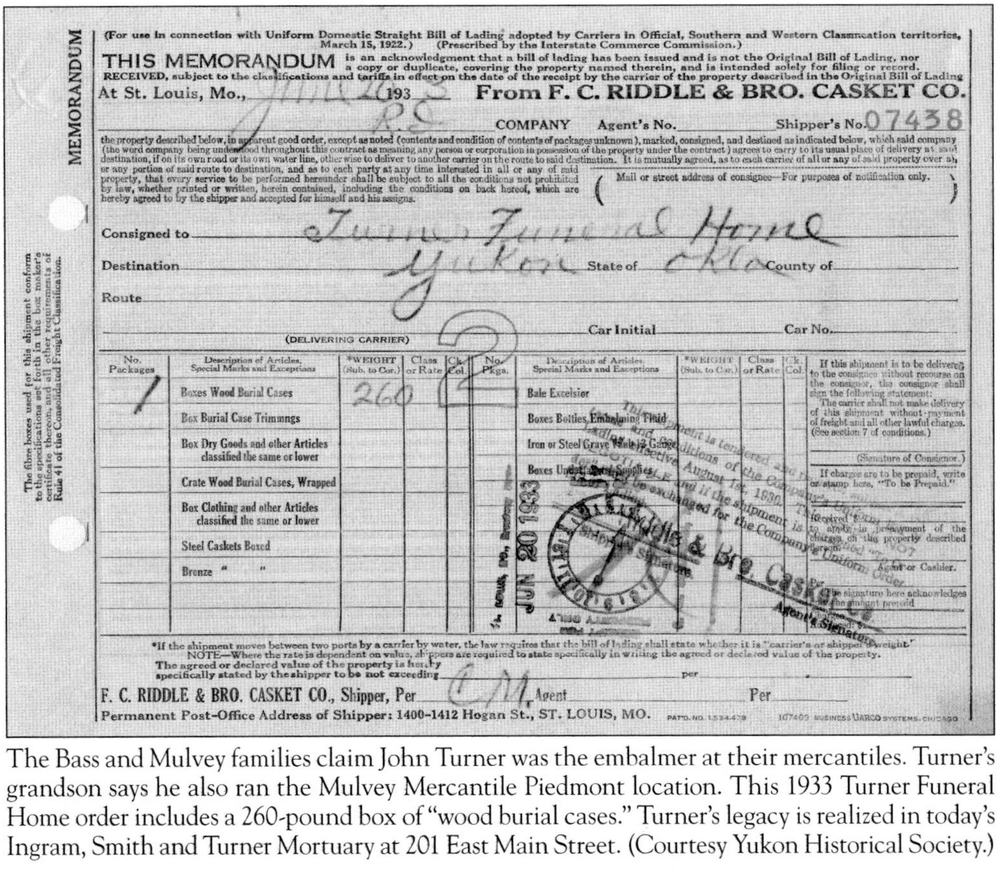

MEMORANDUM

(For use in connection with Uniform Domestic Straight Bill of Lading adopted by Carriers in Official, Southern and Western Classification territories, March 15, 1922.) (Prescribed by the Interstate Commerce Commission.)

THIS MEMORANDUM is an acknowledgment that a bill of lading has been issued and is not the Original Bill of Lading, nor a copy or duplicate, covering the property named therein, and is intended solely for filing or record.

RECEIVED, subject to the classifications and tariffs in effect on the date of the receipt by the carrier of the property described in the Original Bill of Lading

At St. Louis, Mo., 193 From F. C. RIDDLE & BRO. CASKET CO.

COMPANY Agent's No. Shipper's No. 07438

the property described below, in apparent good order, except as noted (contents and condition of contents of packages unknown), marked, consigned, and destined as indicated below, which said company (the word company being understood throughout this contract as meaning any person or corporation in possession of the property under the contract) agrees to carry to its usual place of delivery at said destination, if on its own road or its own water line, otherwise to deliver to another carrier on the route to said destination. It is mutually agreed, as to each carrier of all or any of said property over all or any portion of said route to destination, and as to each party at any time interested in all or any of said property, that every service to be performed hereunder shall be subject to all the conditions not prohibited by law, whether printed or written, herein contained, including the conditions on back hereof, which are hereby agreed to by the shipper and accepted for himself and his assigns.

(Mail or street address of consignee—For purposes of notification only.)

Consigned to Turner Funeral Home

Destination Yukon State of Okla County of

Route

(DELIVERING CARRIER) Car Initial Car No.

No. Packages	Description of Articles, Special Marks and Exceptions	*WEIGHT (Sub. to Cor.)	Class or Rate	Ck. Col.	No. Pkgs.	Description of Articles, Special Marks and Exceptions	*WEIGHT (Sub. to Cor.)	Class or Rate	Ck. Col.
1	Boxes Wood Burial Cases	260				Bale Excelsior			
	Box Burial Case Trimmngs					Boxes Bottles Embalming Fluid			
	Box Dry Goods and other Articles classified the same or lower					Iron or Steel Grave Vault 12 Gauge			
	Crate Wood Burial Cases, Wrapped					Boxes Undertakers Supplies			
	Box Clothing and other Articles classified the same or lower								
	Steel Caskets Boxed								
	Bronze " "								

If this shipment is to be delivered to the consignee without recourse on the consignor, the consignor shall sign the following statement: The carrier shall not make delivery of this shipment without payment of freight and all other lawful charges. (See section 7 of conditions.)

(Signature of Consignor.)

If charges are to be prepaid, write or stamp here, "To be Prepaid."

Received $ to apply in prepayment of the charges on the property described hereon.

Agent or Cashier.

Per

The signature here acknowledges only the amount prepaid

JUN 20 1933

This shipment is tendered and received subject to the classifications and conditions of the Company's Uniform Bill of Lading effective August 1st, 1930. This memorandum ... if the shipment is ... to be exchanged for the Company's Uniform Order ...

F. C. Riddle & Bro. Casket Co.

Agent's Signature

*If the shipment moves between two ports by a carrier by water, the law requires that the bill of lading shall state whether it is "carrier's or shipper's weight."

NOTE—Where the rate is dependent on value, shippers are required to state specifically in writing the agreed or declared value of the property.

The agreed or declared value of the property is hereby specifically stated by the shipper to be not exceeding per

F. C. RIDDLE & BRO. CASKET CO., Shipper, Per C.M. Agent Per

Permanent Post-Office Address of Shipper: 1400-1412 Hogan St., ST. LOUIS, MO. PAT'D. NO. 1534478 107409 BUSINESS UARCO SYSTEMS, CHICAGO

The fibre boxes used for this shipment conform to the specifications set forth in the box maker's certificate thereon, and all other requirements of Rule 41 of the Consolidated Freight Classification.

The Bass and Mulvey families claim John Turner was the embalmer at their mercantiles. Turner's grandson says he also ran the Mulvey Mercantile Piedmont location. This 1933 Turner Funeral Home order includes a 260-pound box of "wood burial cases." Turner's legacy is realized in today's Ingram, Smith and Turner Mortuary at 201 East Main Street. (Courtesy Yukon Historical Society.)

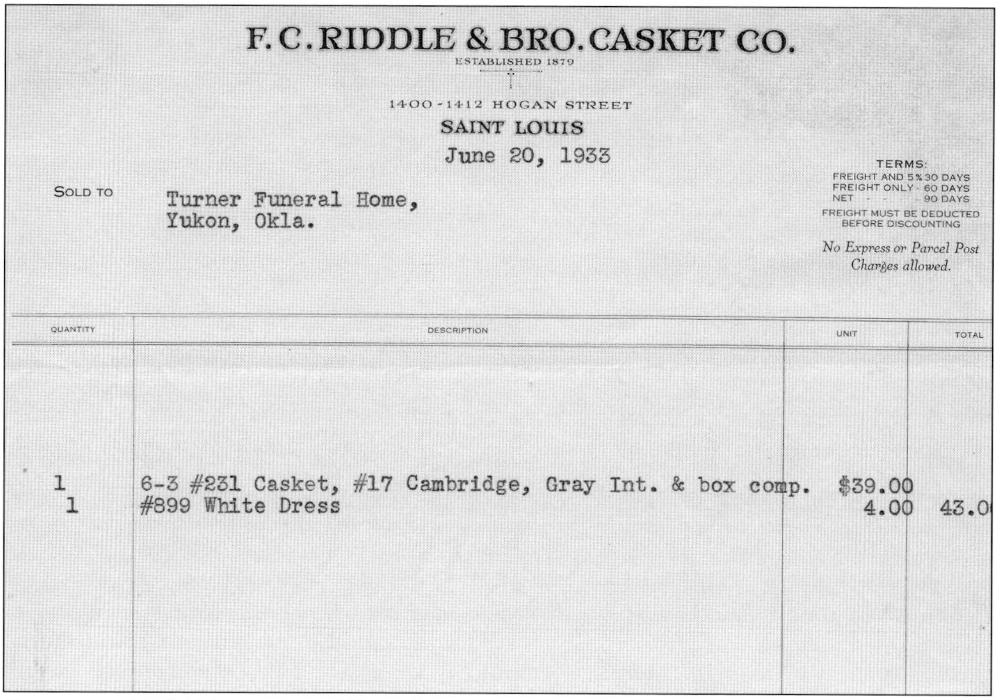

F. C. RIDDLE & BRO. CASKET CO.

ESTABLISHED 1879

1400-1412 HOGAN STREET
SAINT LOUIS
June 20, 1933

SOLD TO Turner Funeral Home,
Yukon, Okla.

TERMS:
FREIGHT AND 5% 30 DAYS
FREIGHT ONLY - 60 DAYS
NET - - - 90 DAYS
FREIGHT MUST BE DEDUCTED BEFORE DISCOUNTING

No Express or Parcel Post Charges allowed.

QUANTITY	DESCRIPTION	UNIT	TOTAL
1	6-3 #231 Casket, #17 Cambridge, Gray Int. & box comp.	$39.00	
1	#899 White Dress	4.00	43.0

Shown is a 1933 bill from F.C. Riddle and Bro. Casket Co. of St. Louis, from which Turner Funeral Home ordered a casket and white dress. Mulvey Mercantile was at 425 West Main Street. At one point, the funeral home was immediately east of Mulvey's. Next to the funeral home was Emma Turner's flower shop, and next to the flower shop was Lena Turner's beauty shop. (Courtesy Yukon Historical Society.)

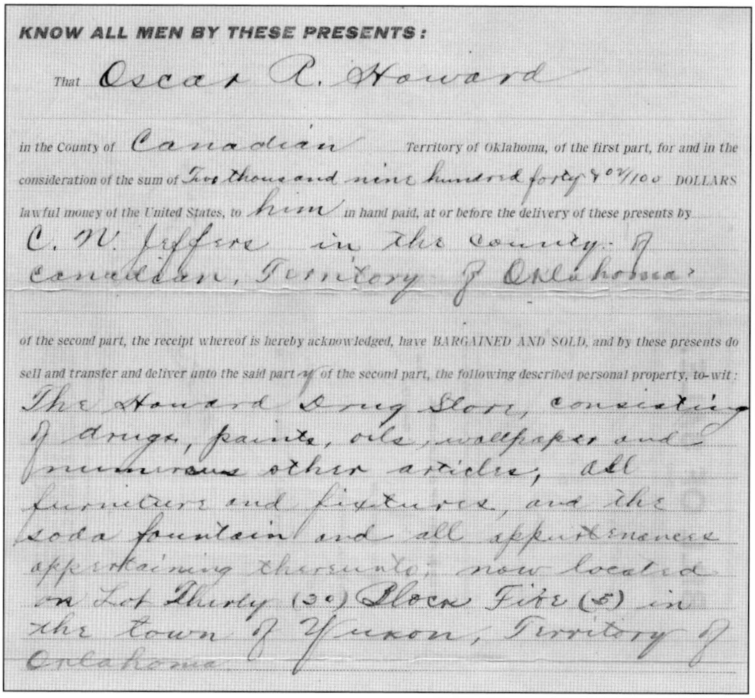

KNOW ALL MEN BY THESE PRESENTS:

That Oscar R. Howard in the County of Canadian Territory of Oklahoma, of the first part, for and in the consideration of the sum of Two thousand nine hundred forty & 00/100 DOLLARS lawful money of the United States, to him in hand paid, at or before the delivery of these presents by C. N. Jeffers in the county of Canadian, Territory of Oklahoma of the second part, the receipt whereof is hereby acknowledged, have BARGAINED AND SOLD, and by these presents do sell and transfer and deliver unto the said party of the second part, the following described personal property, to-wit: The Howard Drug Store, consisting of drugs, paints, oils, wallpaper and numerous other articles, all furniture and fixtures, and the soda fountain and all appurtenances appertaining thereunto, now located on Lot Thirty (30) Block Five (5) in the town of Yukon, Territory of Oklahoma

In 1905, Oscar Howard sold Howard Drug Store to C.N. Jeffers for $2,940. The sale included the store, drugs, paint, oils, wallpapers, furniture, fixtures, the soda fountain, and all related items. (Courtesy Yukon Historical Society.)

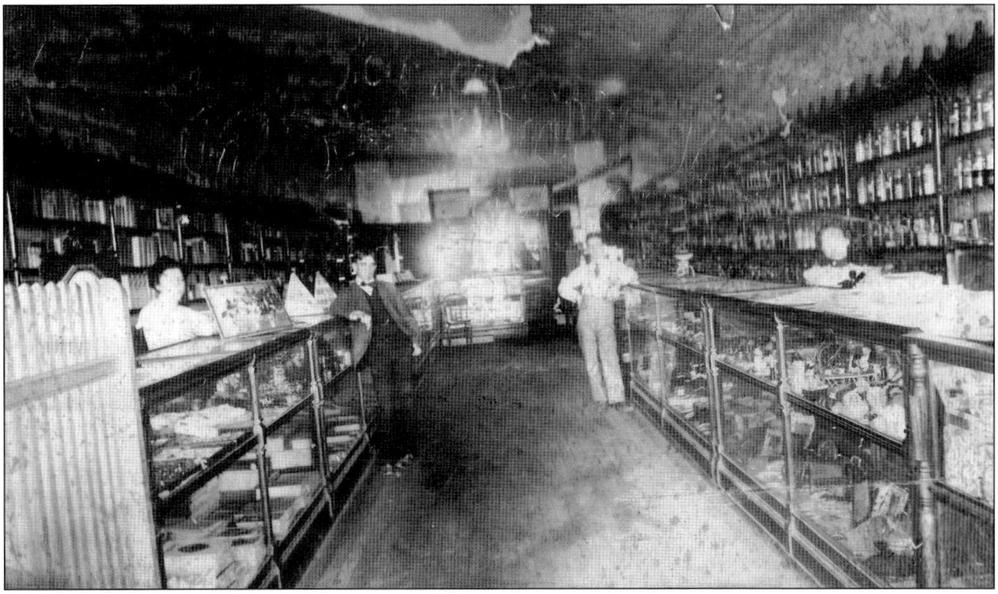

This undated image shows R. Sallie Jeffers on the left and her husband, owner and pharmacist Clyde "Jeff" Jeffers, on the right, with pharmacist Frank Smith inside the Jeffers' Model Drug Store on Spencer Avenue. (Courtesy Yukon Historical Society.)

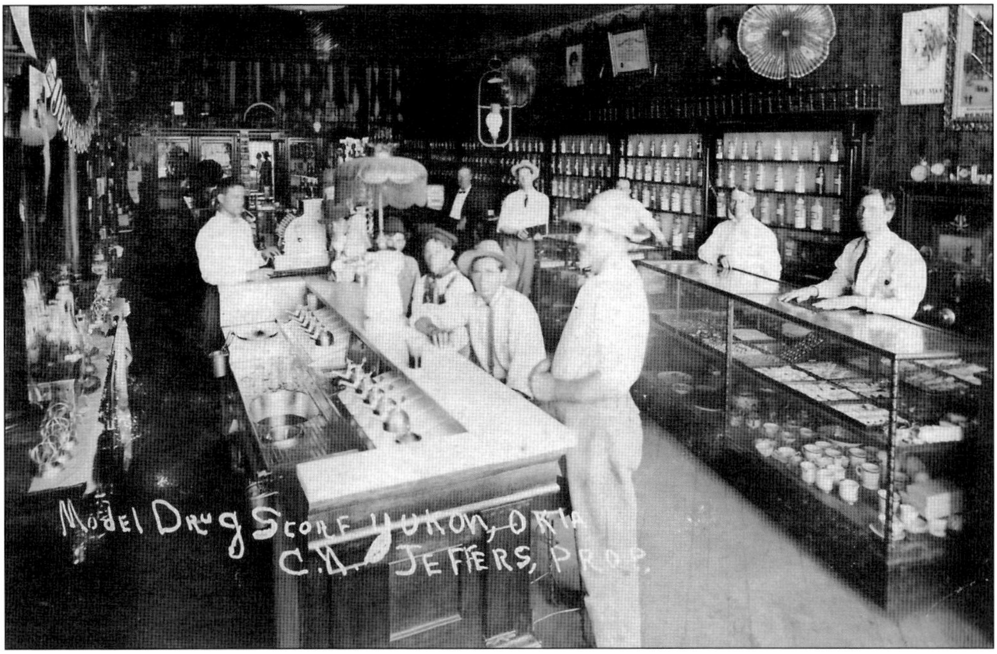

This is the interior of Model Drug Store. One historian claims that C.N. Jeffers originally owned C.N. Jeffers Watch Repair and Jewelry, which later became Model Drug Store. Jeffers also established his Model Confectionery Store at 454 West Main Street in the 1920s. (Courtesy Yukon Historical Society.)

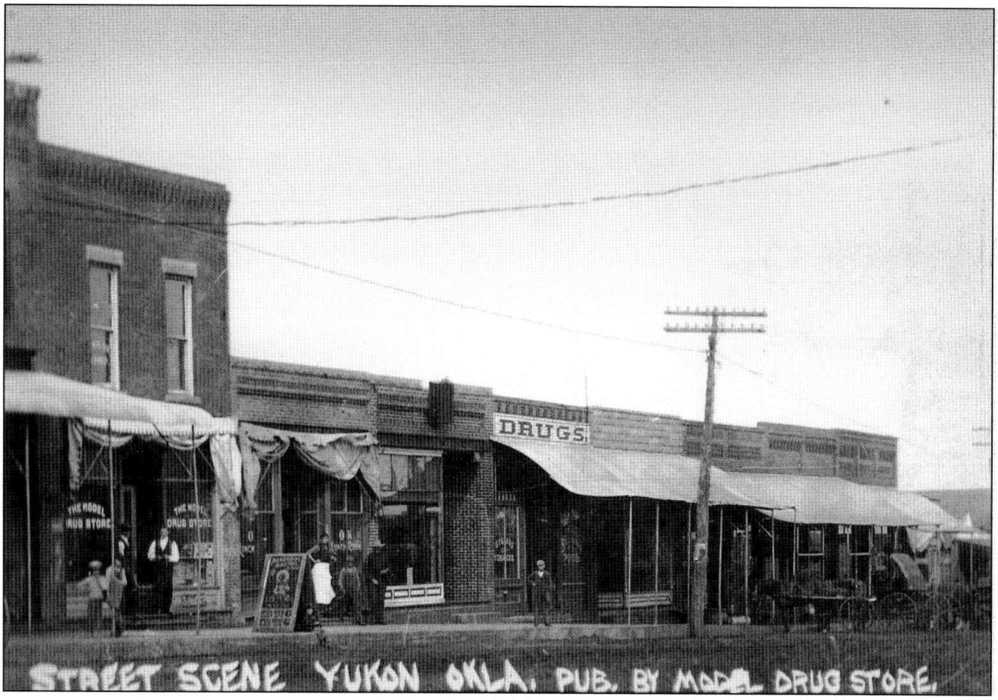

In this undated photograph, Model Drug Store is shown on the far left on the north side of Spencer Avenue. On the second story, above the store, the window reads, "Tailor Shop." Next to the store is the OK Lunch Room. The other businesses run east all the way to the northwest corner of today's Fourth and Main Streets, where buggies and horses are shown waiting out front. (Courtesy Genie Vinson.)

The Model....
Confectionery

HIGH CLASS
CANDIES
CONFECTIONS
FRUITS
NUTS
CIGARS
CIGARETTES
SMOKERS' SUPPLIES

Crystal Ice Cream
Crystal Dainties
Crystal Brickletts

WARM IN WINTER
COOL IN SUMMER

Hot and Cold Drinks in Season

In 1917, Model Drug Store owner C.N. Jeffers gave a kit to each soldier leaving for World War I. Each kit contained a safety razor, toothpaste, and shaving soap. Other merchants followed suit. Women began making kits, bandages, and other items. In this 1923 advertisement, C.N. Jeffers lists the sweets he sold at his other business, Model Confectionery. (Courtesy Phil Carson family.)

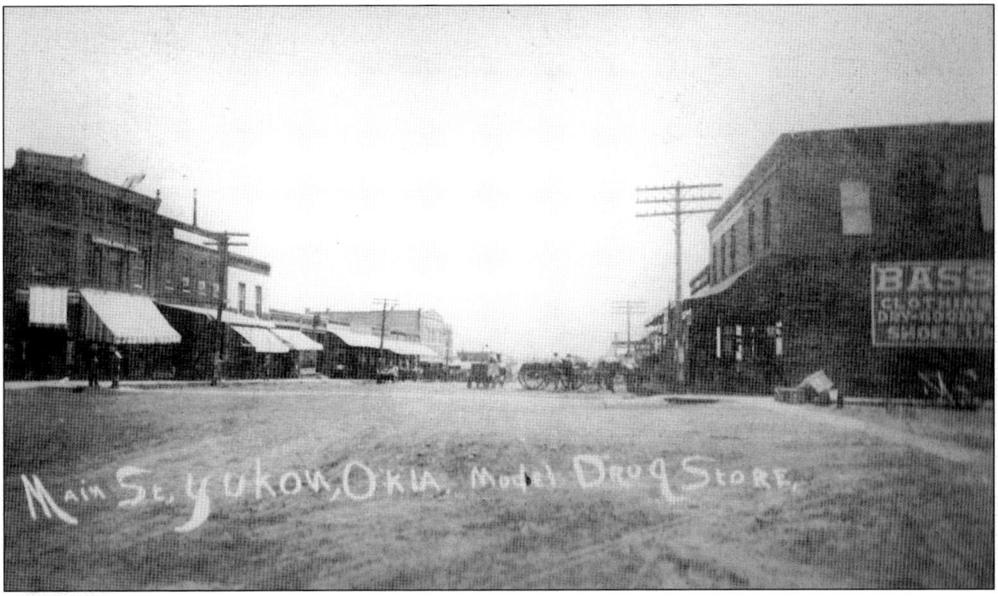

Looking east from Fifth Street and Spencer Avenue, this c. 1910 photograph shows the Bass Building at far right, with the words "Bass," "Clothing," "Dry-Goods," and "Shoes" on the side. The Mulvey Building is at center. Two men chat on the corner at far left. Horses, wagons, and people are in the street. (Courtesy Genie Vinson.)

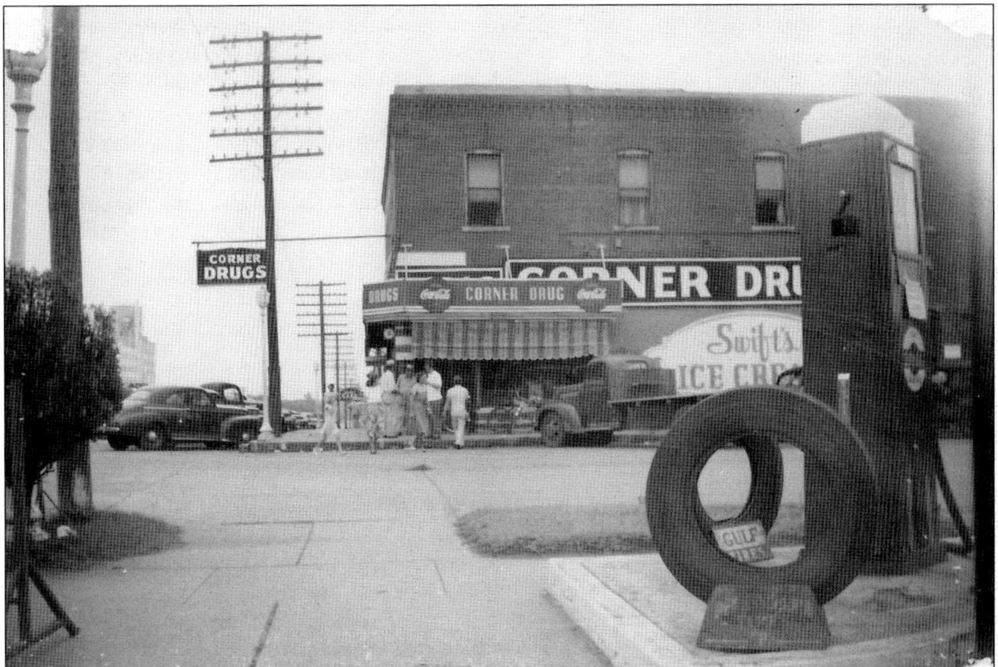

In the 1930s, Corner Drug occupied the retail space in the northwest corner of the Bass Building. Besides the usual drug store items, it had a popular fountain where locals enjoyed ice cream, sodas, and sandwiches. The gas station in the foreground was on the southwest corner of Fifth and Main Streets. (Courtesy Betty Sackett and the Trch family archives.)

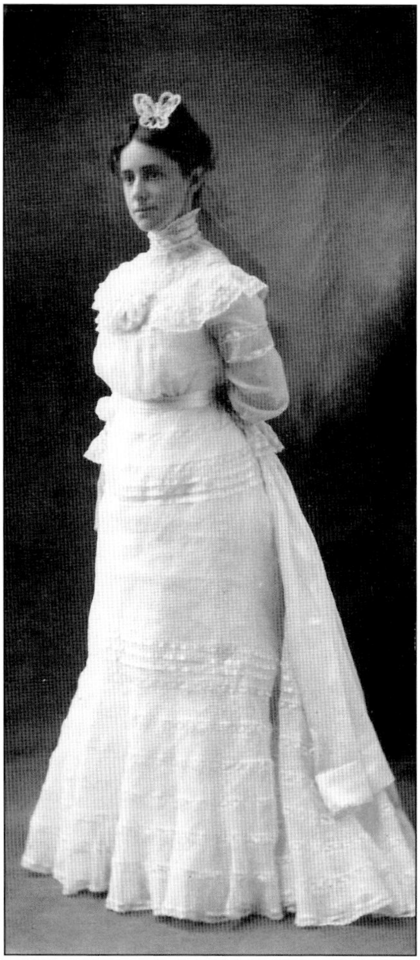

First known as District No. 5 and built around 1890 on land platted to include a school, Spring Creek School's first building was a one-room structure north of Hefner Road and Highway 4. Emma Sanger is shown wearing her 1898 high school graduation dress. She drove her horse and buggy to teach at Spring Creek from 1899 to 1900. She married George Bass. (Courtesy Bass and Ramey families.)

During the 1914–1915 school term, locals completed this cement block, one-room Spring Creek School. They used sand to make the blocks with a block machine. Students walked to school or arrived on horseback or in buggies. A now-giant tree grew out of the girls' outhouse in back. Now private property, the structure stands at the intersection of Hefner Road and Highway 4. (Courtesy Betty Sackett and the Trch family archives.)

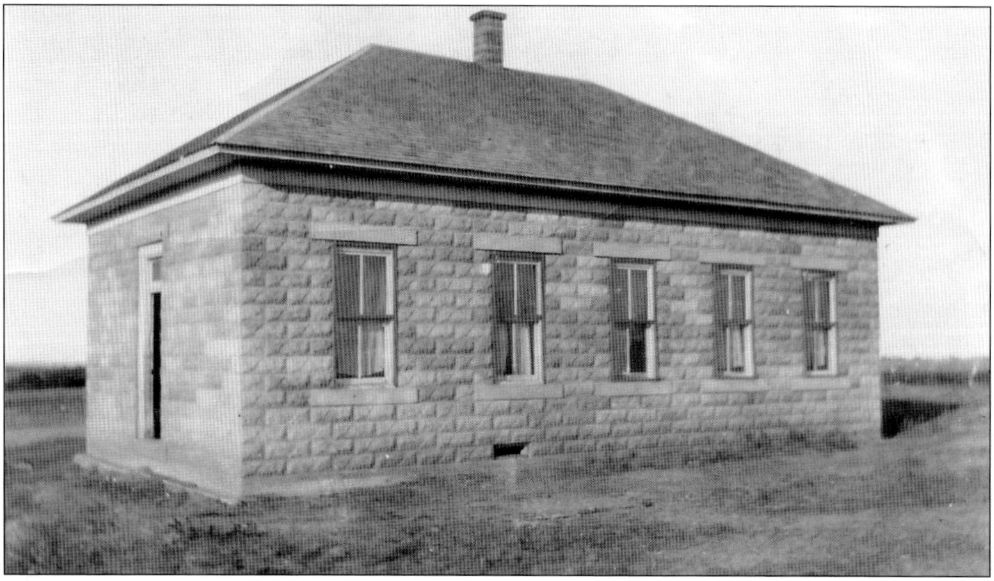

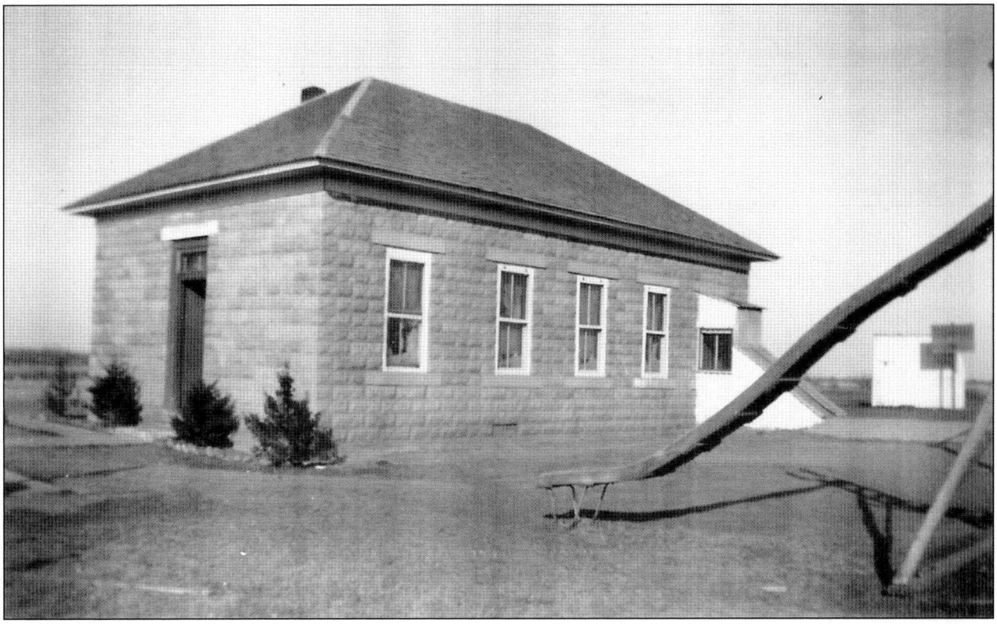

Note the door leading from the school to the underground tornado shelter, built in the 1920s. An 1897 issue of the *Church Bell* daily newspaper, published in El Reno, Oklahoma Territory, includes an advertisement selling "cyclone caves" and "a cyclone policy," calling tornadoes "the Monster Cyclone" and saying no area "will be exempt from this great destroyer of both property and life." (Courtesy Betty Sackett and the Trch family archives.)

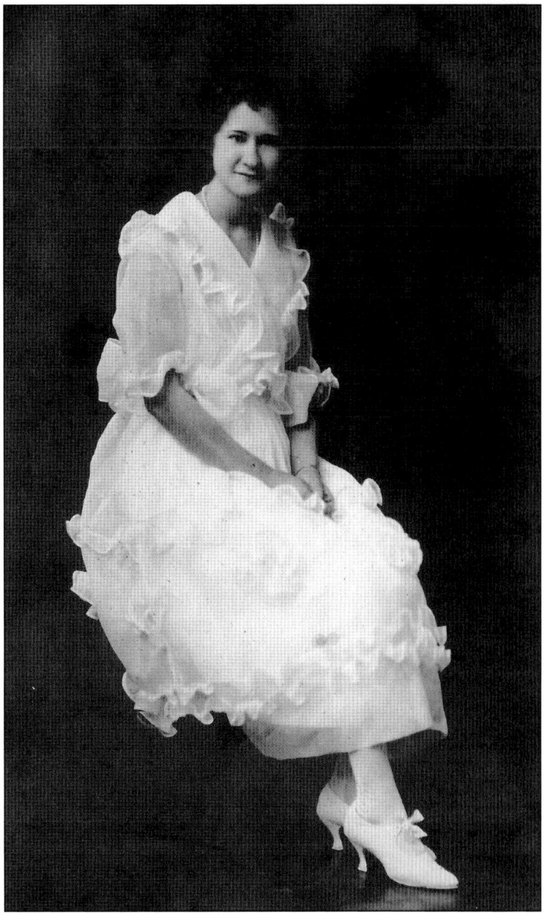

Anna Yeck wears her high school graduation dress. After graduating from Yukon High School in 1921, she attended Edmond's Central State Teachers College, now the University of Central Oklahoma, during summer 1921. She taught at Spring Creek School. Anna was bilingual, and spent extra time helping Czech students learn English. (Courtesy LaVerne and Victor Benda family.)

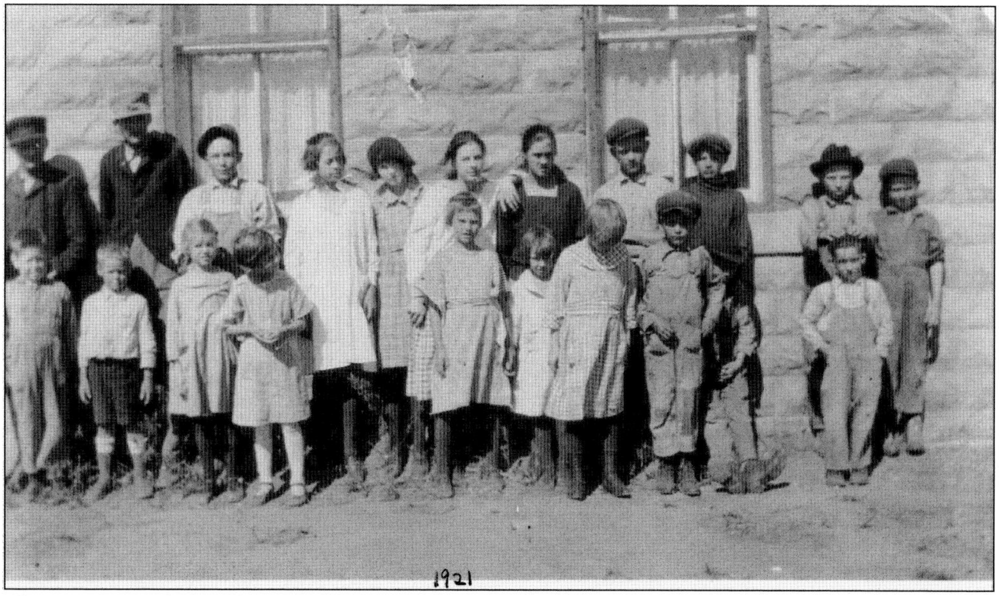

Shown are students who attended Spring Creek School in 1921. Numerous rural schools, just like Spring Creek, peppered the area. After finishing eighth grade, students often entered Yukon schools. After the new block building was erected, Ike Simmons purchased the original, 1890 one-room building, moving it to his farm one mile east and using it to store hay. (Courtesy Betty Sackett and the Trch family archives.)

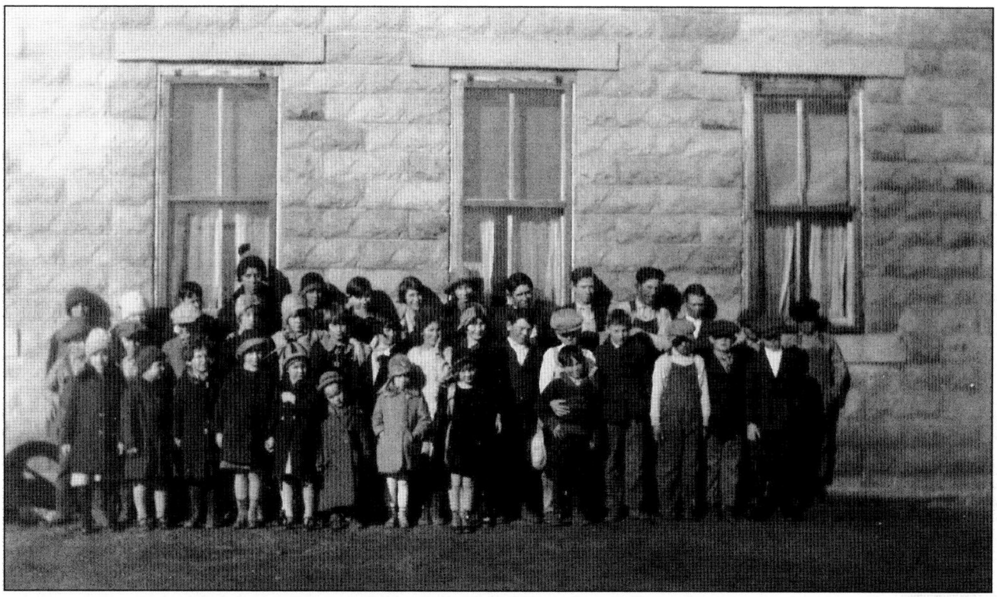

Pictured here are Spring Creek students. On the school grounds, there was a coal house that also served as a shelter for horse feed. There were also two outdoor toilets and a wood house. During winter, older boys took turns bringing fuel in from the coal house so the teacher could build a fire the next morning. Teachers arrived early on cold mornings to get the room warm before the students arrived. (Courtesy Betty Sackett and the Trch family archives.)

This photograph shows students who attended Spring Creek School during the 1932–1933 school year. (Courtesy Betty Sackett and the Trch family archives.)

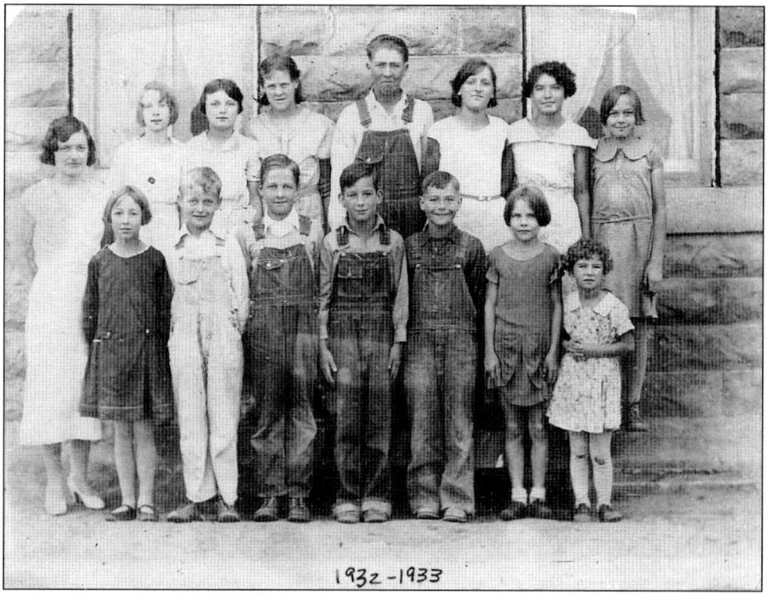

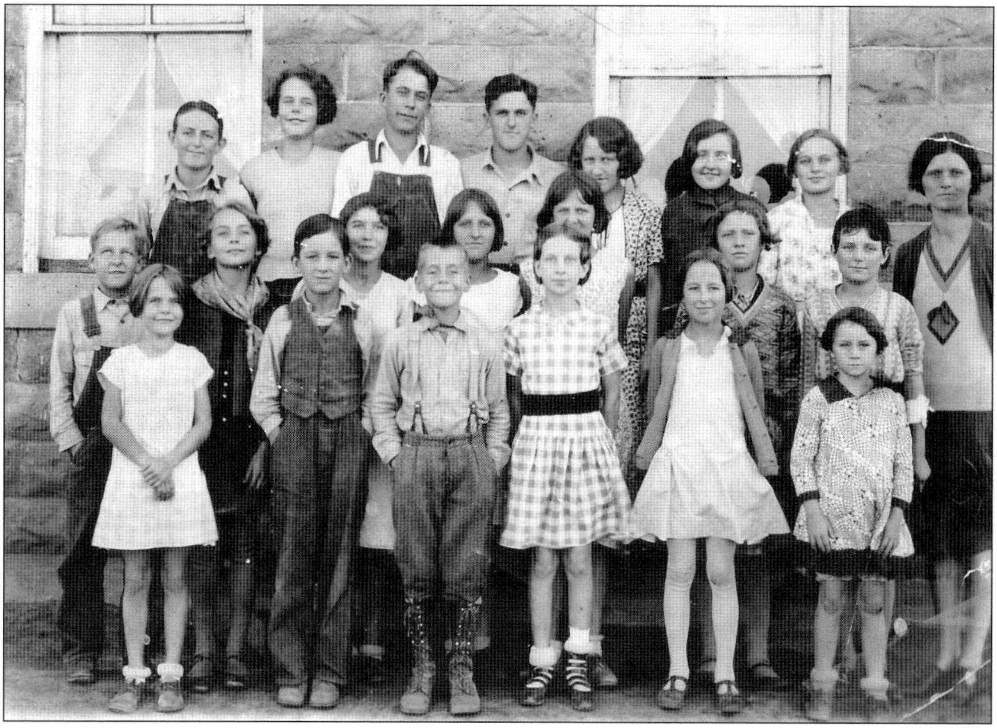

Born on a Canadian County farm in 1918, Adelene Trch stands third from right in the back row in this Spring Creek class photograph. (Trch rhymes with "church.") The school was on Adelene's parents' farm. She attended Spring Creek from first through eighth grades. Teachers at most rural schools taught first through eighth grades. Spring Creek School was annexed to the Yukon School District in July 1947. (Courtesy Betty Sackett and the Trch family archives.)

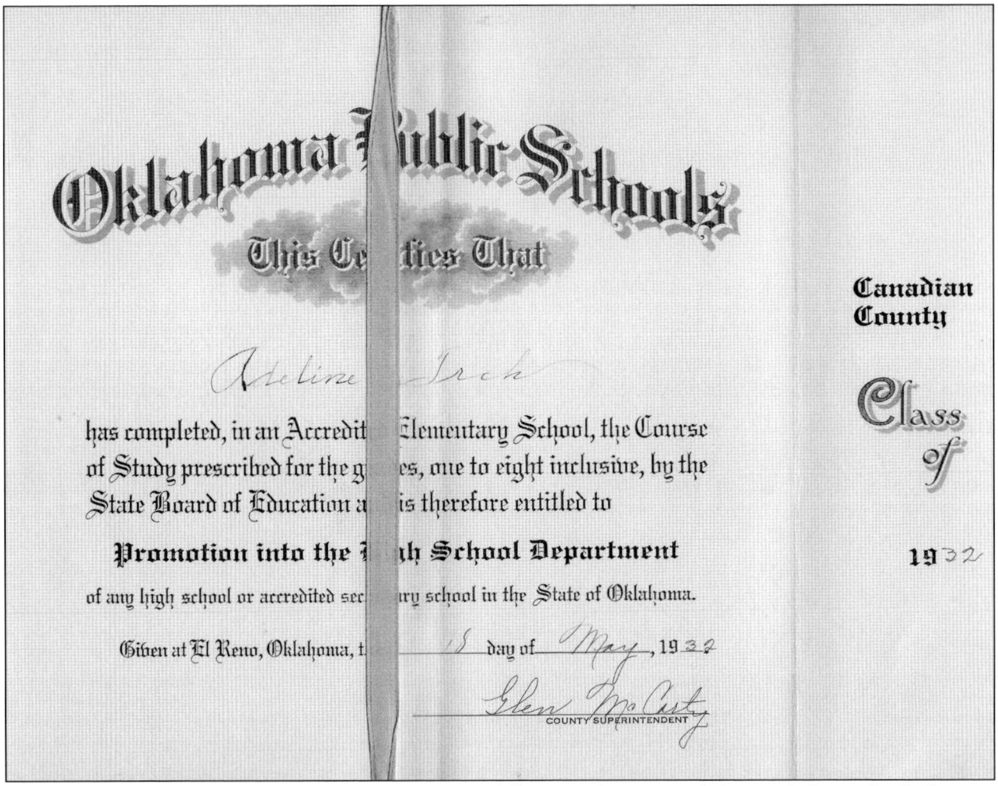

Oklahoma ublic Schools

This Ce tifies That

Canadian County

Class of 1932

Adeline Trch

has completed, in an Accredit Elementary School, the Course of Study prescribed for the g es, one to eight inclusive, by the State Board of Education a is therefore entitled to

Promotion into the gh School Department

of any high school or accredited sec ary school in the State of Oklahoma.

Given at El Reno, Oklahoma, t 15 day of May, 1932

Glen McCarty
COUNTY SUPERINTENDENT

Adelene Trch received this eighth-grade diploma upon graduating from Spring Creek in 1932, although her first name is spelled incorrectly. She then attended Yukon Public Schools for ninth through twelfth grades, graduating in 1936. Not all students continued with their education after eighth grade. The last classes at Spring Creek School were held in 1945. (Courtesy Betty Sackett and the Trch family archives.)

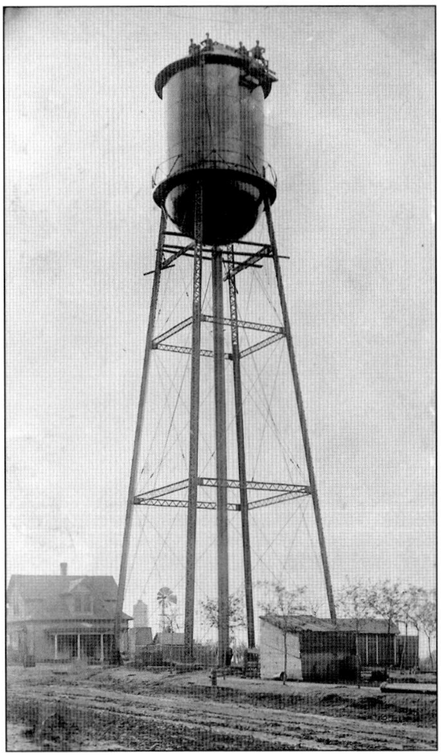

By 1910, Yukon's population was 1,016. On April 16, 1911, the city erected its first water tower on the southwest corner of the Central School yard. Four people are atop the water tower in this 1911 photograph. (Courtesy Yukon Historical Society.)

There were rural schools, such as Spring Creek, tucked in among area farms. But the first school actually located in Yukon was a subscription school, established in 1891 in a Baptist church at Sixth and Main Streets. From 1894 through 1895, the Methodist Episcopal South Church housed the school. This photograph's note simply states that Maud Littier was a Yukon teacher around 1895. (Courtesy Yukon Historical Society.)

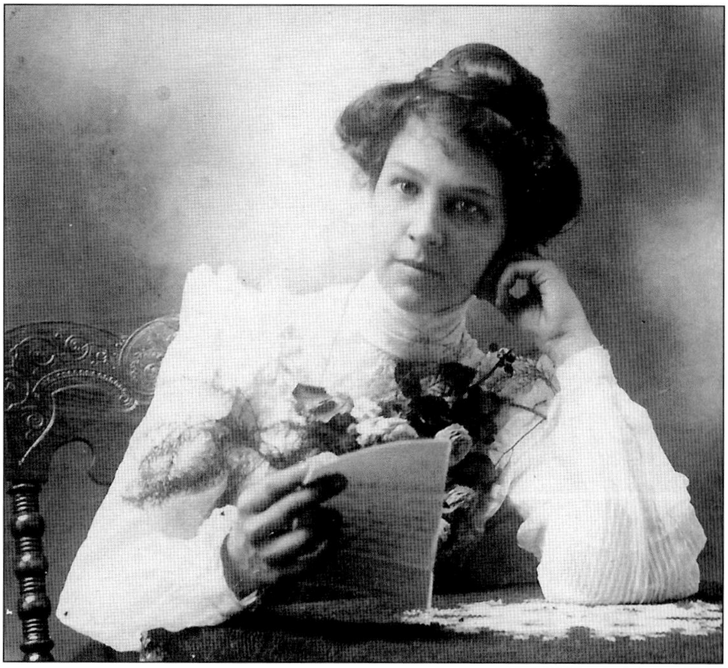

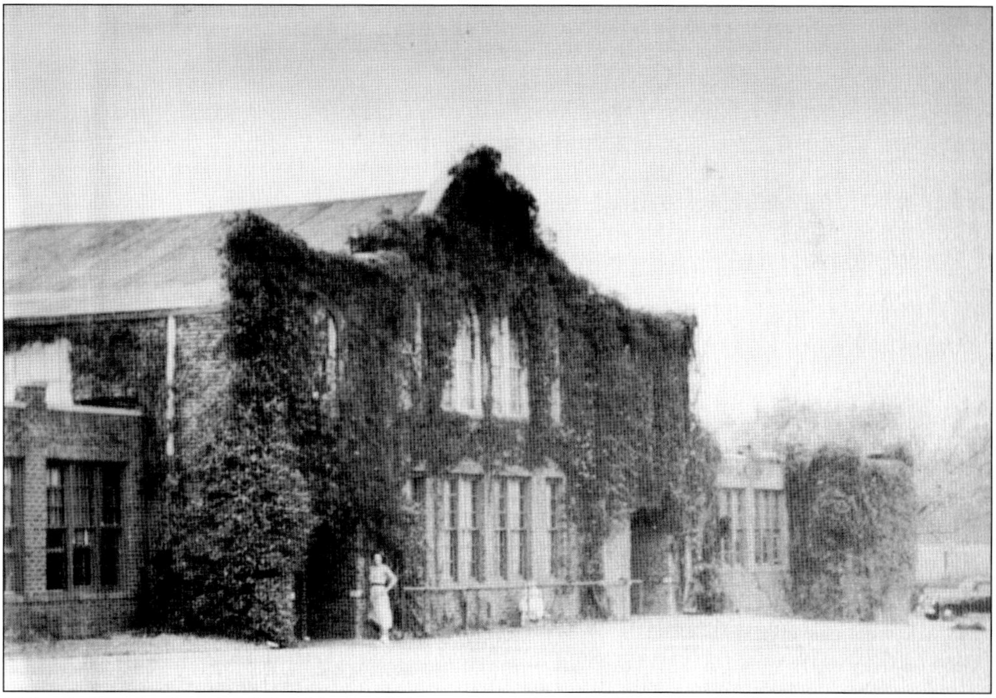

Yukon's first high school building was constructed in 1925 at Ninth and Oak Streets. Locals named the building "The Alamo," referring to its architectural similarity to the famous mission in Texas. (Courtesy Phil Carson family.)

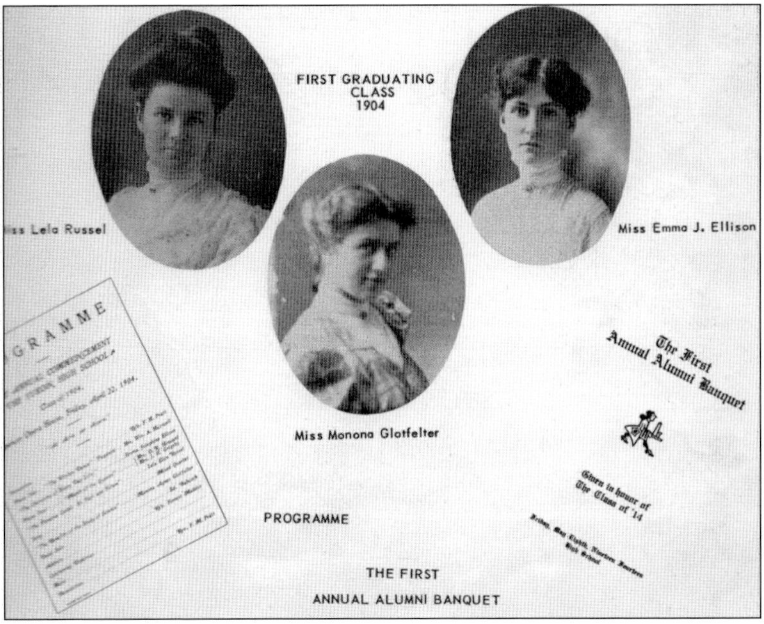

The first high school students graduated in 1904. This yearbook photograph shows all three graduates. Yukon's first school superintendent was Dr. F.M. Sanger, one of Emma Sanger Bass's brothers. He and his wife, Dr. Winnie Sanger, started Yukon High School in 1901. (Courtesy Bass and Ramey families.)

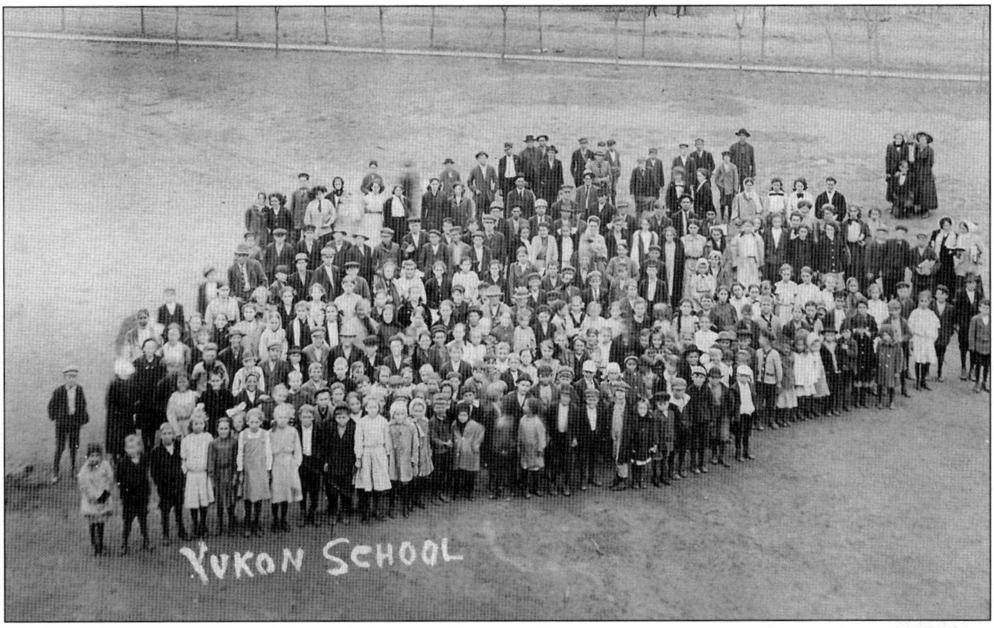

Around 1896, residents voted to build a two-story brick building on land that A.N. Spencer set aside for a school. In 1910, residents voted to build a new building with two stories and a basement. This c. 1910 photograph shows a large group of Yukon school students. (Courtesy Bass and Ramey families.)

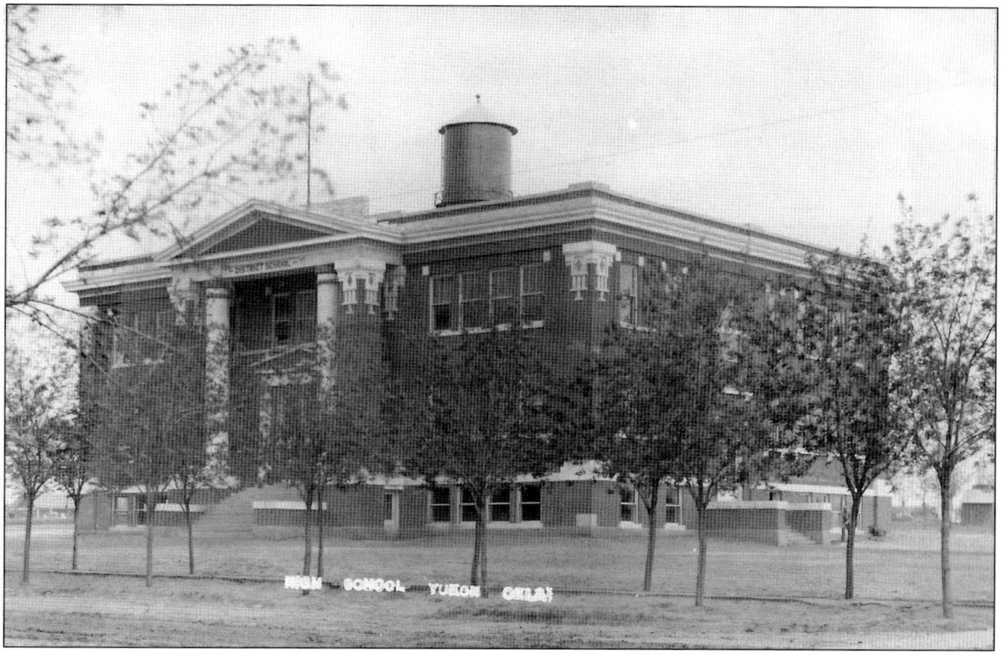

Shown here in 1912 and labeled "High School Yukon Okla," Yukon's District School still stands at Sixth and Oak Streets. Yukon's first water tower is visible behind the school. The building, known as "Old Central," is no longer a school. (Courtesy Genie Vinson.)

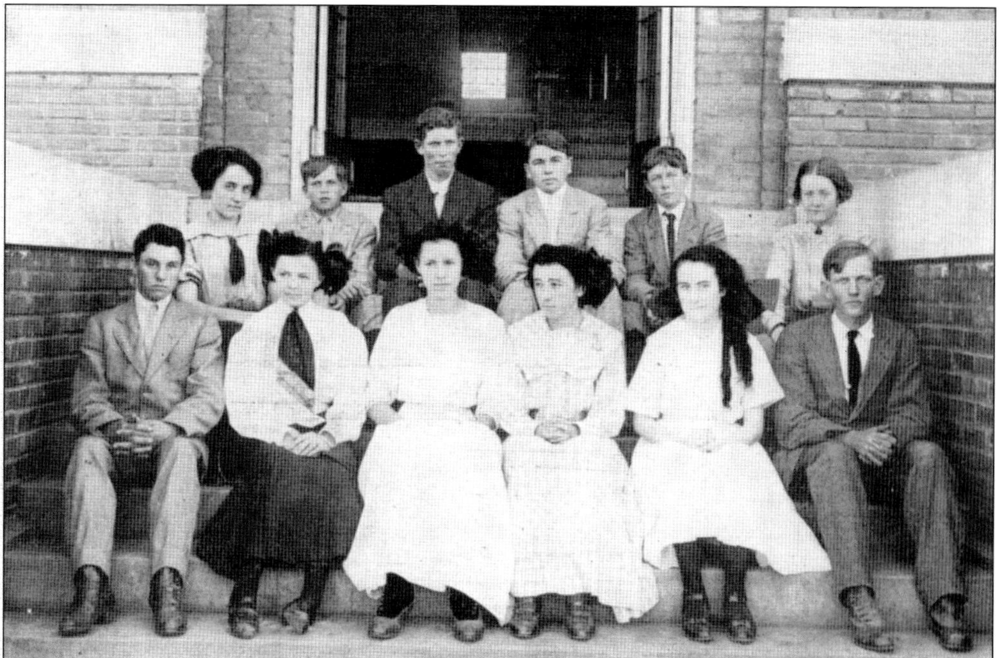

In this 1912 yearbook image, the sophomore class includes Frances Carson, Joe Dobry, Allie Mulvey, and Albert Wheatley, among others. These students were from well-known pioneer families who helped build Yukon. (Courtesy Phil Carson family.)

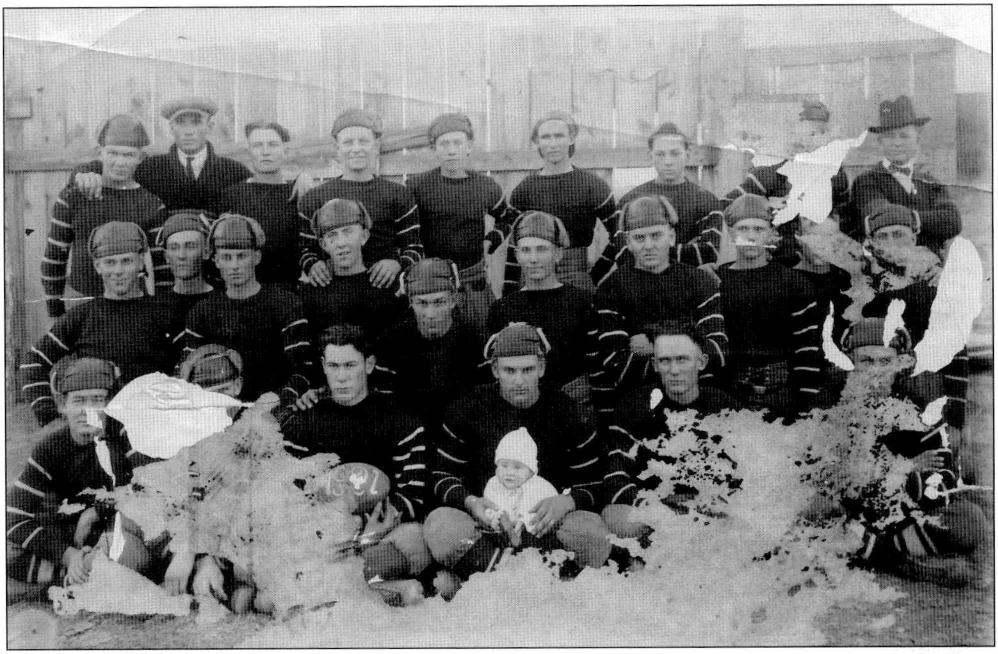

This photograph is likely from around the 1910s or 1920s. In 1912, the first Yukon football team took the field and included students and young businessmen. Note the player holding a baby, and the leather helmets. The players wear Yukon High School jerseys. (Courtesy Yukon Historical Society.)

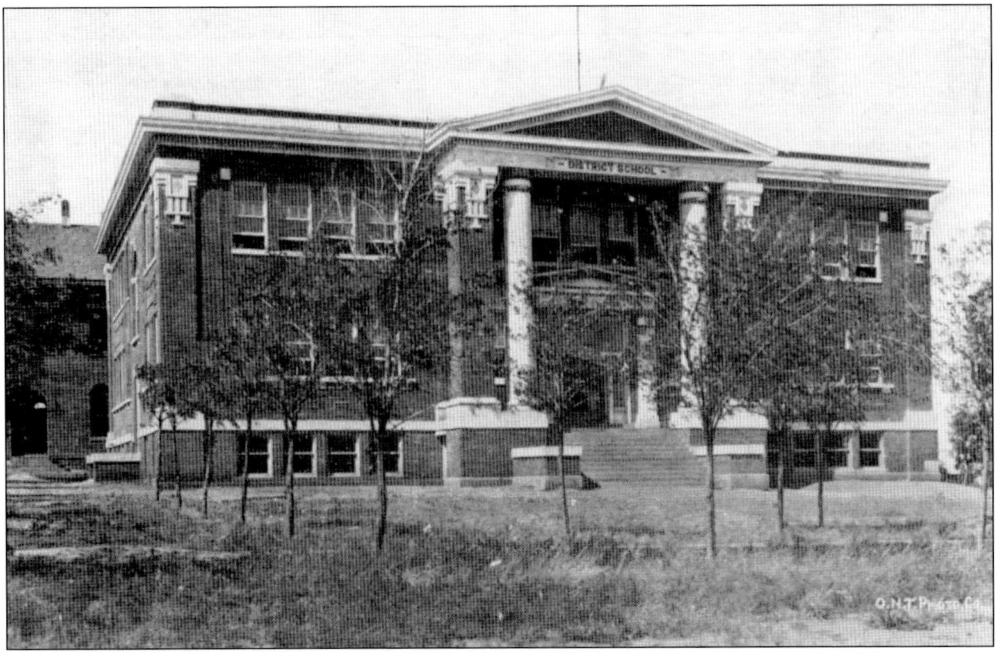

Located at Sixth and Oak Streets, Old Central towers over the area in this undated photograph. Megastar Garth Brooks grew up in Yukon. The home where his family lived is called the Graceland of Yukon. Brooks attended Yukon Public Schools' more modern buildings, and participated in football, baseball, and track and field. (Courtesy Bass and Ramey families.)

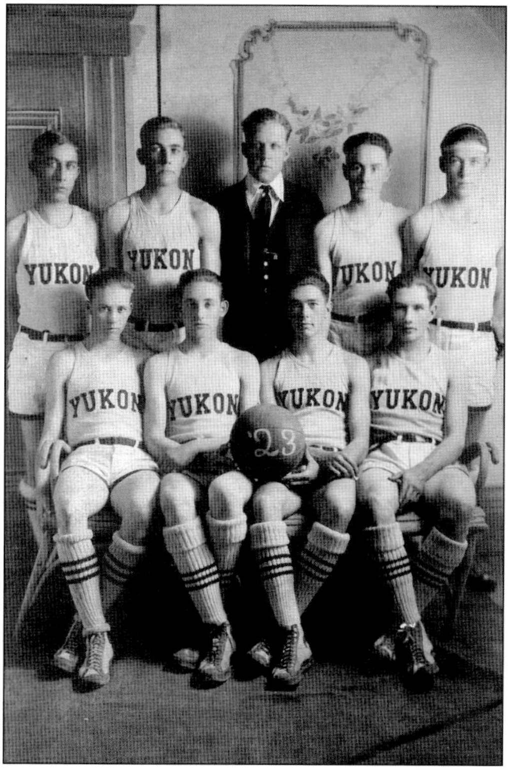

A 1923 Yukon Public School basketball team is shown here. From left to right are (first row) Virgil Compton, Sam Shehan, "Buck" Sanger, and Alva Tharp; (second row) Earl Harris, Roy Allen, coach Ralph Meyers, Charles Wheatley, and George Phillips. Meyers served in many positions in the schools, including as superintendent. (Courtesy Phil Carson family.)

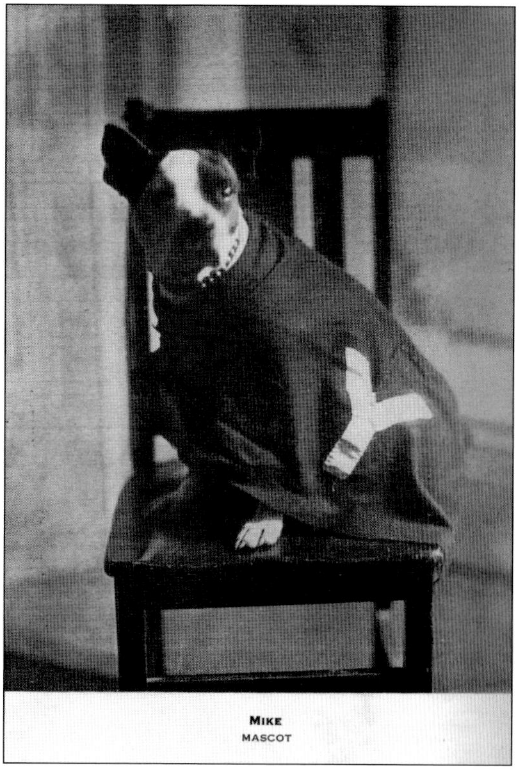

The Yukon Public School District has had numerous mascots. Shown here in a 1923 yearbook image is Mike, an early mascot. Today's Yukon students have the Miller Man as their mascot, representing Yukon's past flour mills. (Courtesy Phil Carson family.)

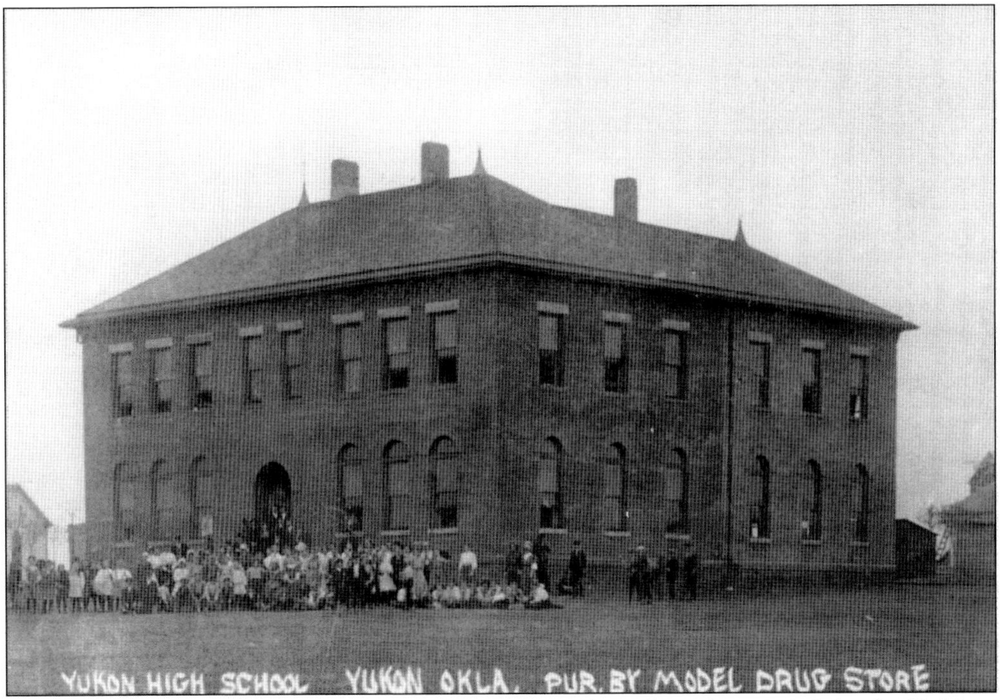

Printed by Model Drug Store, this undated postcard simply reads "Yukon High School." Children and adults are gathered around the school. (Courtesy Yukon Historical Society.)

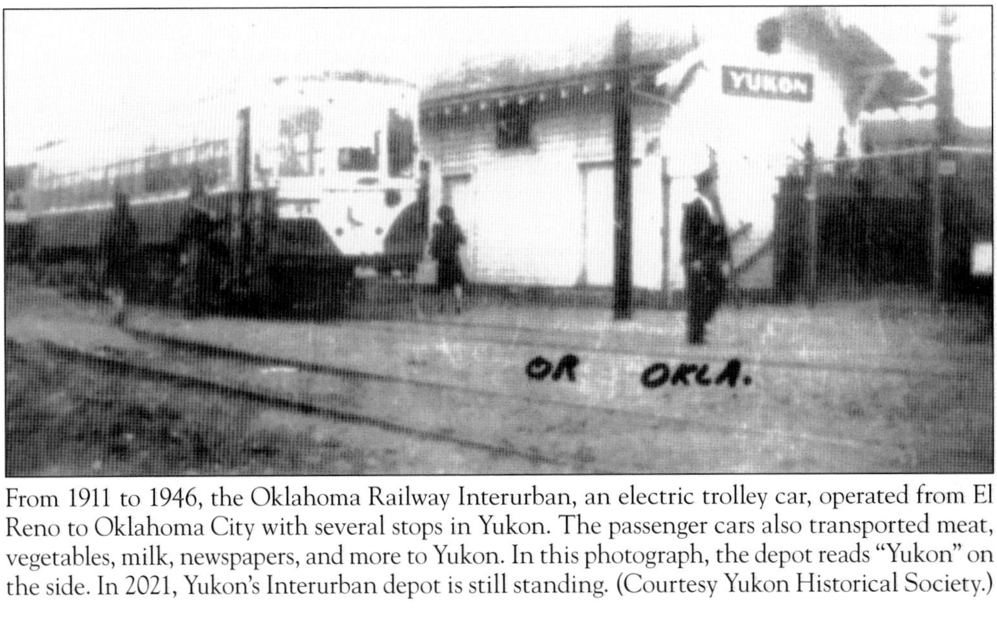

From 1911 to 1946, the Oklahoma Railway Interurban, an electric trolley car, operated from El Reno to Oklahoma City with several stops in Yukon. The passenger cars also transported meat, vegetables, milk, newspapers, and more to Yukon. In this photograph, the depot reads "Yukon" on the side. In 2021, Yukon's Interurban depot is still standing. (Courtesy Yukon Historical Society.)

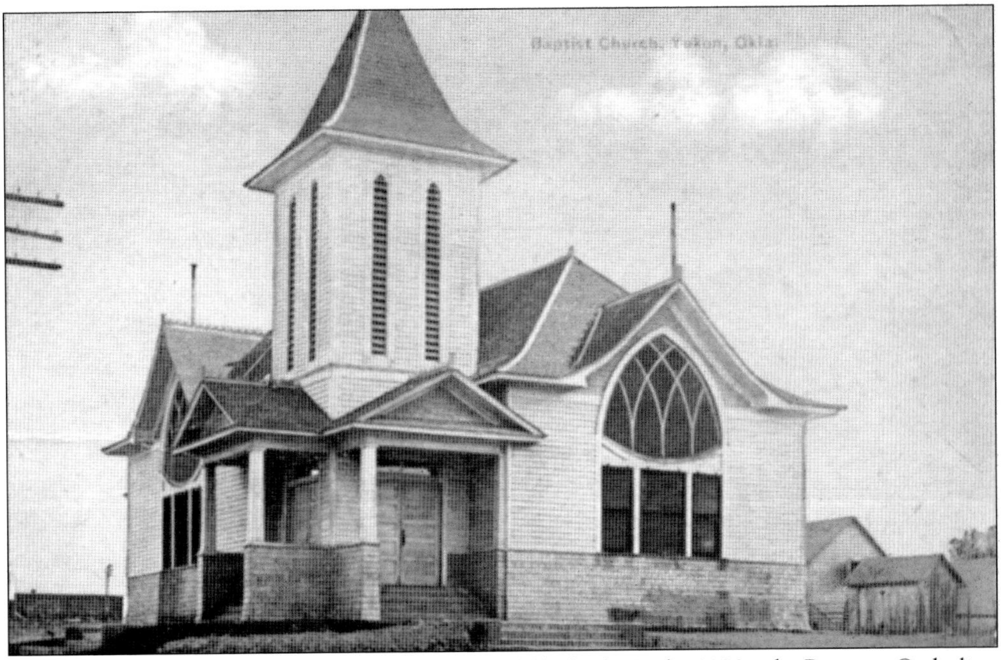

A.N. Spencer donated lots on which churches could be built. In the 1890s, the Baptists, Catholics, Methodists, and the Christian Church built Yukon's first four small churches. First to build in 1891, this painting shows the First Baptist Church in 1912. (Courtesy Yukon Historical Society.)

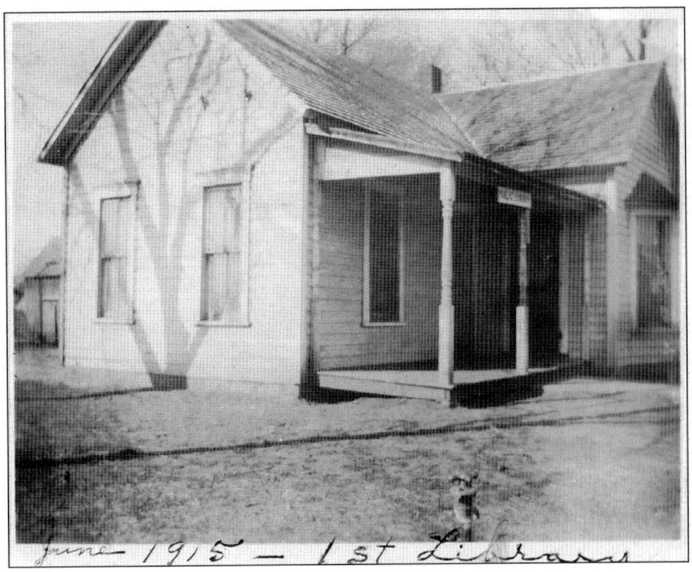

Originally named the Franklin Library Club, the Ladies Library Club raised funds through oyster suppers, ice-cream suppers, plays, and donations. In 1915, they purchased this three-room house on Elm Street and used the living room for the first public library. The librarian lived in the other two rooms. When they hired school librarian Mabel Fry in 1931, the library's hours expanded. (Courtesy Yukon Historical Society.)

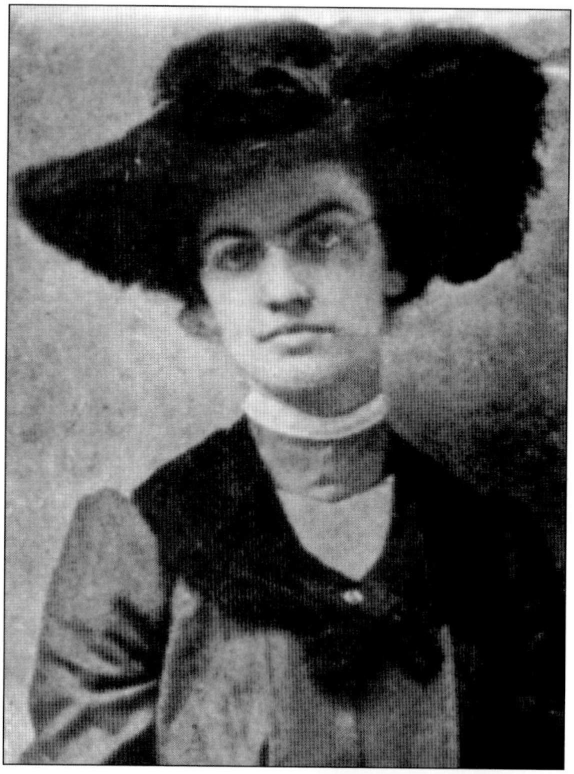

A Kansan born in 1884, Mabel Fry arrived in Yukon in December 1889. She was instrumental in organizing school music programs and worked as the high school librarian. For almost 50 years, Fry served as librarian for the Yukon Library, which was later named after her. She placed books that she thought were naughty or dirty under her desk so they could not be checked out. (Courtesy Yukon Historical Society.)

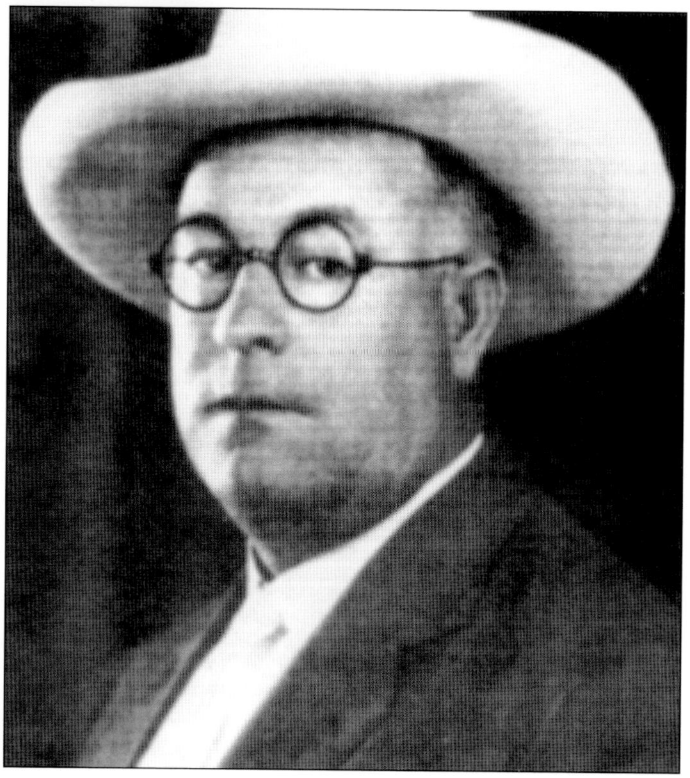

Isaac Alexander Floyd Jr., known as "Pop" Floyd, was born in 1885. He was a fearless crime fighter who worked in law enforcement in Indian Territory and southern Oklahoma, and at the Oklahoma State Penitentiary in McAlester. He served as Yukon's city marshal from 1931 until his death in 1959. (Courtesy Betty Sackett.)

Two

Flour, Suds, and Progress

Yukon was founded by Americans. They had European ancestors, but they were rough-and-tumble, true-grit Americans who considered the frontier available for the taking. They were brimming with ideas, and they saw the prairie as a blank slate, a place to experiment and bring their dreams to fruition.

However, European upheaval, and government persecution of Europeans, played a major role in Yukon's growth. In particular, a large Bohemian population gravitated to the area. Some had already suffered badly under the weight of the Austro-Hungarian Empire's yoke, or they had relatives who had endured horrible pain and suffering. Leaving their homelands behind and making the long and arduous journey across the Atlantic and into a foreign world was no small undertaking. It took guts and a hearty constitution.

Word of free land made its way to Europe. A few Bohemians made the Land Run of 1889, nabbing homesteads in the future Yukon. By 1899, large numbers of Bohemians were entering the area. They were hard at work, and founded their first lodge by 1899. Over time, the Bohemian population grew.

During the mid-20th century, due to political situations in Europe, the name "Bohemians" shifted to "Czechs."

Czechs in Yukon accomplished a lot. Many were farmers, and as sodbusters, they worked hard to create massive farms, raise livestock, and provide for their families. Others were entrepreneurs and businessmen. As a result, Yukon became home to farms, ranches, the Yukon Mill and Grain Company, the Dobry Flour Mills, and so much more.

At one point, Yukon started scooping up area farms, making them part of the growing town and giving their children access to Yukon schools. Yukon had a town band from 1908 to 1912. Electricity came to Yukon before other rural towns. The first cars belonged to men such as John Kroutil, Frank Kroutil, A.F. Dobry, George Bass, and twins Odie and Mike Mulvey.

Last but not least, Yukon gained the title "Czech Capital of Oklahoma."

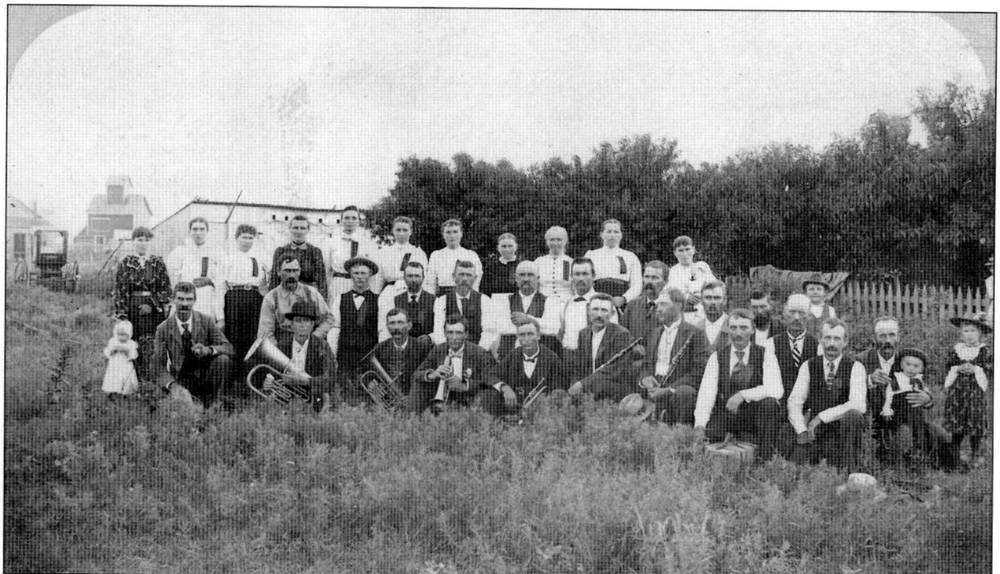

Yukon is home to Lodge Jan Žižka, organized in July 1899 in the yard of Karel Bruza's Yukon home. As the 67th member of the multi-state Czechoslovakian organization Západní Česko-Bratrská Jednota (ZČBJ), the lodge's early meetings were held in various members' homes. This July 1899 photograph in Yukon, Oklahoma Territory, shows charter members of Lodge Jan Žižka wearing badges. (Courtesy Yukon Czech Hall.)

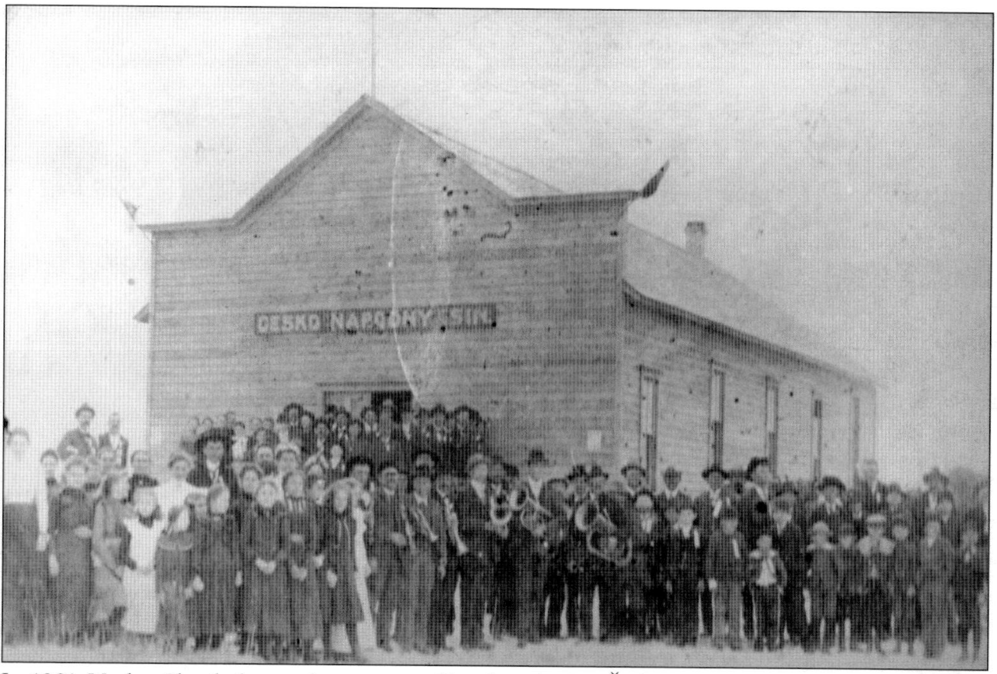

In 1901, Vaclav Slavik donated two acres of land to the Jan Žižka and T.J. Sokol lodges. Shown is the small hall built as a meeting place. In 1924, this building was razed in order to erect a larger one. Much of the wood from the original hall was used in the new building. (Courtesy Yukon Czech Hall.)

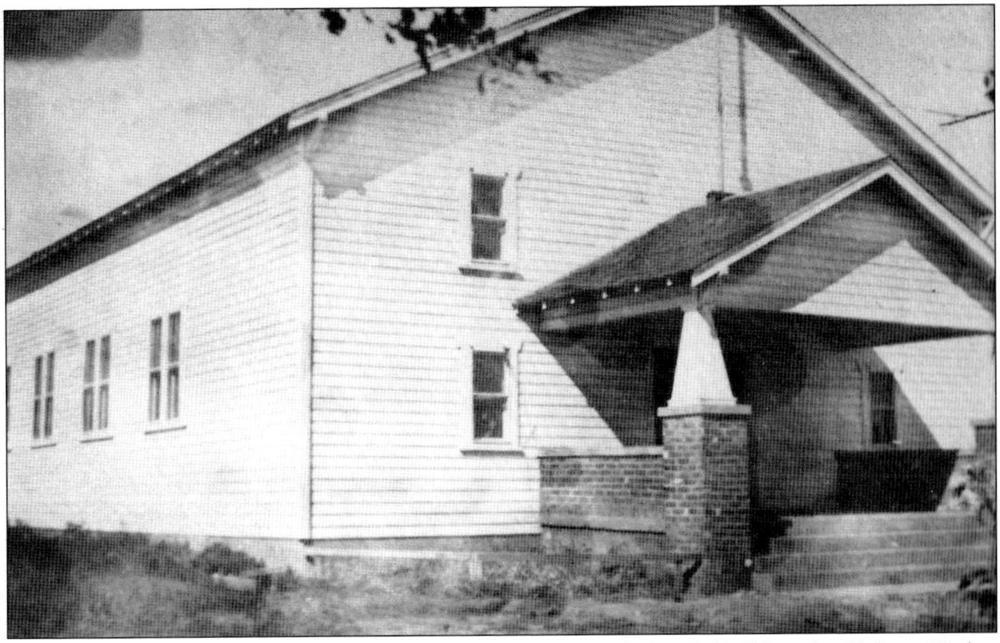

In 1924, volunteers built the current Czech Hall at 205 North Czech Hall Road in Yukon. With a May 1925 grand opening, the hall was named Bohemian Hall. Tony Blecha, whose parents were born in Bohemia, played his accordion as part of the band that played the first polka dance at the grand opening. Music is important to Czech heritage. (Courtesy Yukon Czech Hall.)

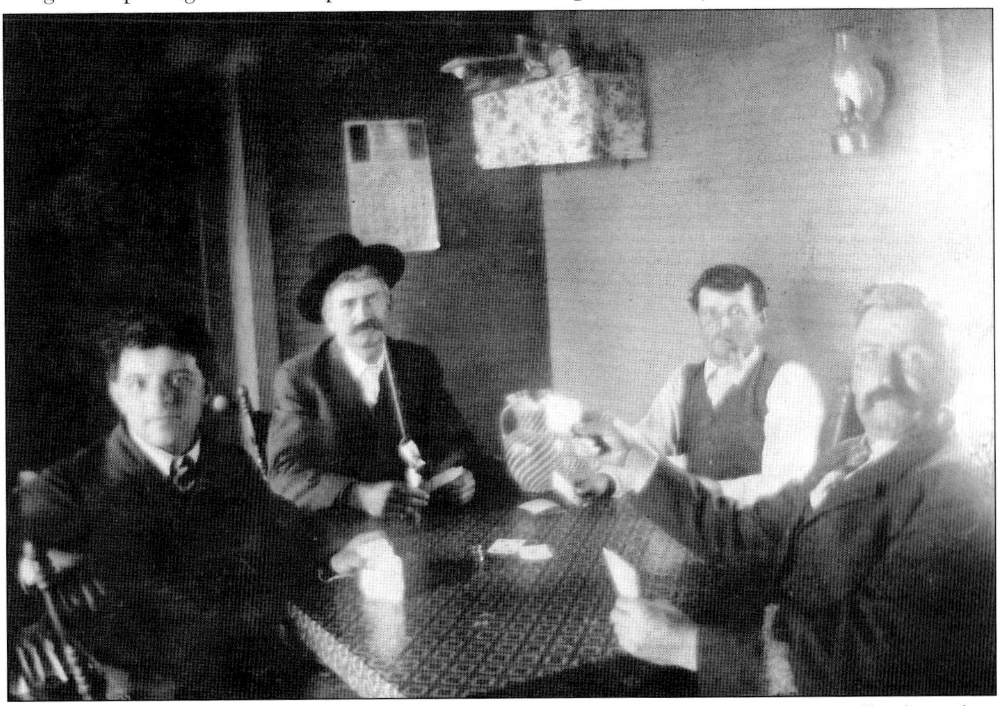

These men playing cards are likely gathered in the basement of the current Czech Hall, where they often played cards one night each week. At the same time, the women socialized upstairs, and young Sokol members practiced their gymnastics and drills. (Courtesy LaVerne and Victor Benda family.)

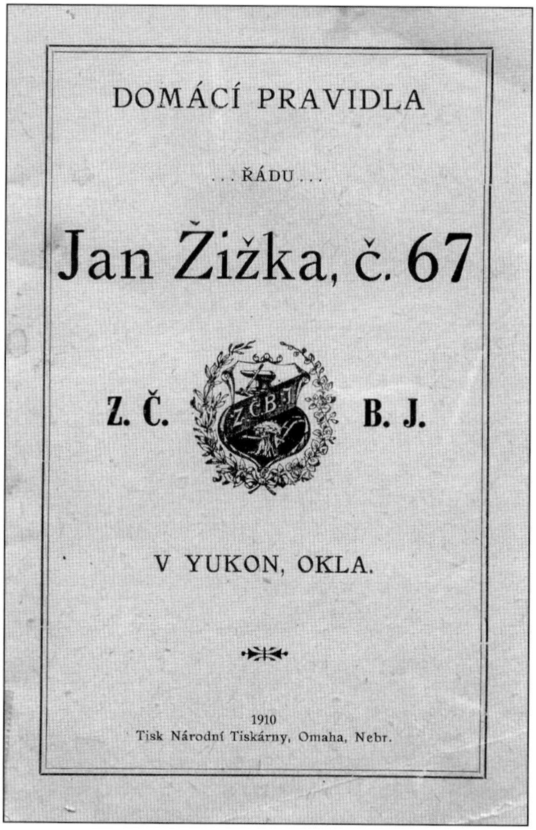
DOMÁCÍ PRAVIDLA

. . . ŘÁDU . . .

Jan Žižka, č. 67

Z. Č. B. J.

V YUKON, OKLA.

1910
Tisk Národní Tiskárny, Omaha, Nebr.

Through time, the Czech Hall building received various updates and additions and expanded with more land. In 1945, people began calling the venue "Czech Hall," or "Yukon Czech Hall," rather than Bohemian Hall. In 1970, the Oklahoma Historical Society honored the hall as an official historic site. In November 1980, it was listed in the National Register of Historic Places. (Courtesy Yukon Czech Hall.)

Early meetings at Czech Hall were conducted in the Czech language. But since 1945, the English language has been spoken at meetings. This Czechoslovakian primer, printed in Chicago, was used to teach the Czech language. (Courtesy Yukon Czech Hall.)

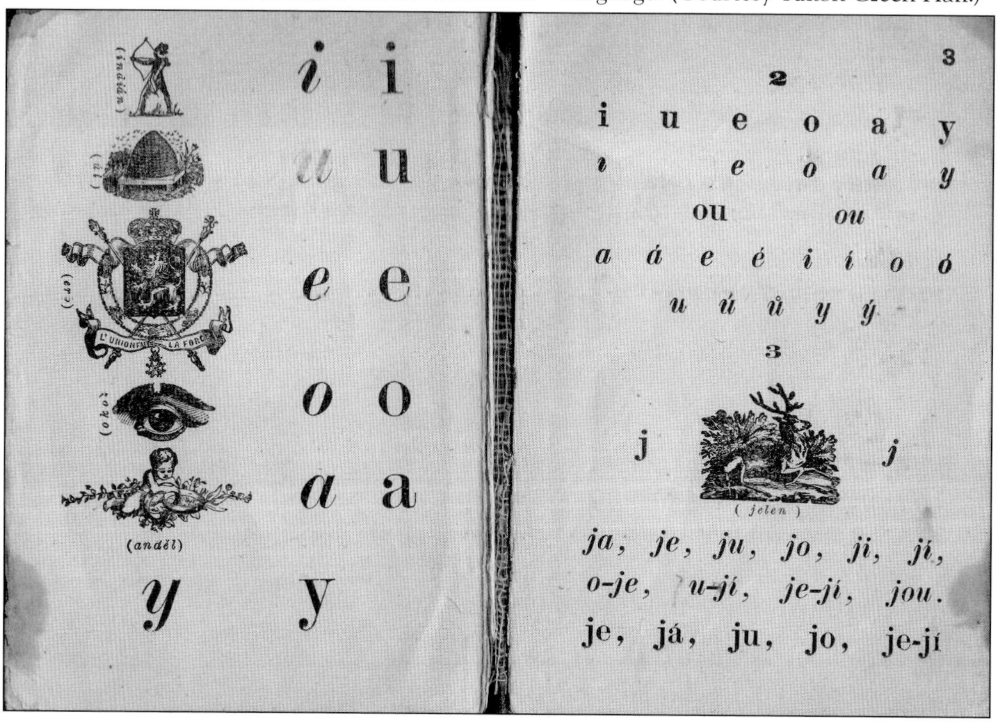

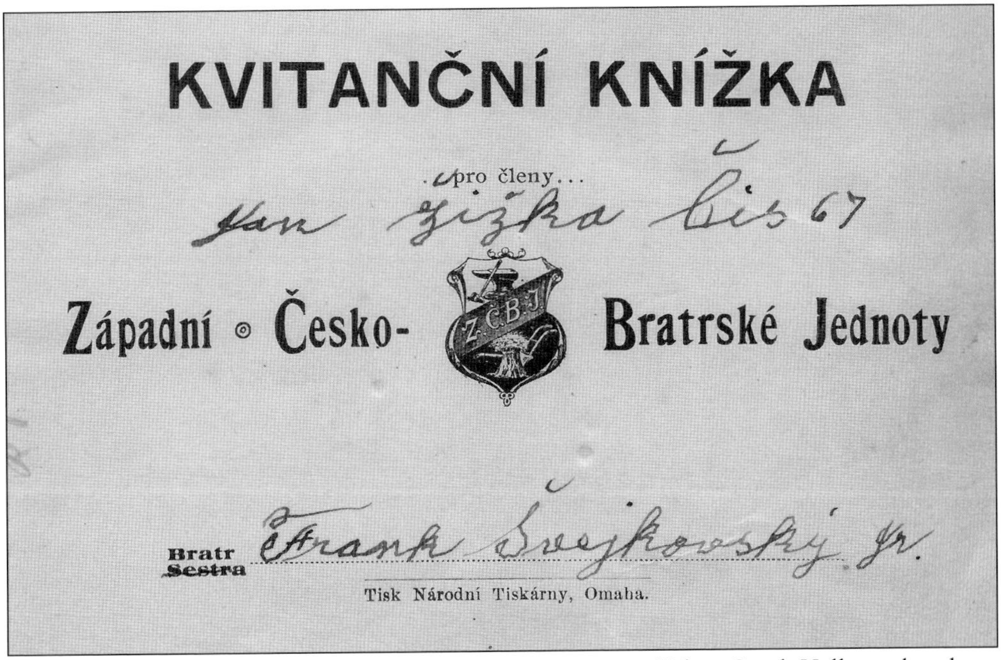

KVITANČNÍ KNÍŽKA

pro členy...

Jan Žižka čís 67

Západní Česko- Z.Č.B.J. Bratrské Jednoty

Bratr ~~Sestra~~ Frank Švejkovský Jr.

Tisk Národní Tiskárny, Omaha.

This receipt is written in the Czech language. For many years, Yukon Czech Hall members have been preserving their cultural memorabilia and displaying items museum-style in Czech Hall. (Courtesy Yukon Czech Hall.)

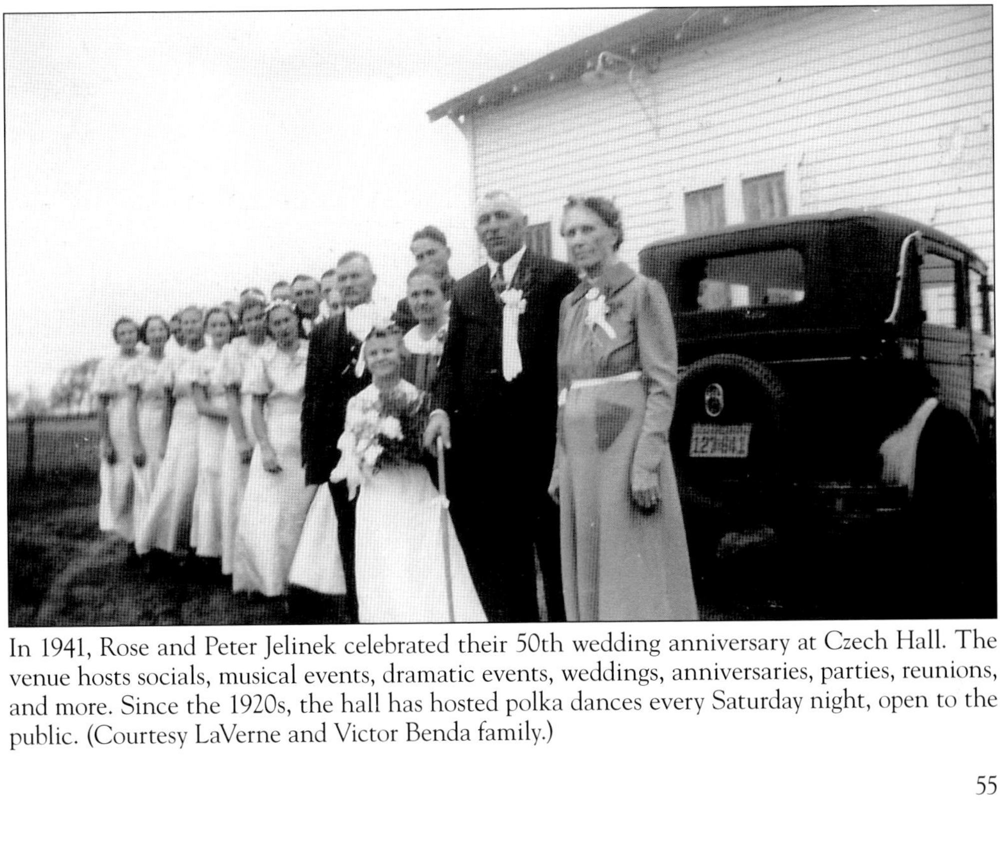

In 1941, Rose and Peter Jelinek celebrated their 50th wedding anniversary at Czech Hall. The venue hosts socials, musical events, dramatic events, weddings, anniversaries, parties, reunions, and more. Since the 1920s, the hall has hosted polka dances every Saturday night, open to the public. (Courtesy LaVerne and Victor Benda family.)

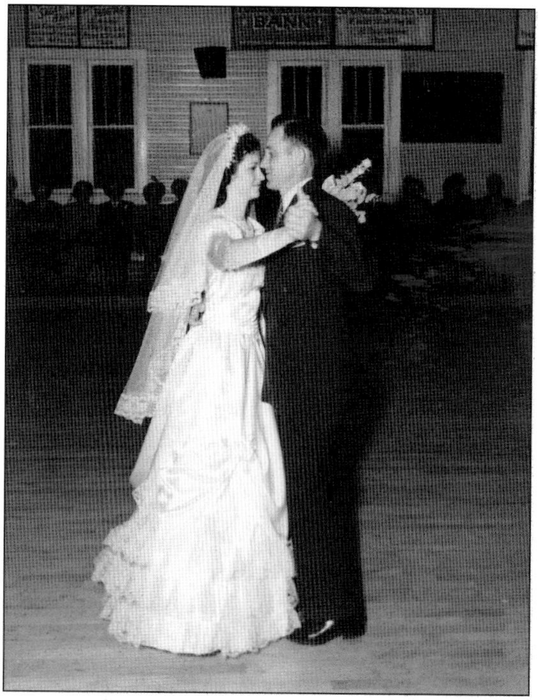

LaVerne Svejkovsky and Victor Benda married in 1949 and are shown dancing at Czech Hall. His parents and her grandparents were born in Bohemia. For over a century, many members of the Czech community have met their spouses at Czech Hall. (Courtesy LaVerne and Victor Benda family.)

In this undated photograph, Czech-American youth are likely gathered at the original Czech Hall. The girls in front wear sashes that read, from left to right, "Truth," "Love," and "Loyalty," the motto of the ZČBJ organization. (Courtesy Yukon Czech Hall.)

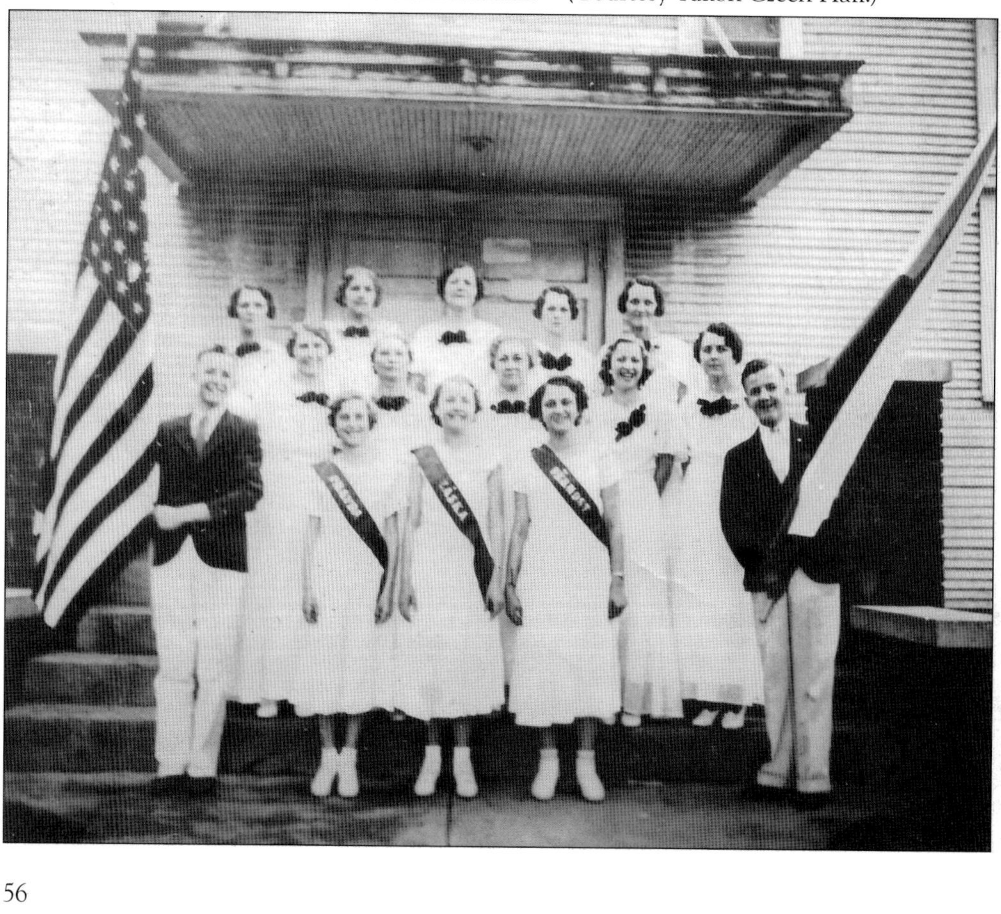

Shown is a very old script for a play that was performed at Czech Hall. Czech Hall remains a place for maintaining the Czech heritage, including language classes, lodge meetings, and public polka dances, and housing historical memorabilia. (Courtesy Yukon Czech Hall.)

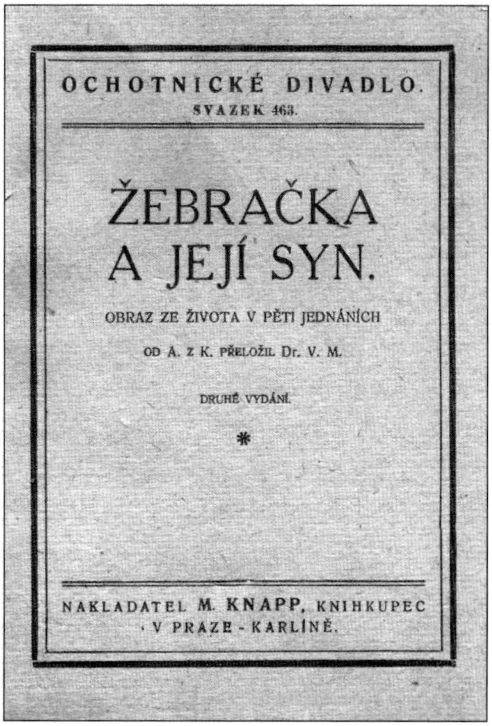
OCHOTNICKÉ DIVADLO.
SVAZEK 463.

ŽEBRAČKA A JEJÍ SYN.

OBRAZ ZE ŽIVOTA V PĚTI JEDNÁNÍCH

OD A. Z K. PŘELOŽIL Dr. V. M.

DRUHÉ VYDÁNÍ.

NAKLADATEL M. KNAPP, KNIHKUPEC
V PRAZE - KARLÍNĚ.

In Europe, Bohemian villages had their own distinct dances. The Austro-Hungarian Empire was persecuting Bohemians. In the 1800s, Bohemians took folk dances from multiple villages and put them together, creating the Beseda. This c. 1940s photograph shows the Yukon Sokol Beseda dance group. (Photograph by Gordon Dinsmore, courtesy LaVerne and Victor Benda family.)

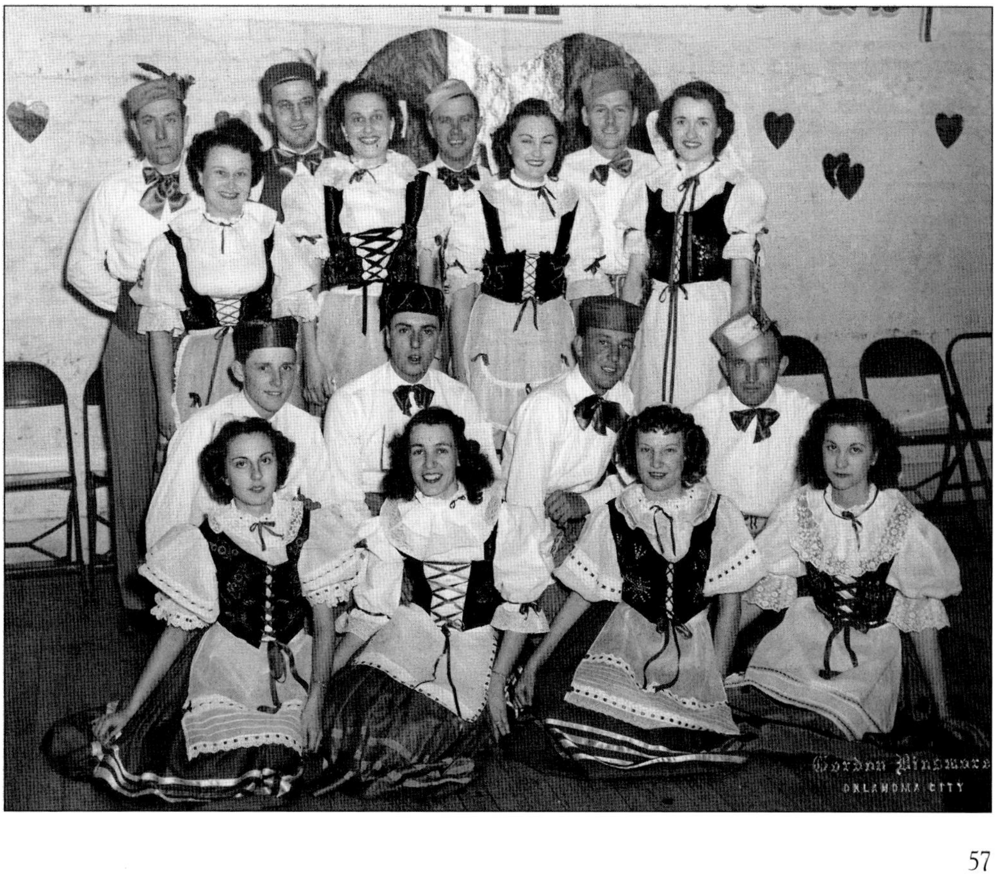

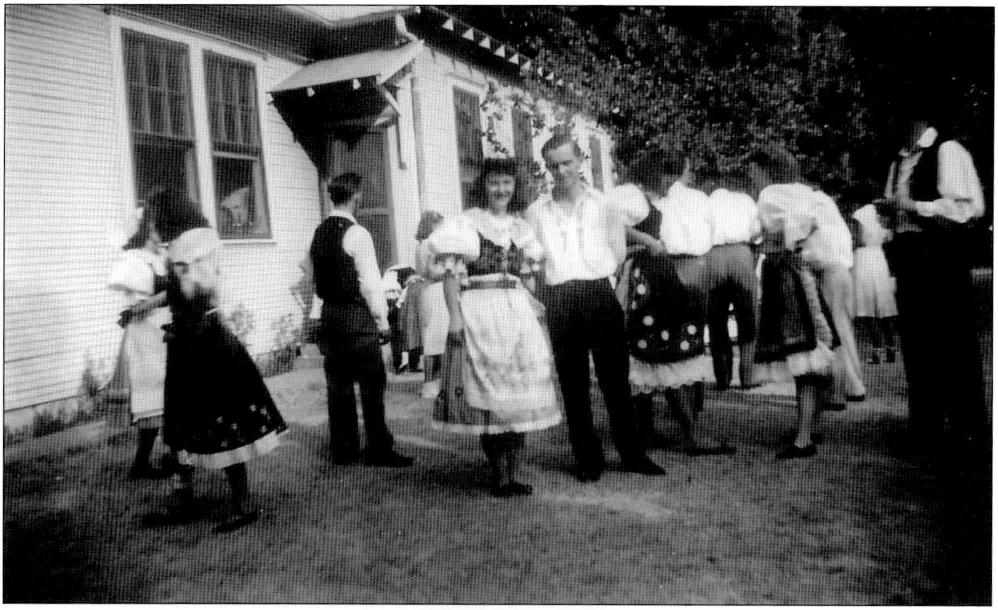

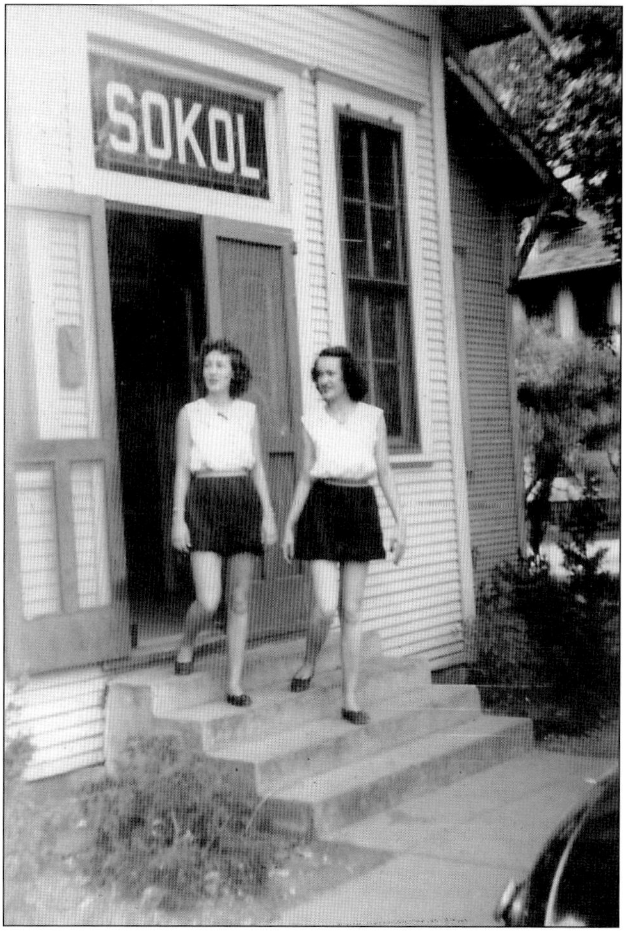

Yukon Sokol Beseda dancers perform around the 1940s. In the early 1900s, a man came from Bohemia to the Yukon Sokol lodge and taught the 16-minute Beseda dance, a medley of intricate dances and songs. Requiring four couples, the dance represents Bohemian unity. Yukon Sokol Beseda dancers traveled and performed at Czechoslovakian celebrations and festivals. Yukon's Czechs still accurately teach and perform the Beseda. (Courtesy LaVerne and Victor Benda family.)

Bohemians formed Sokol to unite under Austro-Hungarian rule. Sokol's motto is "A sound mind in a sound body." Members competed in gymnastics and marching drills and enjoyed social activities. Yukon Sokol was formed in 1894 and continues today. On the left is LaVerne Svejkovsky with Betty Jane Kouba in May 1947, at a regional Czech gymnastics competition. (Courtesy LaVerne and Victor Benda family.)

Sokols traveled to learn Sokol gymnastics and drills, returning home to teach their own members. This photograph likely shows Lidy F. Stejskal, who was a member and instructor at Yukon Sokol. He farmed in the Yukon area and volunteered at Czech Hall Saturday night dances. (Courtesy Yukon Czech Hall.)

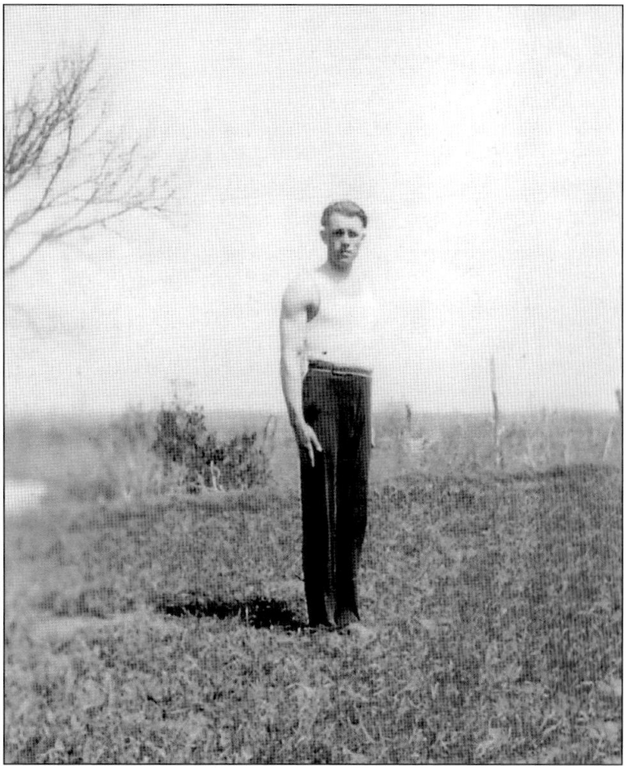

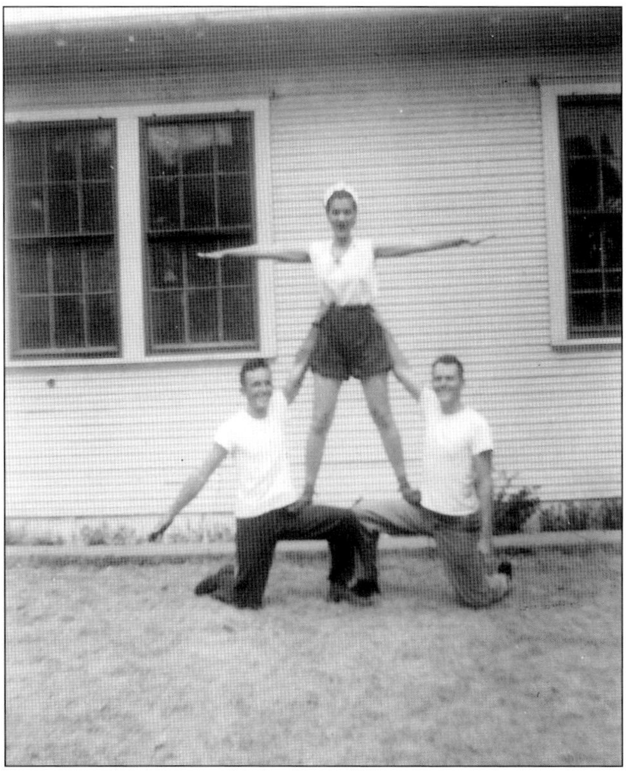

Three members of Yukon Sokol's gymnastics unit practice a routine. (Courtesy LaVerne and Victor Benda family.)

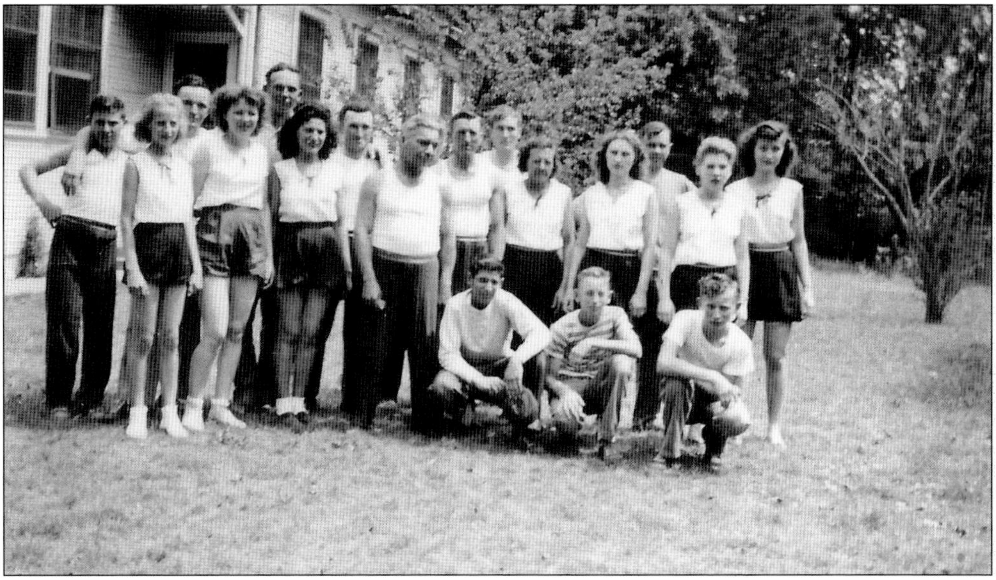

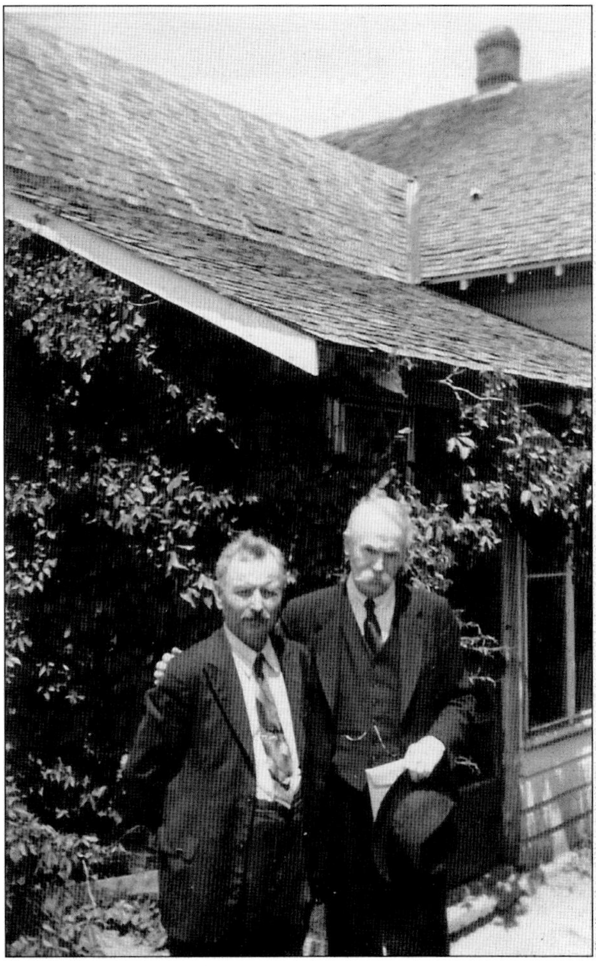

Yukon Sokol's gymnastics unit poses for a picture. Units traveled for competitions against other Sokol units. (Courtesy LaVerne and Victor Benda family.)

After Hitler invaded Czechoslovakia and prior to the declaration of World War II, the Czech government was in exile. Vojta Benês (right) toured America to alert Czech communities to events transpiring in Czechoslovakia. Benês is pictured here with Pavel Maly after speaking at Czech Hall in 1939. (Courtesy Yukon Czech Hall.)

In 1893, A.N. Spencer and associates established a small grain elevator by the train tracks on the south side of Spencer Avenue. The business was sold several times. In the same year, the Kroutils, from Bohemia, arrived in Yukon with their sons John and Frank. John and Frank had numerous siblings, including their sister Mary Ann. This 1912 Yukon High School yearbook photograph shows John Kroutil when he was school board treasurer. (Courtesy Phil Carson family.)

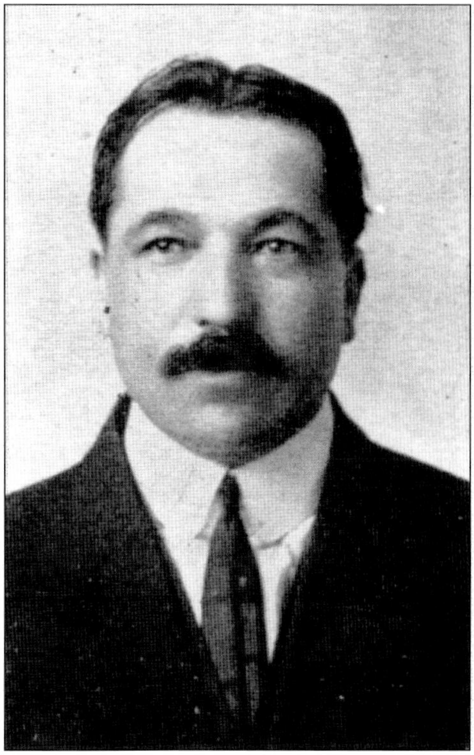

Mary Ann Kroutil married Anton F. "A.F." Dobry, both from Bohemia. In 1902, John and Frank Kroutil and A.F. Dobry bought the small grain elevator. They established the Yukon Mill and Grain Company, with John Kroutil as president. In this early photograph, there are two men on the right. Also to the right is Third Street, where the Yukon Mill office building still stands today. (Courtesy Yukon Historical Society.)

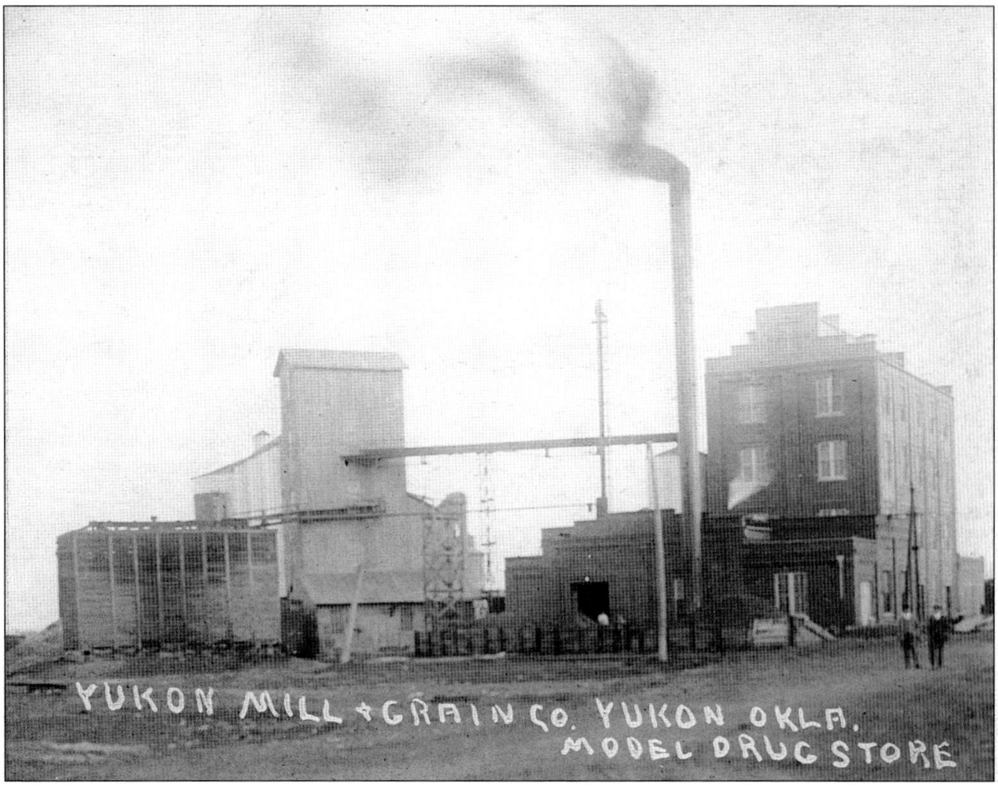

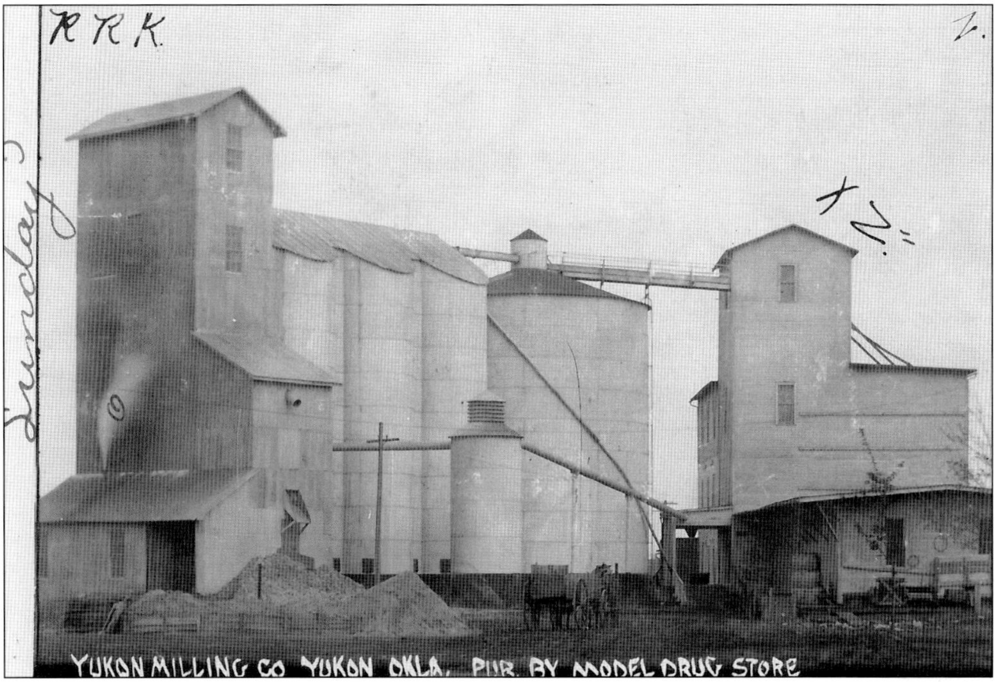

This early Yukon Mill and Grain Company photograph shows a still-small structure on the south side of Main Street, which is also Route 66. At some point early on, the business also established a grain elevator in Piedmont, so Piedmont farmers would not have to bring their grain all the way to Yukon. The Piedmont elevator was on the east side of Highway 4, just a few blocks south of Monroe Avenue. (Courtesy Yukon Historical Society.)

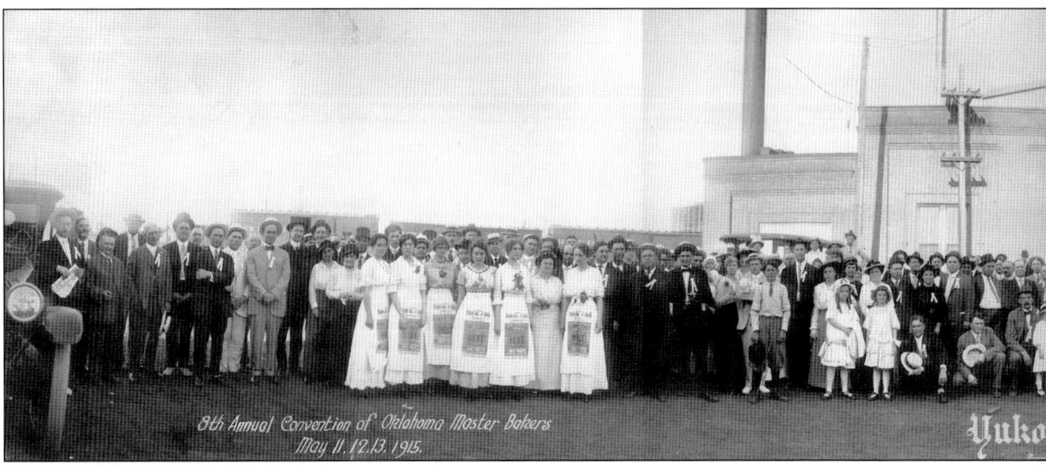

The writing on this photograph reads, "8th Annual Convention of Oklahoma Master Bakers, May 11, 12, 13, 1915," and "Gift of Yukon Mill and Grain Co." Above the ampersand at center, wearing a dark suit and hat, is John Kroutil. The women at left are wearing aprons with the Yukon's Best

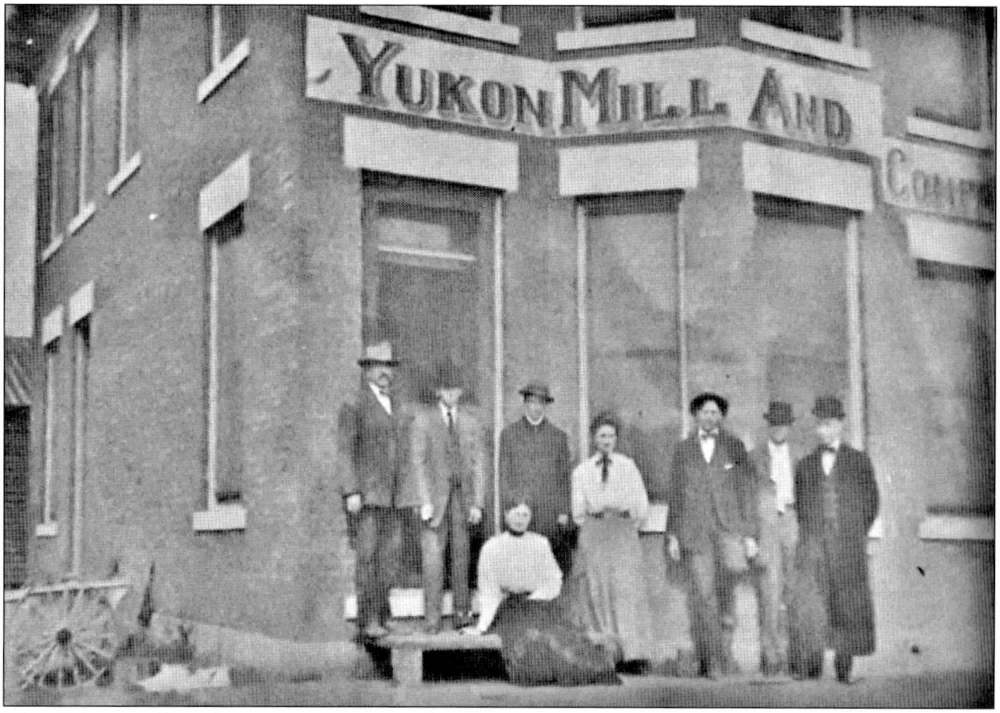

The Yukon Mill and Grain Company office building at 301 West Elm Street is seen here. Sam Carson sold the property to the company and then moved his home and business to Carson Corner around 1904. The historic building still stands, and is now home to other businesses. (Courtesy Eve Plumb.)

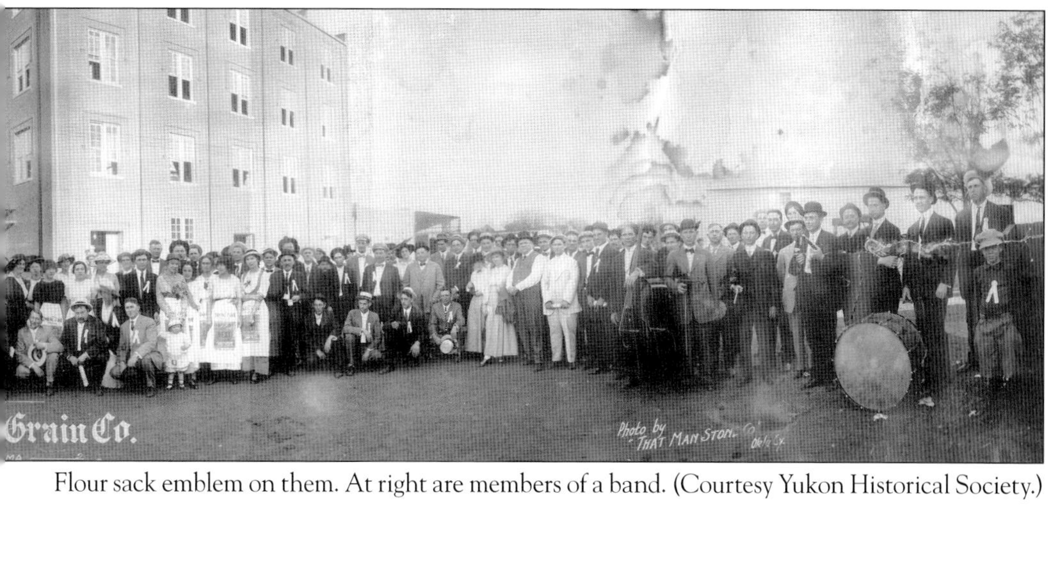

Flour sack emblem on them. At right are members of a band. (Courtesy Yukon Historical Society.)

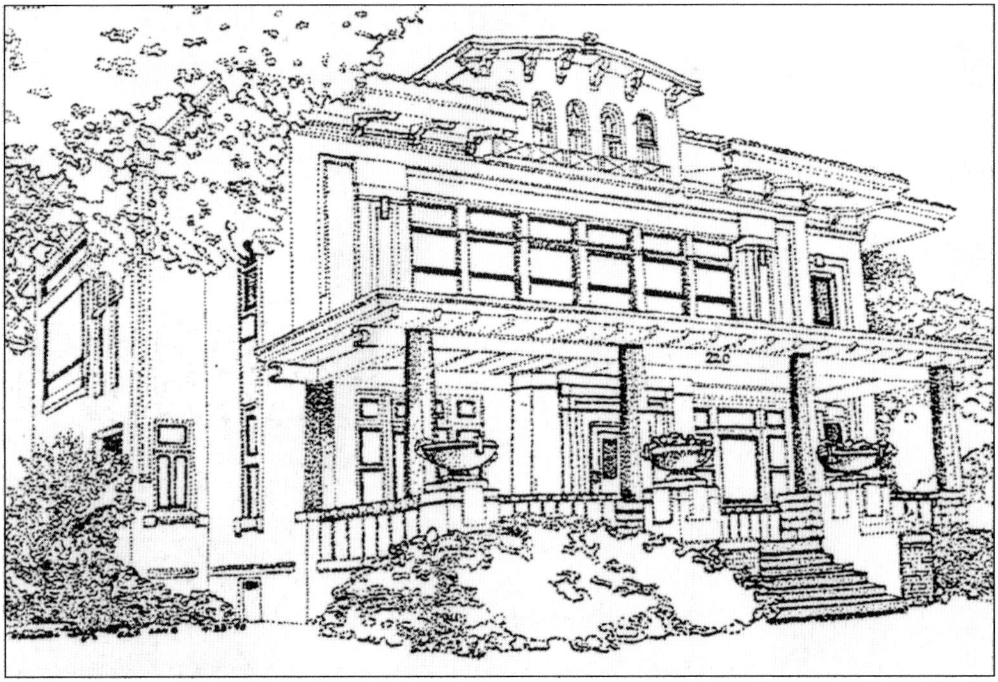

In 1917, John Kroutil built this home for $75,000, still located on Fifth Street. The elaborate, massive Kroutil Mansion had a basement ballroom. It was one of Yukon's first huge homes. Others followed, building their grand homes near Kroutil Mansion. The homes had concrete carriage steps next to the street so people could easily step down out of a carriage. (Courtesy Yukon Chamber of Commerce.)

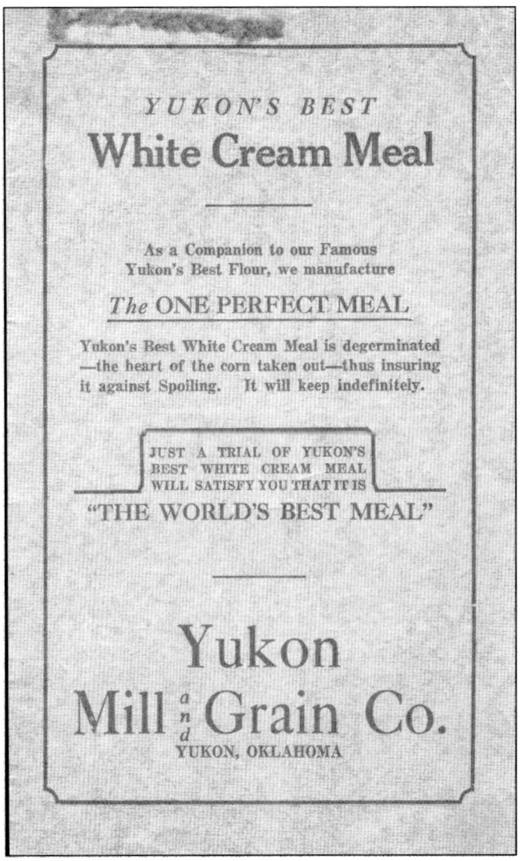

YUKON'S BEST

White Cream Meal

As a Companion to our Famous Yukon's Best Flour, we manufacture

The ONE PERFECT MEAL

Yukon's Best White Cream Meal is degerminated —the heart of the corn taken out—thus insuring it against Spoiling. It will keep indefinitely.

JUST A TRIAL OF YUKON'S BEST WHITE CREAM MEAL WILL SATISFY YOU THAT IT IS

"THE WORLD'S BEST MEAL"

Yukon Mill and Grain Co.

YUKON, OKLAHOMA

Inside a recipe book, Yukon Mill and Grain Company promotes White Cream Meal. In 1907, Oklahoma reached statehood, and John Kroutil established the Yukon Electric Company, supplying electricity for his mill workers. He provided electricity for Yukon from around 1910 to 1960. Small-town Yukon was unique in Oklahoma. (Courtesy Yukon Historical Society.)

The Farmers and Merchants Bank was established in 1904 on Spencer Avenue. In 1912, the Yukon National Bank opened with John Kroutil as president until his 1954 death. Early on, the bank bought Farmers and Merchants Bank. Shown is a 1946 Yukon High School yearbook advertisement for Yukon National Bank. (Courtesy Yukon Historical Society.)

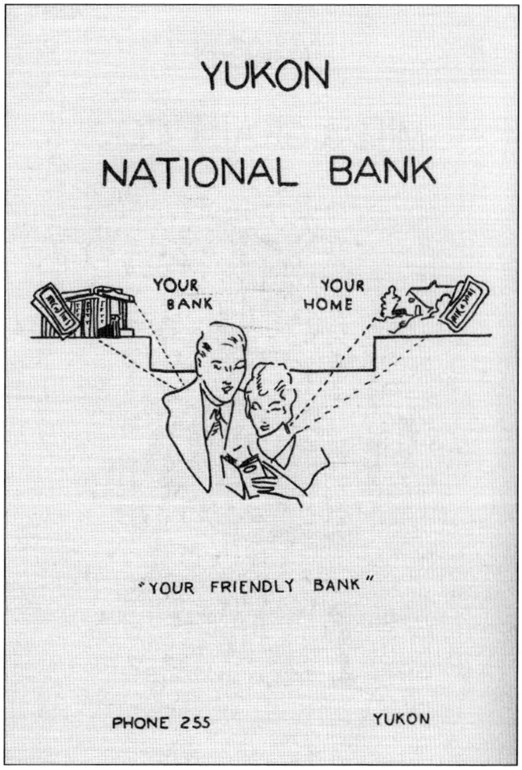

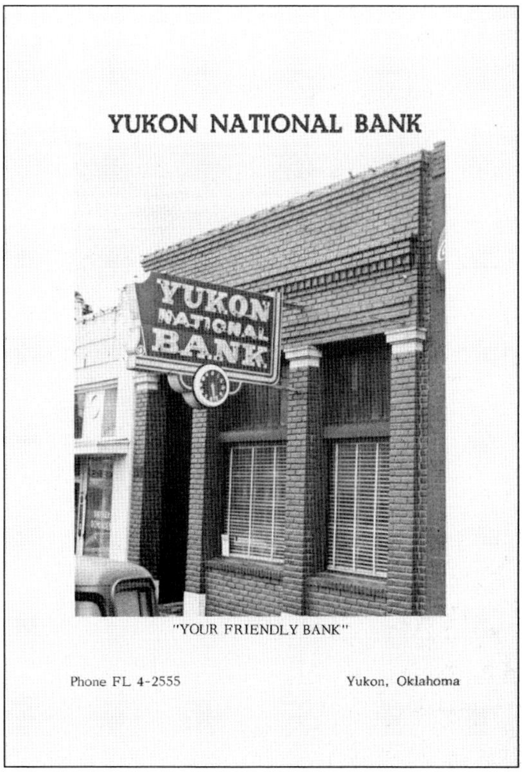

Yukon National Bank has been family owned and operated since 1912, and in 2021, it is still owned by Kroutil family descendants. Shown is an early Yukon High School yearbook advertisement for the bank. (Courtesy Yukon Historical Society.)

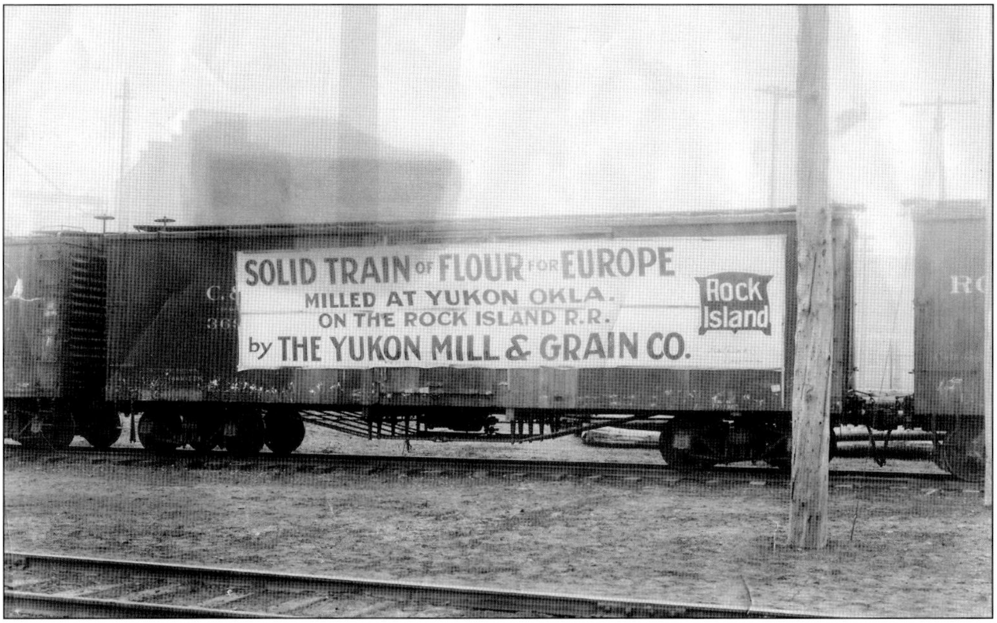

Sitting next to the railroad tracks that cross Main Street, the Yukon Mill and Grain Company shipped flour nationwide and to various European nations. This 1920 photograph shows a Rock Island train car loaded with flour bound for Europe. During World War II, the company shipped flour to Holland. (Courtesy Yukon Historical Society.)

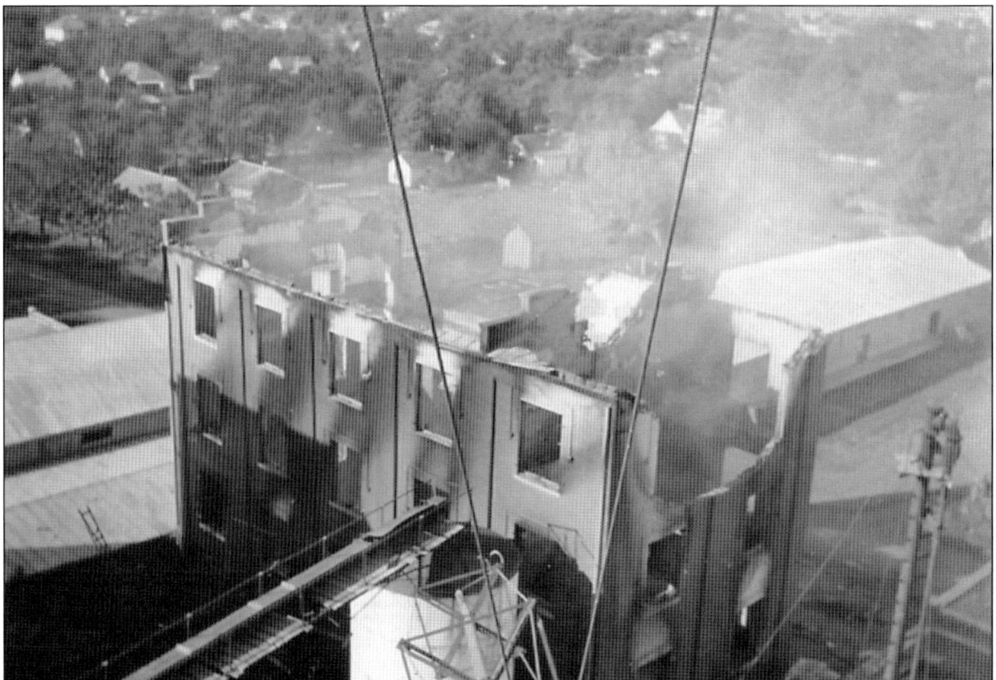

On October 3, 1921, at 11:00 p.m., a fire ignited due to an explosion in the flour bin, and the Yukon Mill and Grain Company burned to the ground. A photographer snapped this picture while the structure was still smoking. (Courtesy Yukon Historical Society.)

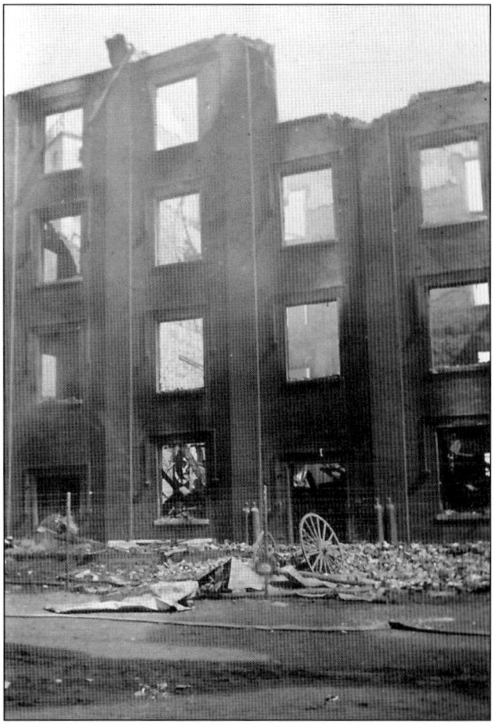

Oklahoma City and El Reno fire departments arrived to help fight the 1921 Yukon Mill and Grain Company blaze. In 1922, the location was rebuilt, becoming the largest independent flour mill in the southwestern United States, capable of producing 2,000 barrels of flour daily. (Courtesy Yukon Historical Society.)

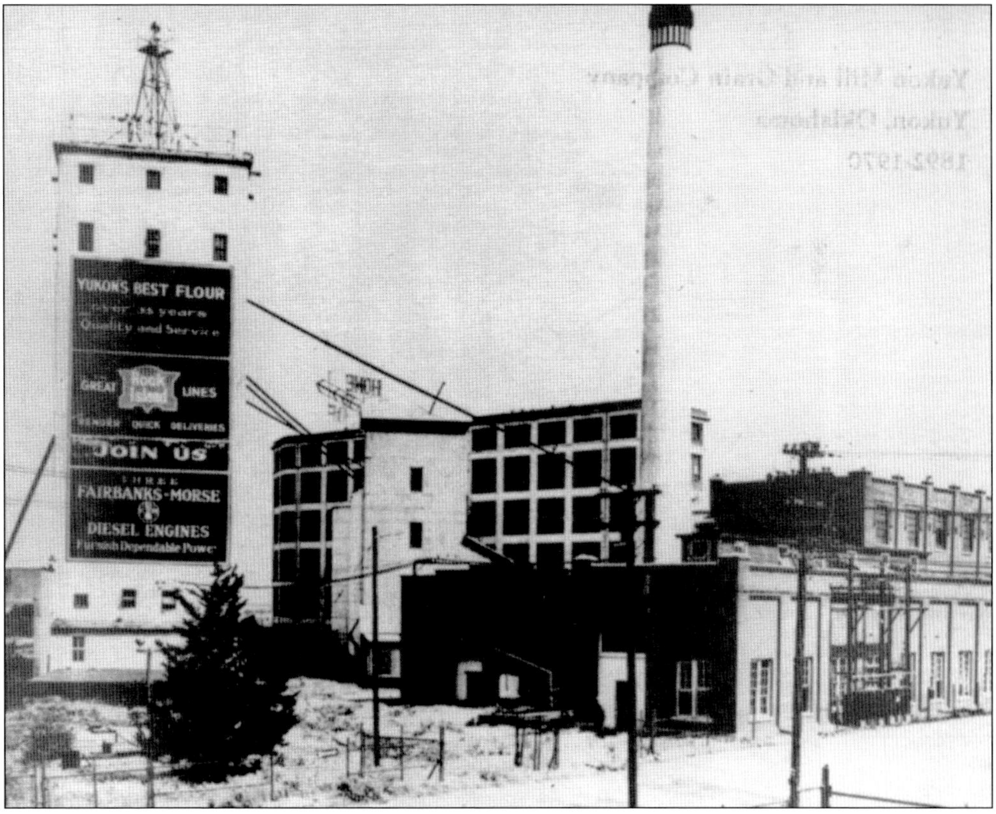

Yukon Mill and Grain Company is still on the south side of Main Street, or Route 66, in 2021. In this early photograph, the words on the building read, "Yukon's Best Flour," "Join Us," "Great Rock Island Lines Render Quick Deliveries," and "Three Fairbanks-Morse Diesel Engines Furnish Dependable Power." (Courtesy Yukon Historical Society.)

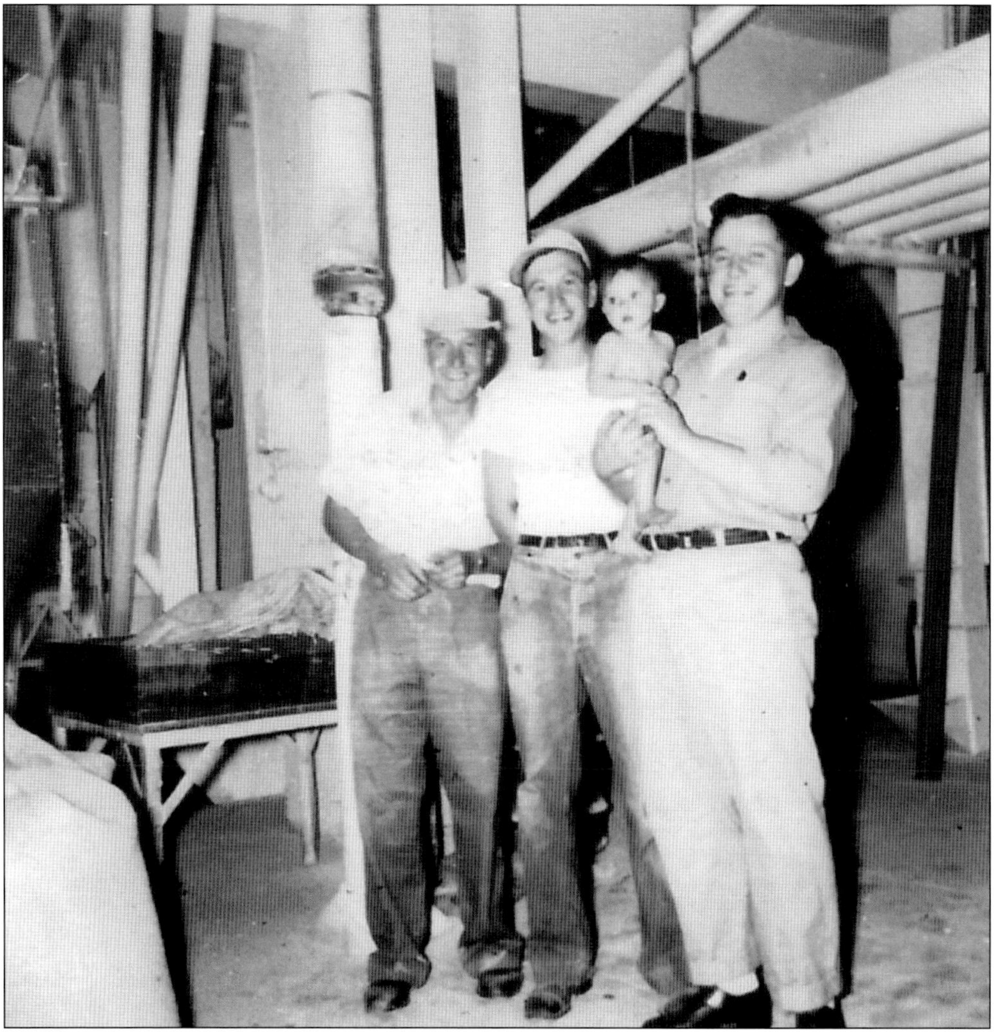

Frank Kroutil died in 1932, and John Kroutil died in 1954. Their sons Raymond and Norman continued to operate the Yukon Mill and Grain Company but sold out to Shawnee Milling Company in 1970. In this 1948 photograph, from left to right, David Rudisell, Bill Rudisell, Gene Hudson, and Gary Rudisell are pictured inside on the first floor. (Courtesy Yukon Historical Society.)

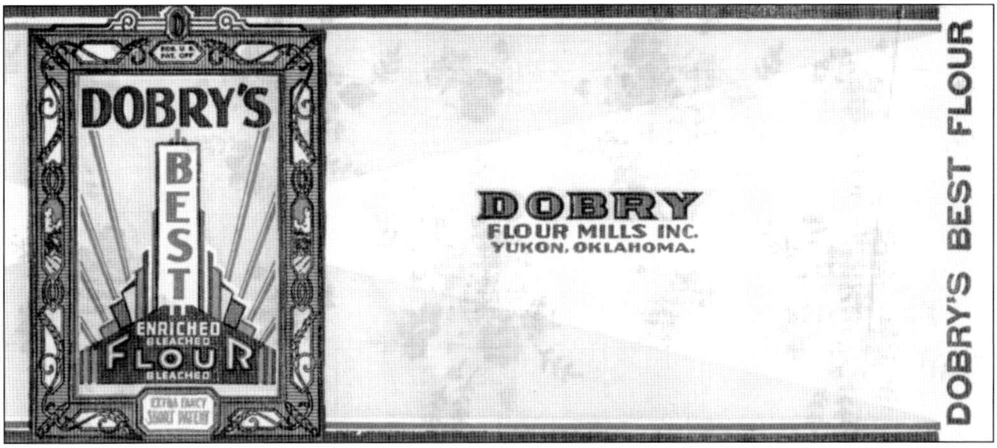

In 1933, Mary Ann and A.F. Dobry and their family sold their share of the Yukon Mill and Grain Company to the Kroutil family. The Dobrys built their own mill across the street on the north side of Main Street, which is Route 66. This photograph shows early Dobry Flour Mills memorabilia. (Courtesy Yukon Historical Society.)

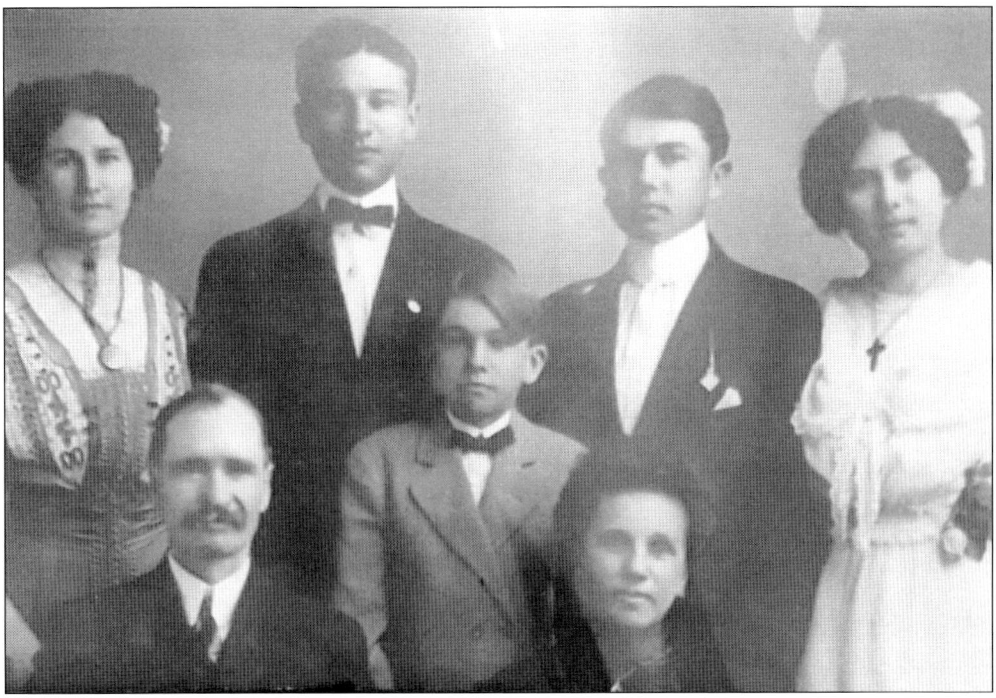

Anton F. "A.F." Dobry and his wife, Mary Ann Kroutil Dobry, were born in Bohemia in 1862 and 1870, respectively. They are pictured here with their children Vernie, Theophile "T.D.," Joseph, Mary, and John. T.D. Dobry was actress Eve Plumb's grandfather. (Courtesy Eve Plumb.)

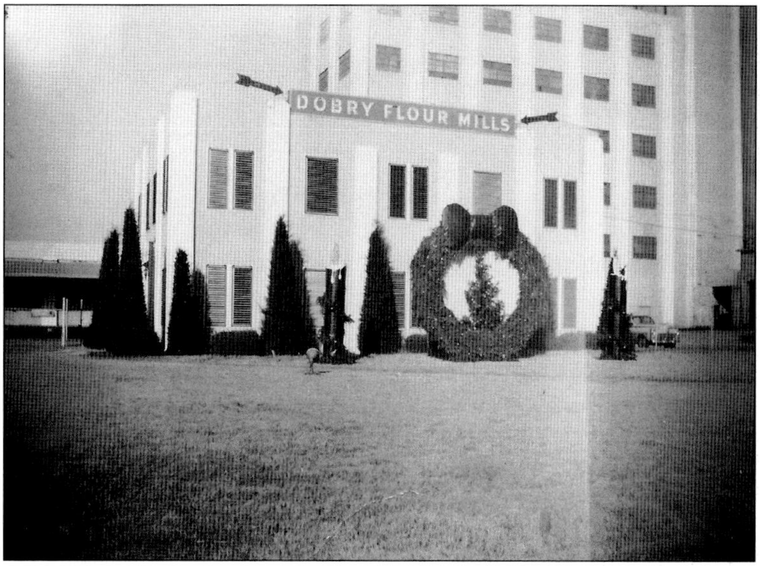

In 1933, with their children, Mary Ann and A.F. Dobry built their six-story masonry structure, Dobry Flour Mills, at 221 West Main Street on the north side of Route 66. This 1930s image shows Dobry Flour Mills with the office out front. The office structure no longer exists. (Courtesy Betty Sackett and the Trch family archives.)

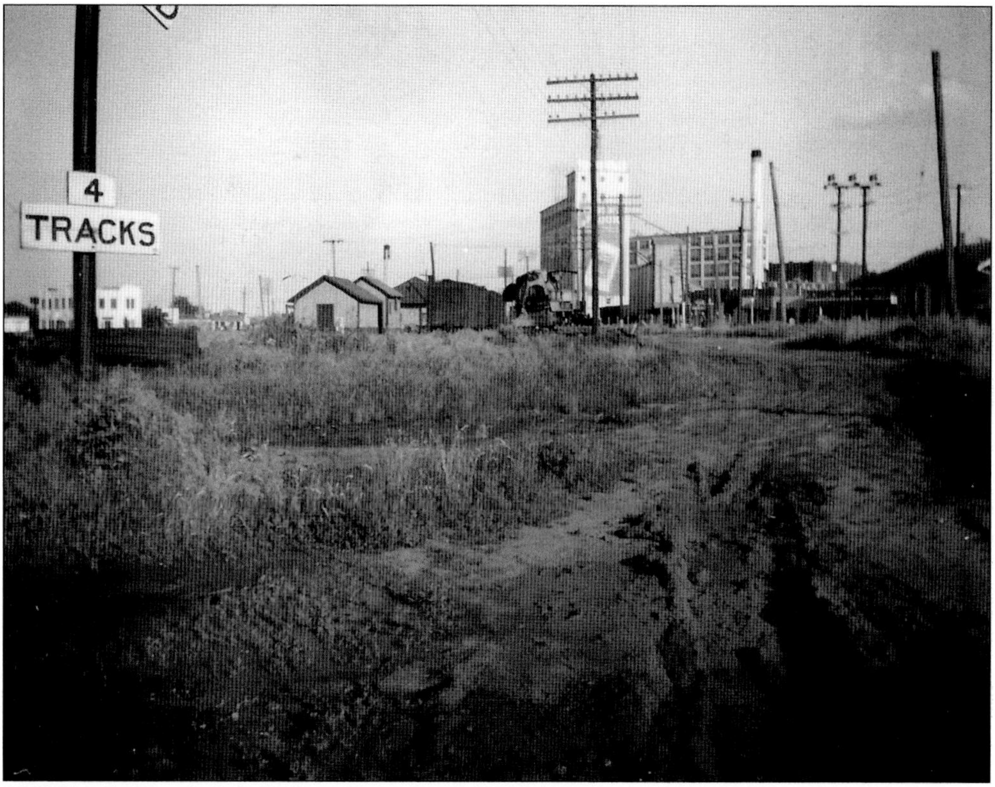

With her husband, A.F. Dobry, Mary Ann's brothers John and Frank Kroutil established the Yukon Mill and Grain Company. Other Kroutil siblings were involved in the business, including Thomas Kroutil and Robert Kroutil. The Dobry and Kroutil families split. This 1930s photograph shows the two milling companies, Dobry Flour Mills and the Yukon Mill and Grain Company, after the split. (Courtesy Betty Sackett and the Trch family archives.)

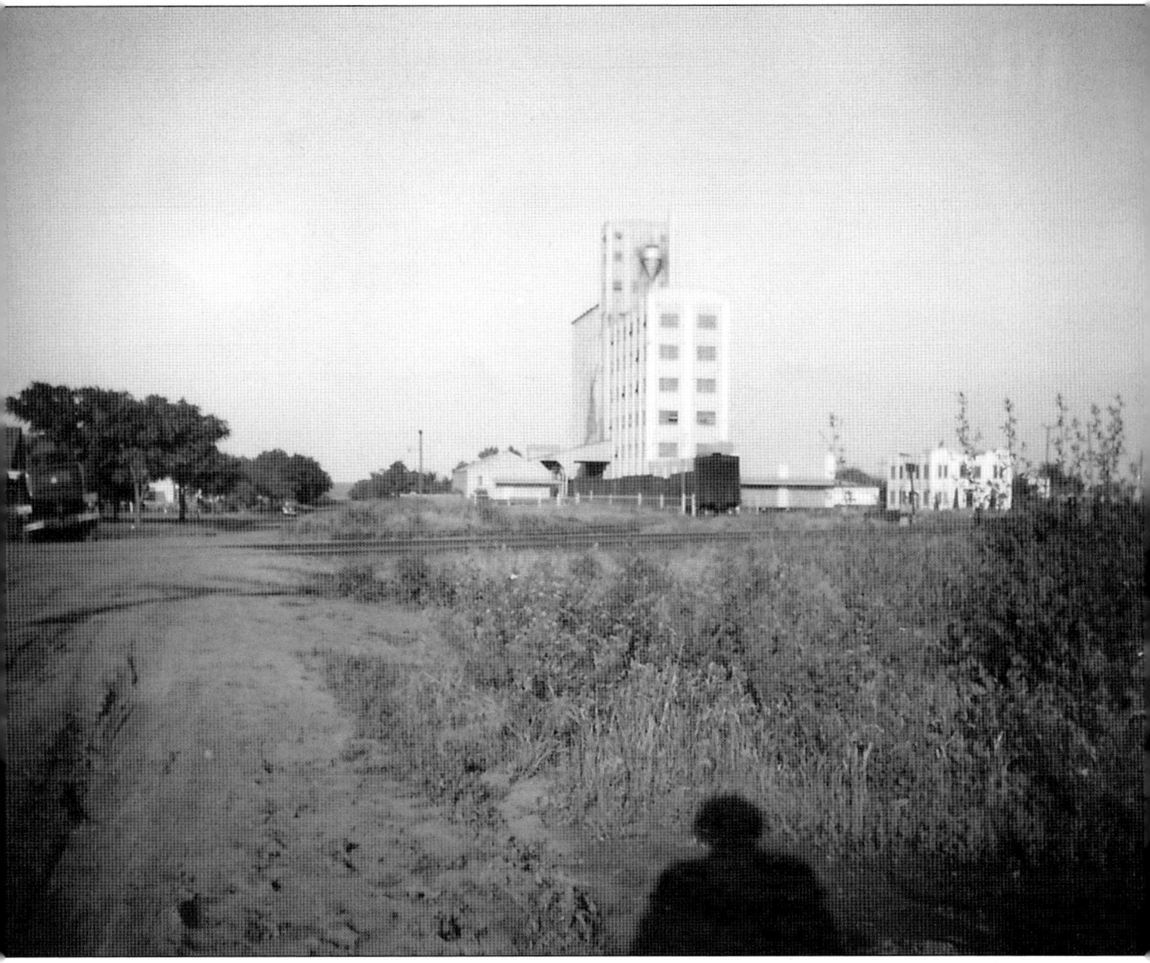

Dobry Flour Mills continued in operation until 1972, when it was sold to Mid-Continent. Although the structure still stands in 2021, it apparently is no longer in use. This 1930s photograph shows the Dobry Flour Mills on the north side of Main Street. (Courtesy Betty Sackett and the Trch family archives.)

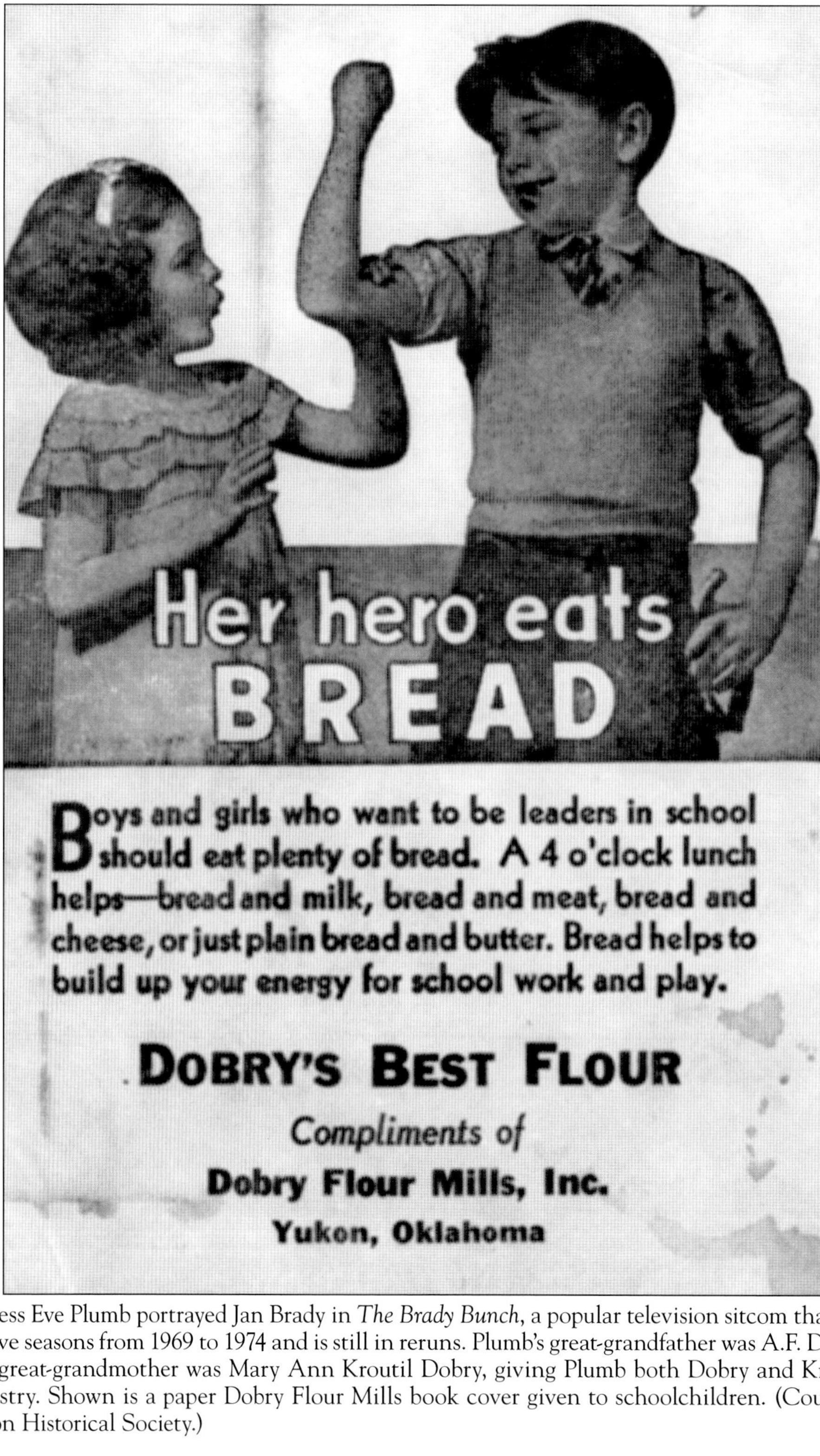

Actress Eve Plumb portrayed Jan Brady in *The Brady Bunch*, a popular television sitcom that ran for five seasons from 1969 to 1974 and is still in reruns. Plumb's great-grandfather was A.F. Dobry. Her great-grandmother was Mary Ann Kroutil Dobry, giving Plumb both Dobry and Kroutil ancestry. Shown is a paper Dobry Flour Mills book cover given to schoolchildren. (Courtesy Yukon Historical Society.)

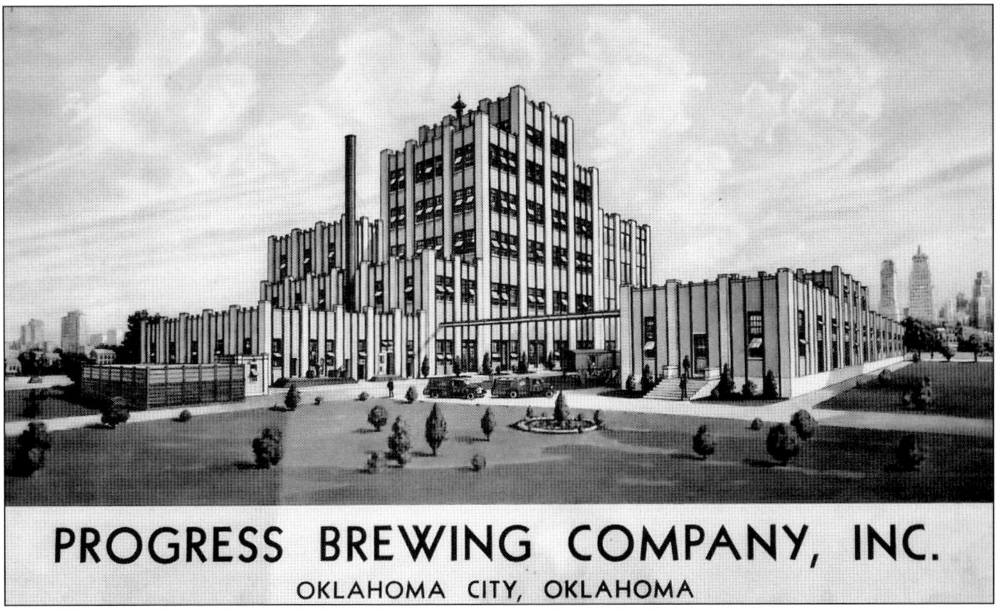

John Kroutil and Gustave F. Streich started brewing beer in a barn east of today's Kimbell Park. The barn is long gone. Rumors are that brewing initially began in the basement of the John Kroutil Mansion. This lithograph is an architectural rendering of what the Progress Brewing facility would look like on completion. (Courtesy Kathryn Kroutil Wright family.)

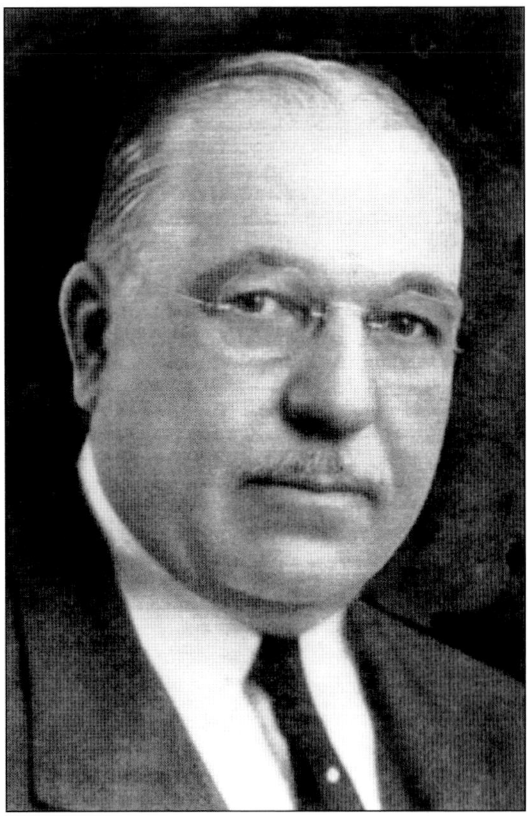

John Kroutil was an entrepreneur ahead of his time, and his ideas provided jobs and promoted a strong economy. He launched Progress Brewing, and took advantage of television when it first became popular to promote Progress Beer through televised wrestling matches. (Courtesy Betty Sackett.)

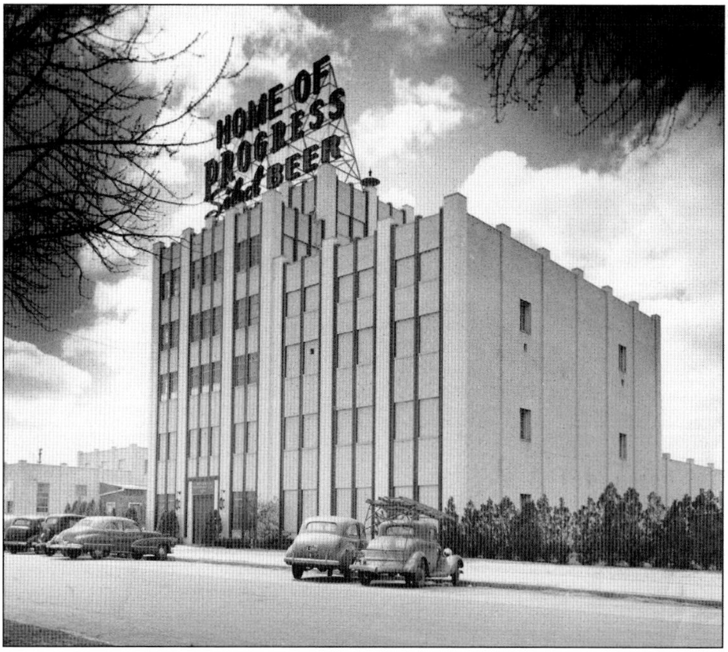

On December 5, 1933, Prohibition ended, and beer and wine under 3.2 percent alcohol became legal in Oklahoma. In 1933 or 1934, John Kroutil and Gustave F. Streich opened Progress Brewing in Oklahoma City, the first legal beer brewing operation in Oklahoma. This photograph shows the Progress facility in Oklahoma City before additions were made. (Courtesy Kathryn Kroutil Wright family.)

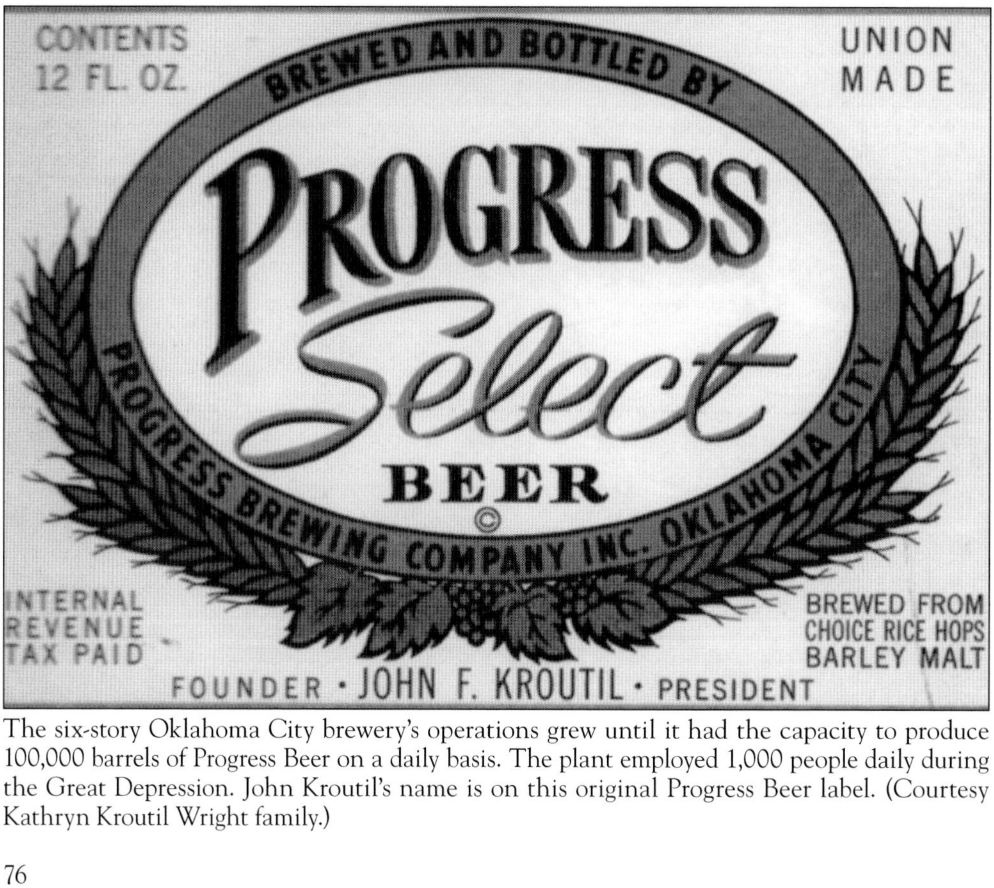

The six-story Oklahoma City brewery's operations grew until it had the capacity to produce 100,000 barrels of Progress Beer on a daily basis. The plant employed 1,000 people daily during the Great Depression. John Kroutil's name is on this original Progress Beer label. (Courtesy Kathryn Kroutil Wright family.)

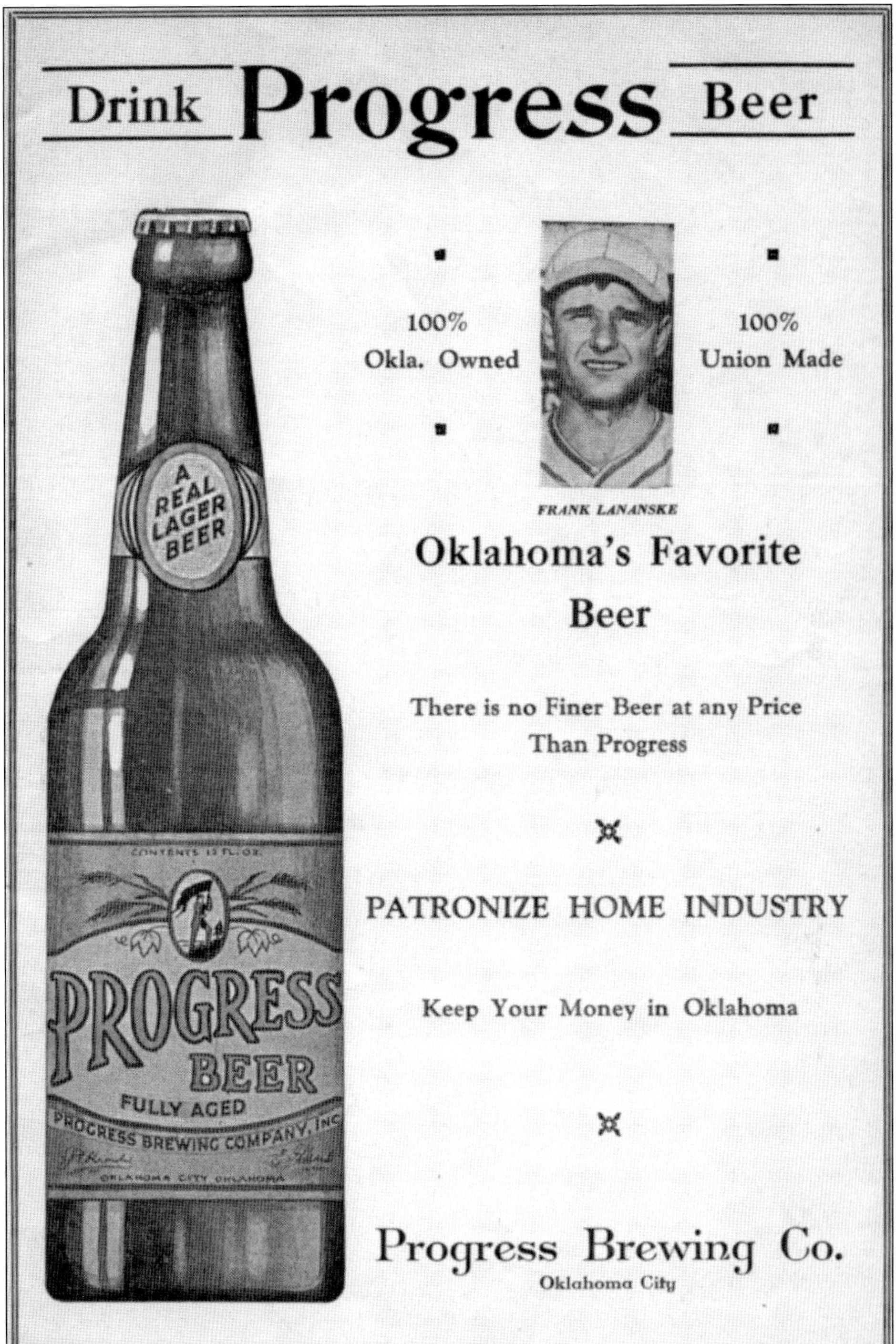

John Kroutil brought grain for Progress Beer to Yukon via the railroad. He was using gravity flow in beer production close to 100 years ago. Progress Beer bottle caps, arriving in large, wooden kegs, were manufactured in Chicago. This Progress Beer advertisement was in a 1938 baseball scorecard. (Courtesy Kathryn Kroutil Wright family.)

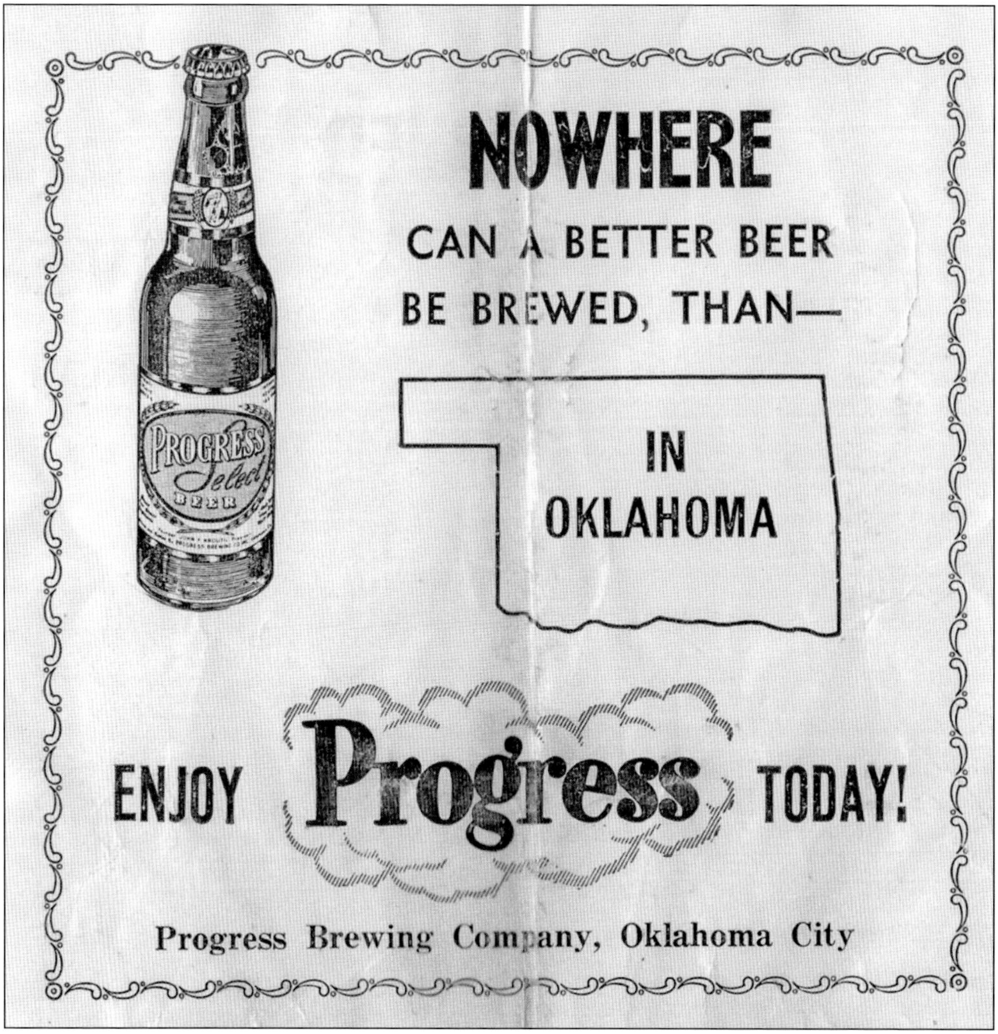

Progress Brewing was one of only three licensed post-Prohibition breweries in Oklahoma, and the longest-lived. In 1954, John Kroutil died, and the brewery was sold to Lone Star Brewery, which produced Progress Beer until 1974. This advertisement is from a 1949 Future Farmers of America livestock show and rodeo program. (Courtesy Kathryn Kroutil Wright family.)

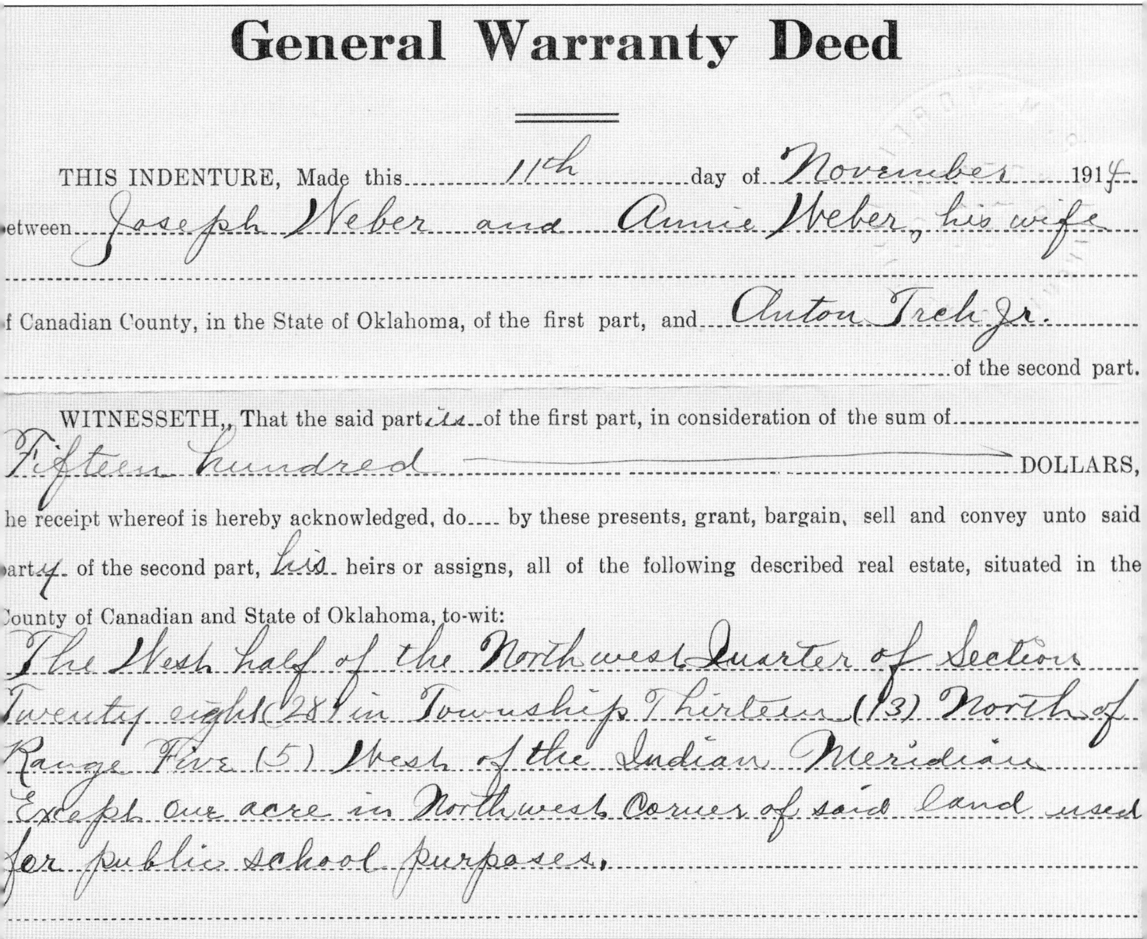

General Warranty Deed

THIS INDENTURE, Made this 11th day of November 1914 between Joseph Weber and Annie Weber, his wife of Canadian County, in the State of Oklahoma, of the first part, and Anton Trch Jr. of the second part.

WITNESSETH, That the said parties of the first part, in consideration of the sum of Fifteen hundred DOLLARS, the receipt whereof is hereby acknowledged, do by these presents, grant, bargain, sell and convey unto said party of the second part, his heirs or assigns, all of the following described real estate, situated in the County of Canadian and State of Oklahoma, to-wit:

The West half of the Northwest Quarter of Section Twenty eight (28) in Township Thirteen (13) North of Range Five (5) West of the Indian Meridian Except one acre in Northwest Corner of said land used for public school purposes.

This 1914 deed documents Anton Trch Jr. buying his first Yukon farm for $1,500 from the Webers. The land was originally platted to include a section where a school would be built. In 2021, the Trch farmlands along Highway 4 are still owned by the family. (Courtesy Betty Sackett and the Trch family archives.)

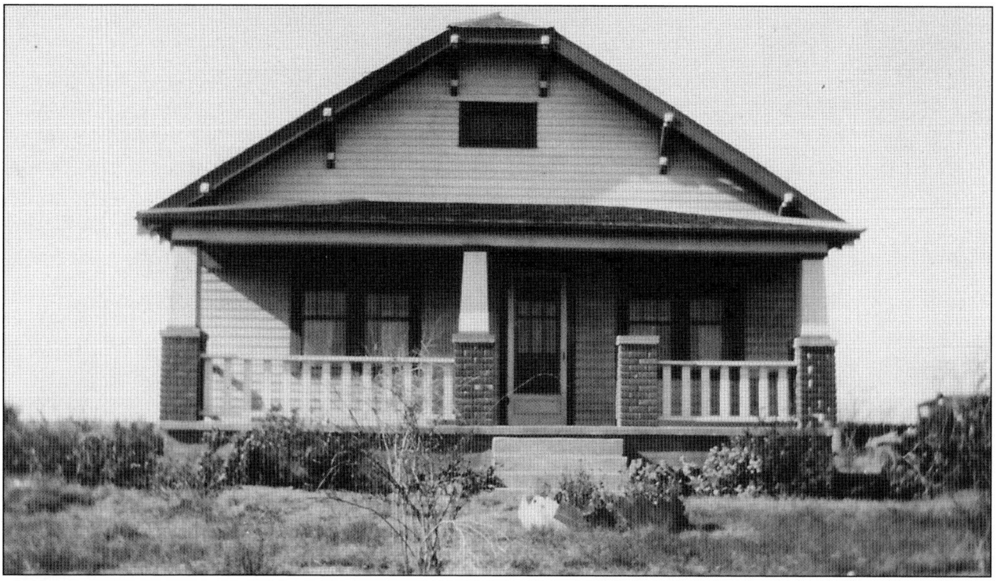

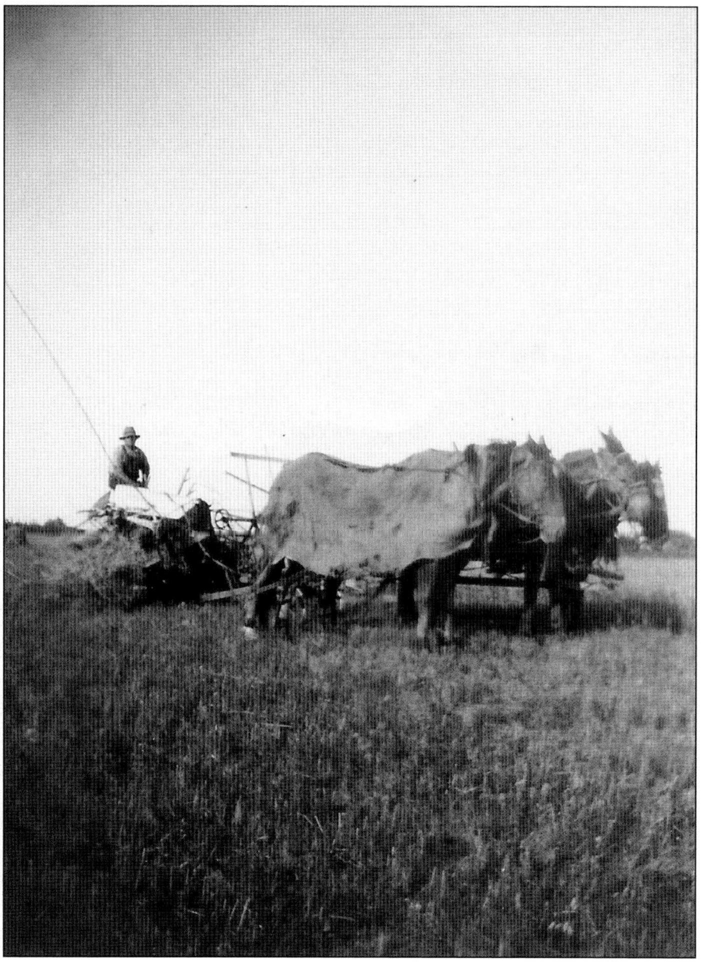

In 1922, Emma and Anton Trch Jr. built their farmhouse, shown here in the 1930s. Several teachers who taught at Spring Creek School lived with the Trch family. In 2021, Trch descendants still own the house on Highway 4. (Courtesy Betty Sackett and the Trch family archives.)

Anton Trch Jr. uses three horses to pull his farm equipment in the 1930s. Anton produced wheat. Wheat producers and horses remain a big part of the Yukon area and its economic base. Horse ranches still dot the area, and golden wheat farms carpet the prairie. (Courtesy Betty Sackett and the Trch family archives.)

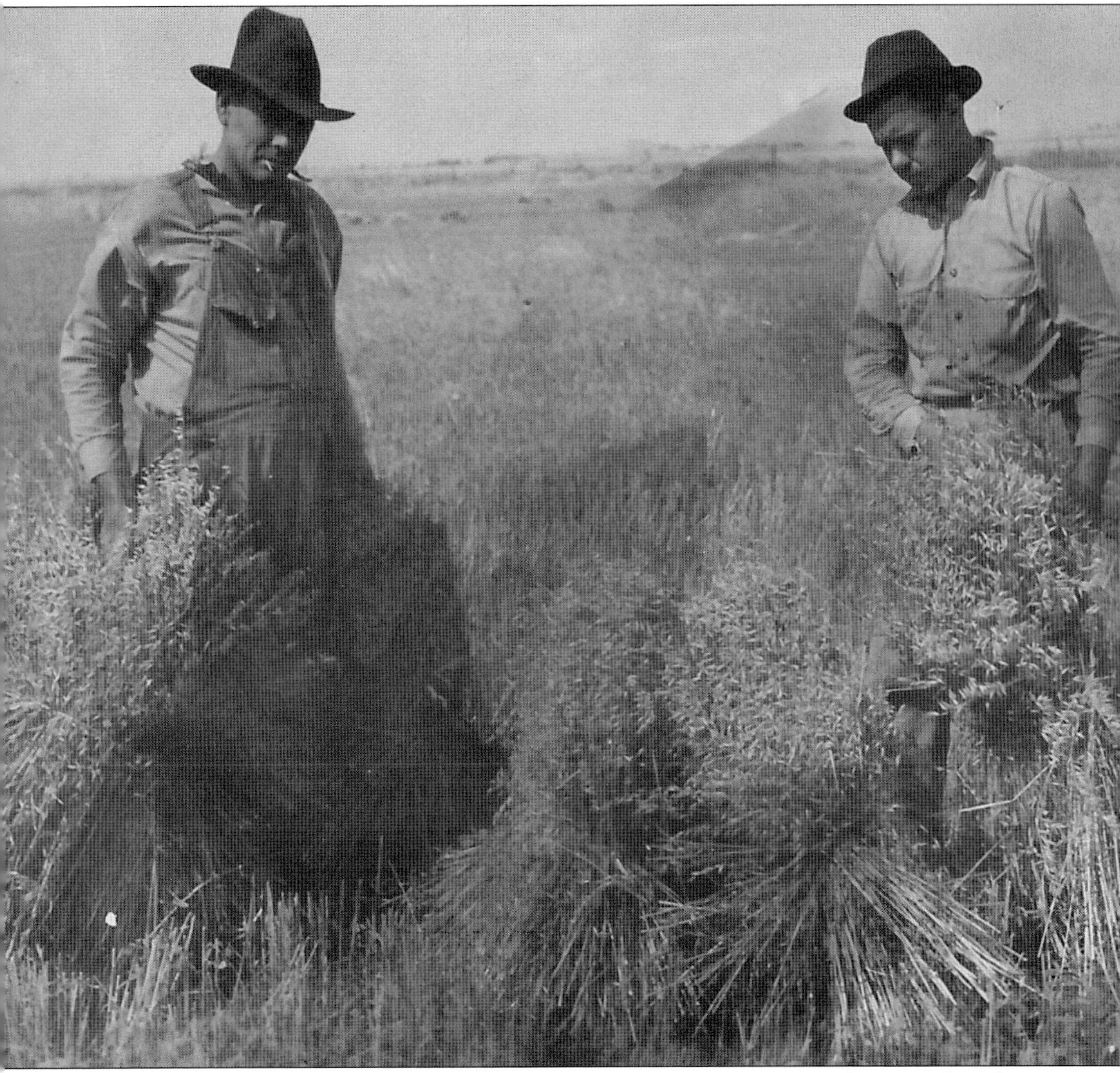

These Yukon farmers are shocking wheat. In this case, the term refers to gathering or bundling wheat in the fields. Even in 2021, wheat farms are a prevalent part of the Yukon and Canadian County agricultural community. Some wheat farms stretch as far as the eye can see, and many are owned and worked by multiple generations of families. (Courtesy Yukon Historical Society.)

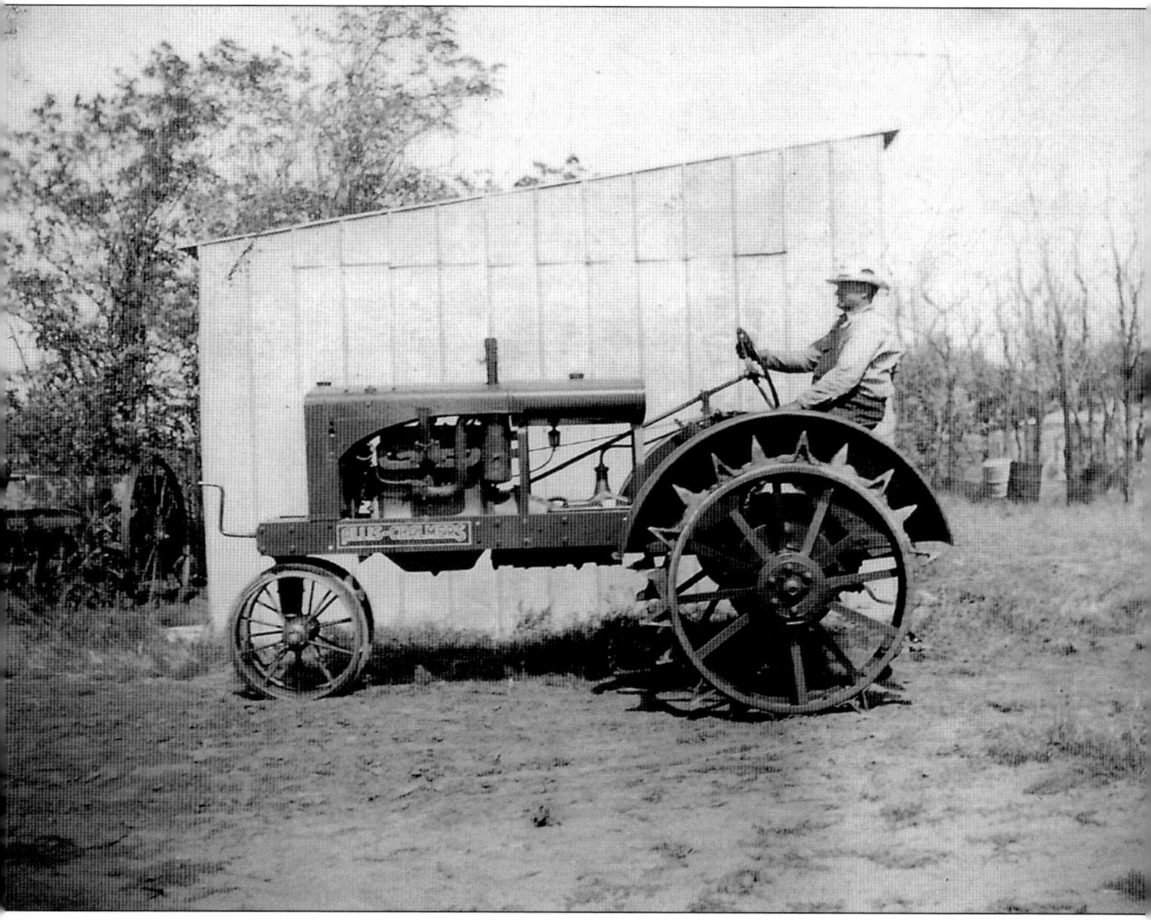

In the 1930s, Anton Trch Jr. upgraded from horse-drawn farm equipment to this tractor. All of Yukon's livery stables were gone before 1940. The auto industry grew in Yukon, with dealers including Cornwell, Clapper, Fitzgerald, Hamilton, Hart, Cooper, Cone, and more, as well as automobile repair shops. (Courtesy Betty Sackett and the Trch family archives.)

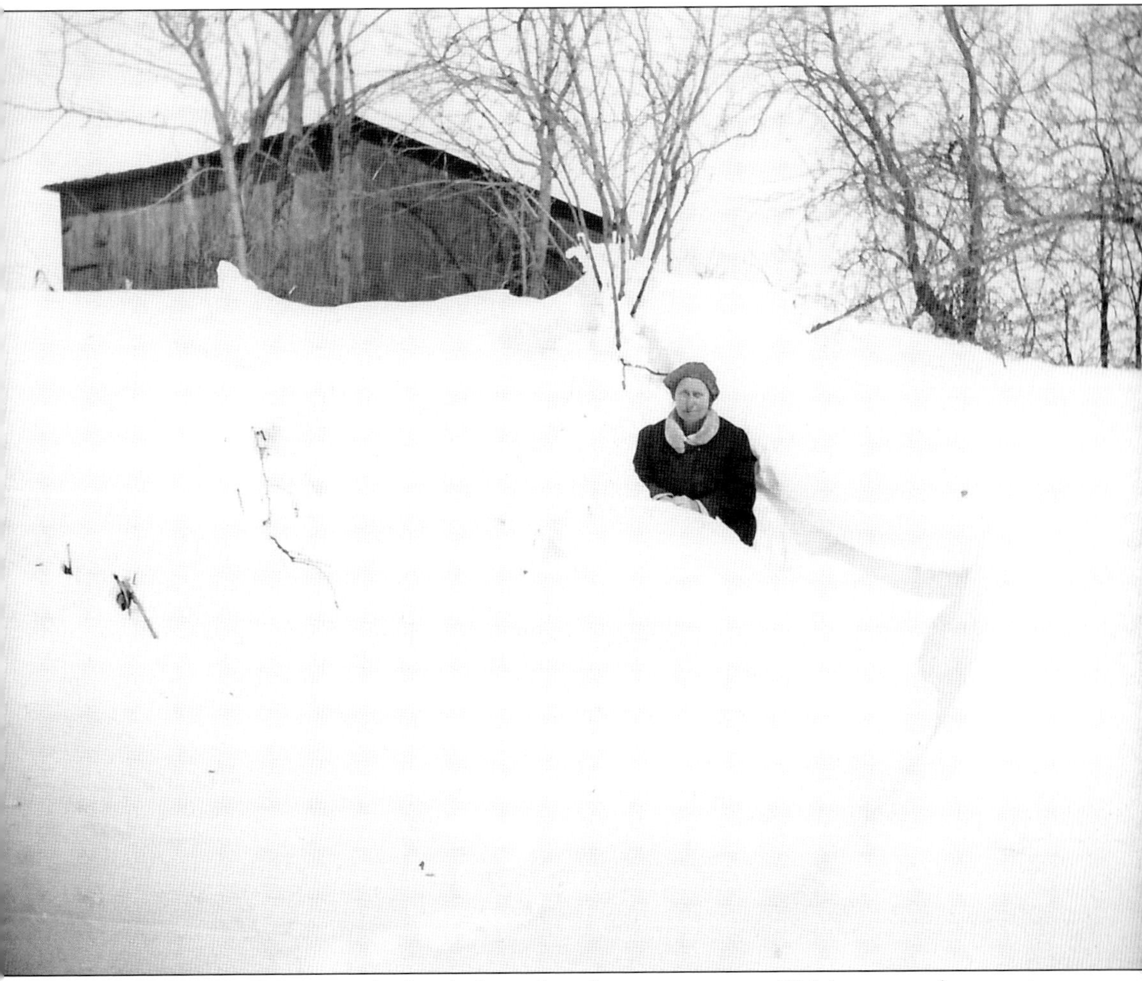

In 1936, Emma Trch poses on the family farm after a heavy snowstorm. Oklahoma weather remains unpredictable, and is especially hard on farmers and their livelihood. Emma and her husband, Anton, produced hay, cattle, chickens, and geese on their farm. (Courtesy Betty Sackett and the Trch family archives.)

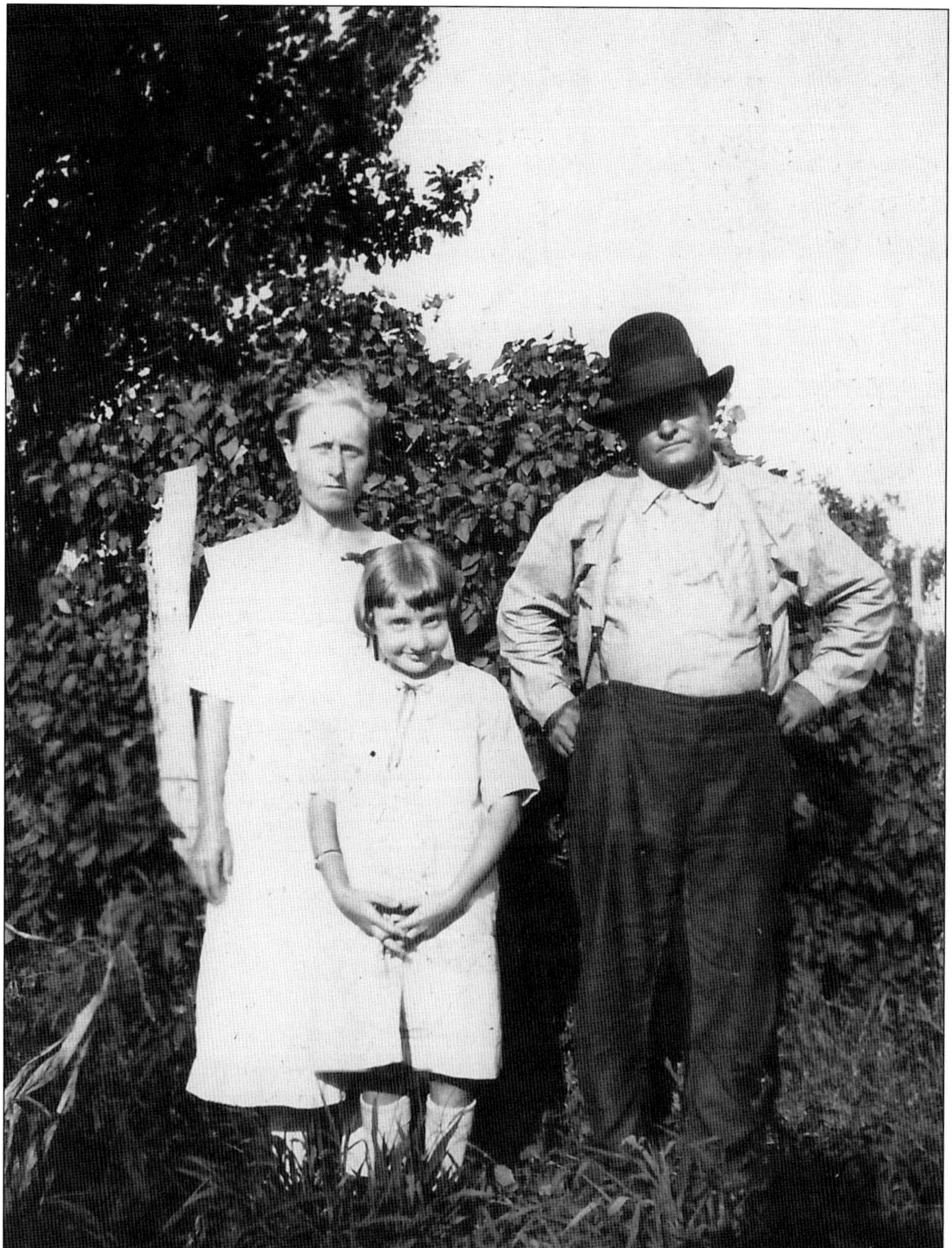

Emma and Anton Trch Jr., both born in Bohemia, stand with their daughter Adelene, who was born in 1918 on a Canadian County farm. She married Theodore Zoubek, the son of Rosa (Blecha) and Frank Zoubek. Theodore was born in Bohemia, and Rosa's parents were as well. (Courtesy LaVerne and Victor Benda family.)

Shown is the future Betty Sackett, as three-year-old Betty Zoubek with her doll in 1948, enjoying the Yukon farm where her Trch grandparents lived. Betty's parents were Adelene and Theodore Zoubek. All of her grandparents had Bohemian ancestry. (Courtesy Betty Sackett and the Trch family archives.)

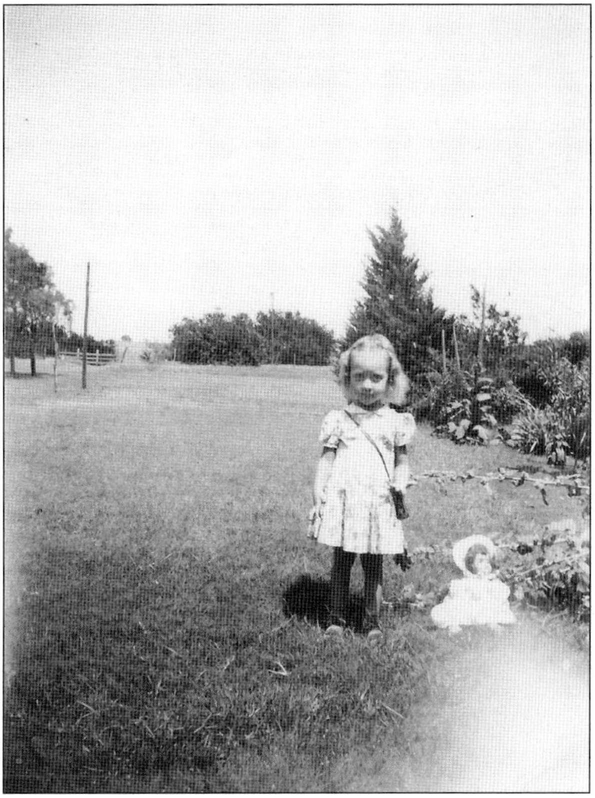

This 1930s photograph shows a huge pile of hay on the Trch Farm in Yukon. A cow grazes on the right, and farm equipment sits idle on the left. Massive numbers of hay bales are still a common site on Yukon's many farms. (Courtesy Betty Sackett and the Trch family archives.)

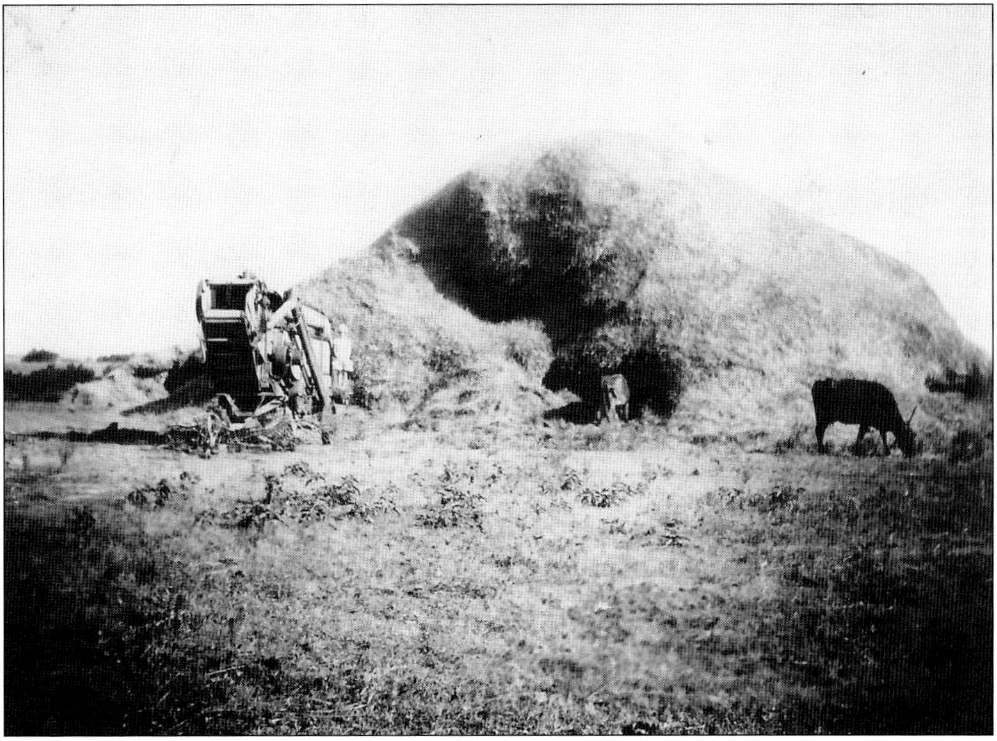

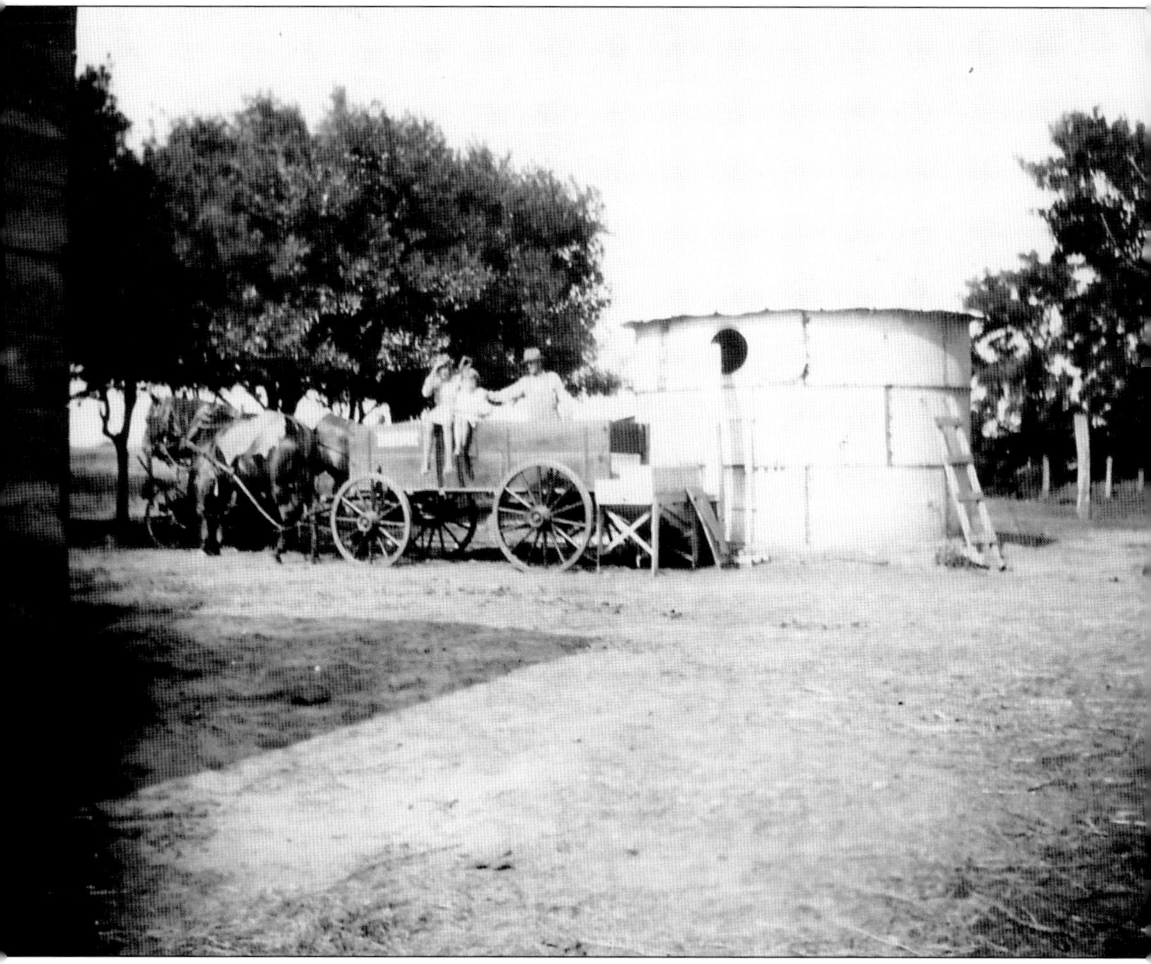

Shown is a 1930s photograph of the Trch Farm in Yukon. Common sites in the area, the cone-topped structure is a granary where Anton Trch Jr. stored his grain. A horse-drawn wagon, carrying unidentified people, sits to the left. (Courtesy Betty Sackett and the Trch family archives.)

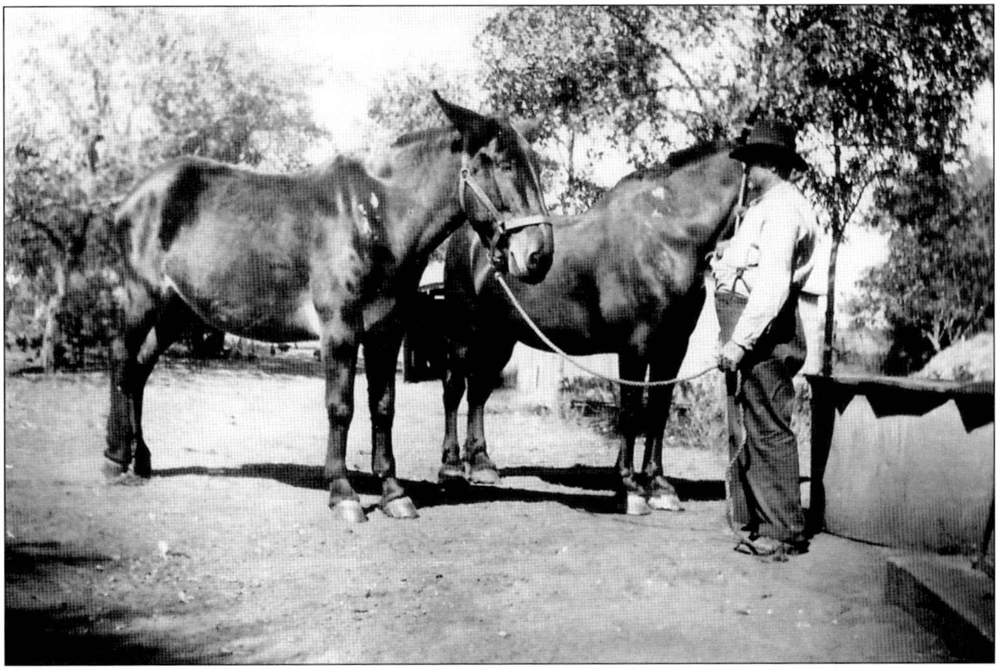

Anton Trch Jr. stands with two horses on his Yukon farm in the 1930s. The Great Depression lasted approximately 10 years, from 1929 until about 1940. But low prices of farm products caused farm communities such as Yukon to feel the hard times earlier and harder. (Courtesy Betty Sackett and the Trch family archives.)

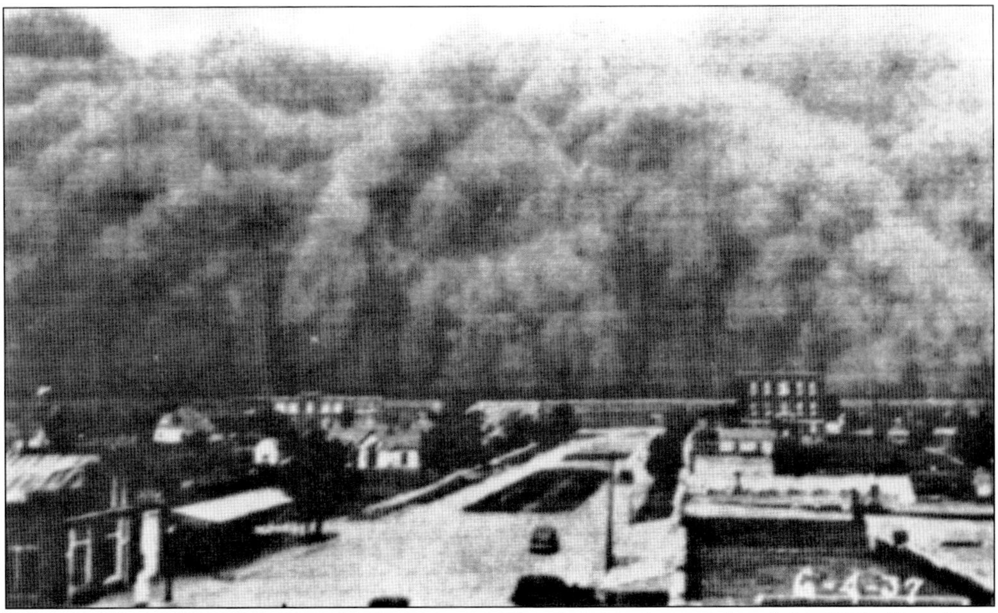

The drought-stricken Southern Plains region suffered under the weight of the 1930s Dust Bowl era. The horrible dust storms arrived during an already crippling Great Depression, impacting every aspect of life and the economy. Dust Bowl pneumonia was not uncommon, taking lives. Yukon was not spared. This photograph shows a dust storm rolling over Yukon on June 4, 1937. (Courtesy Betty Sackett.)

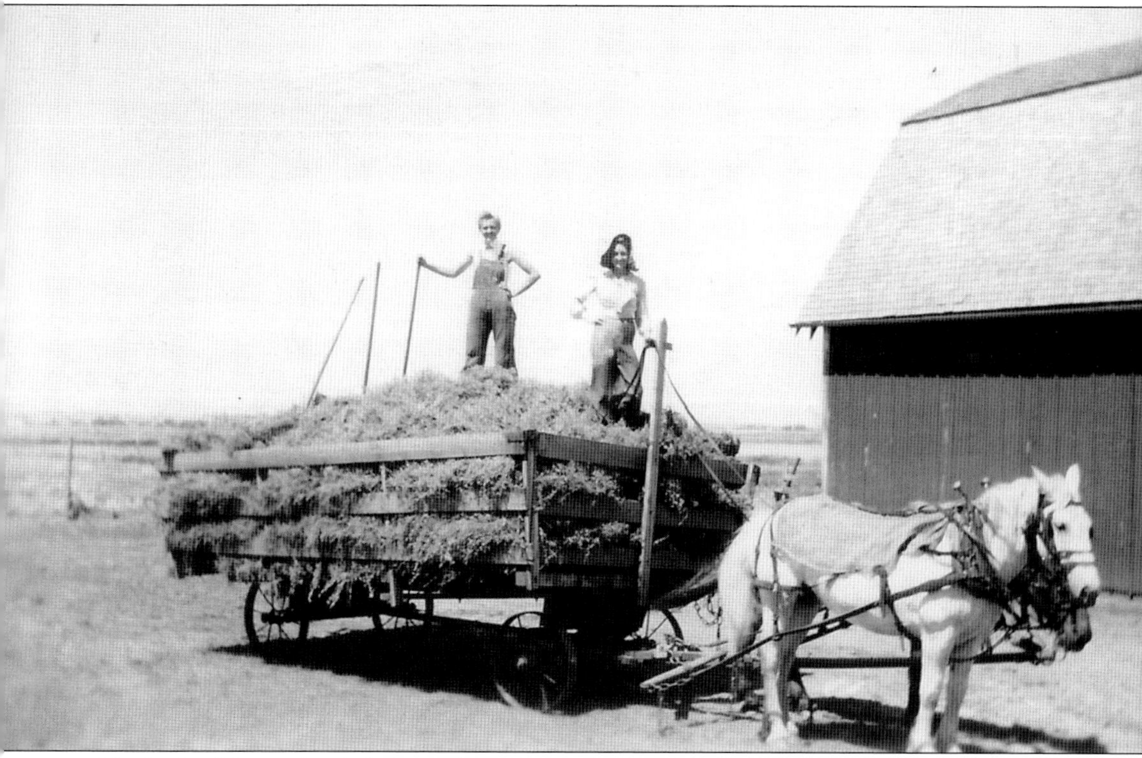

The back of this undated photograph reads, "We're putting up alfalfa." Many area Czechoslovakian families were farmers, and many of their descendants are still farming their ancestors' original lands. There are still groupings of Czechoslovakian families with their lands adjoining or close to each other in and around Yukon. (Courtesy LaVerne and Victor Benda family.)

From left to right are Edward, Bill, and Margaret Svejkovsky as very young children around 1901. They were three of 12 siblings. In many cases, the writing on the back of photographs of Czechoslovakian families is in the Czech language. (Courtesy LaVerne and Victor Benda family.)

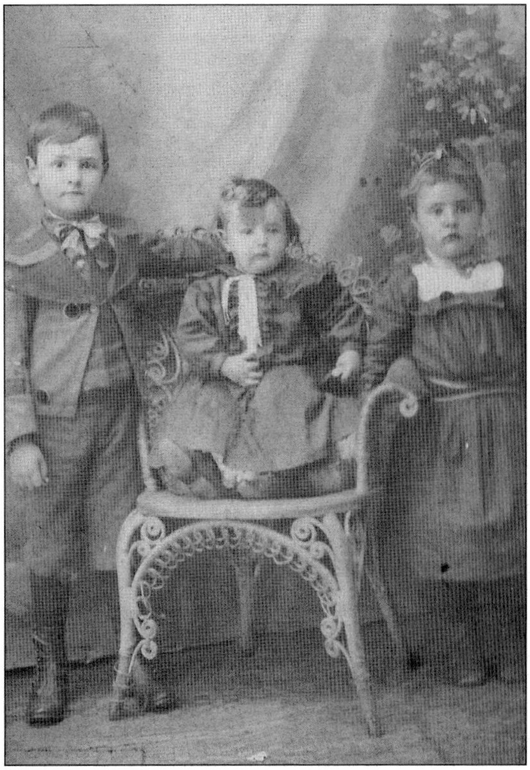

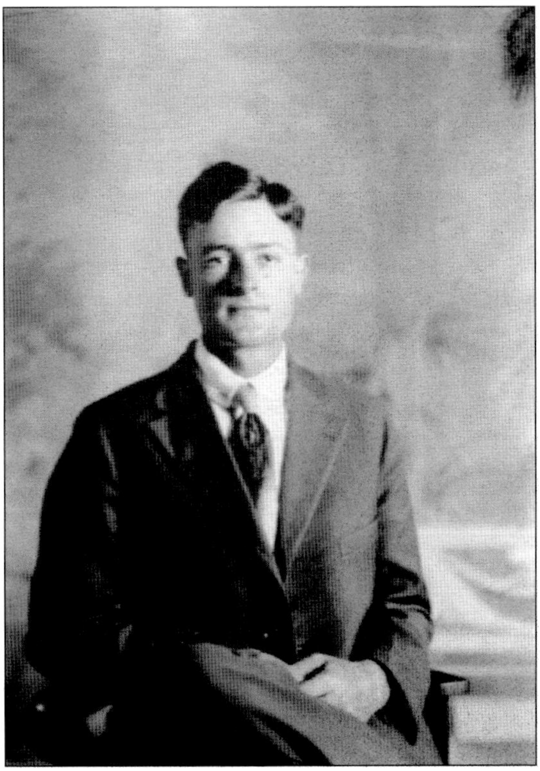

This 1918 portrait shows Edward Svejkovsky at about age 24. Svejkovsky graduated from Yukon High School. (Courtesy LaVerne and Victor Benda family.)

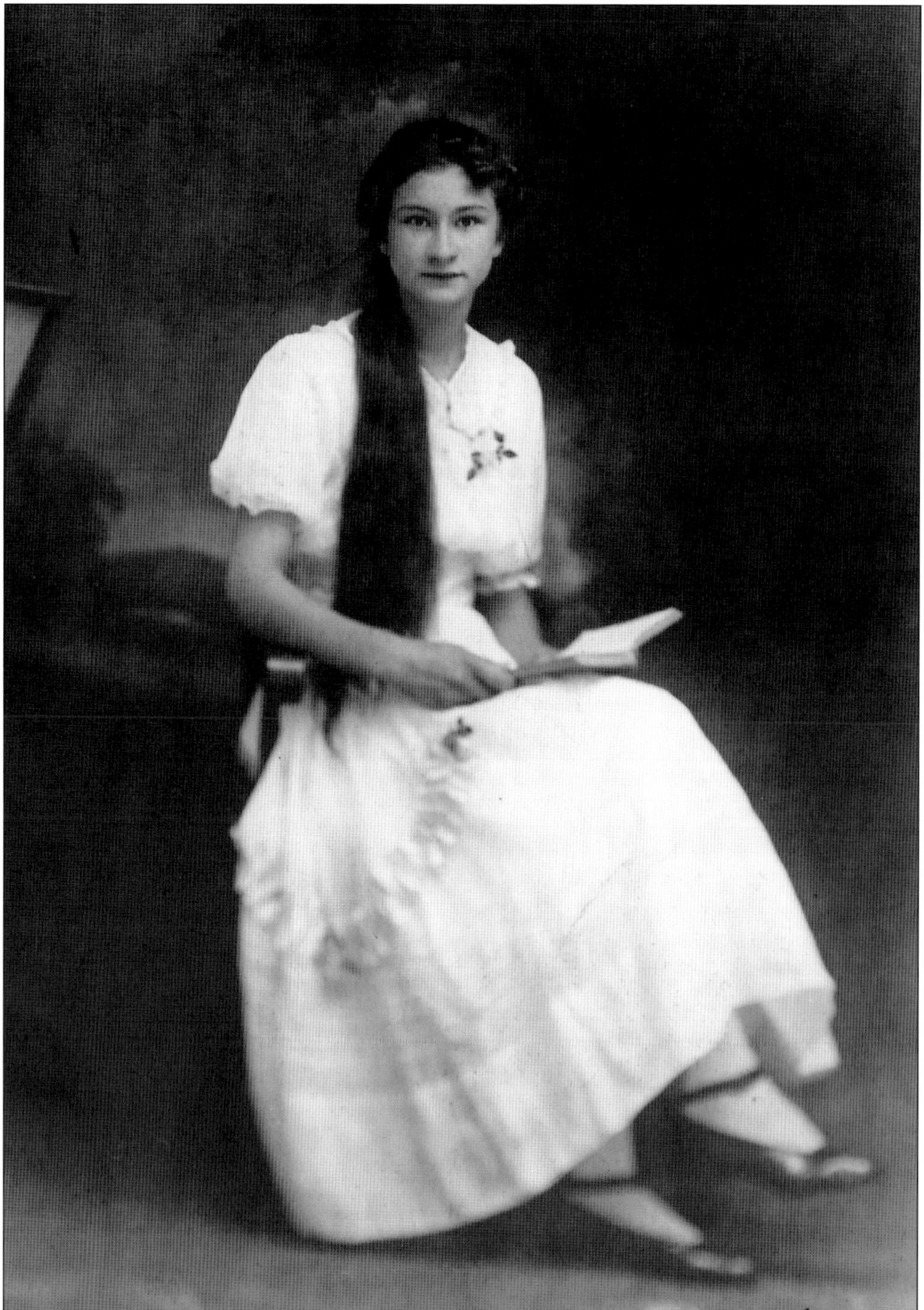

Anna Yeck was an only child who graduated from Yukon Public Schools in 1921. She attended Edmond's Central State Teachers College, now the University of Central Oklahoma. Her parents were born in Bohemia. (Courtesy LaVerne and Victor Benda family.)

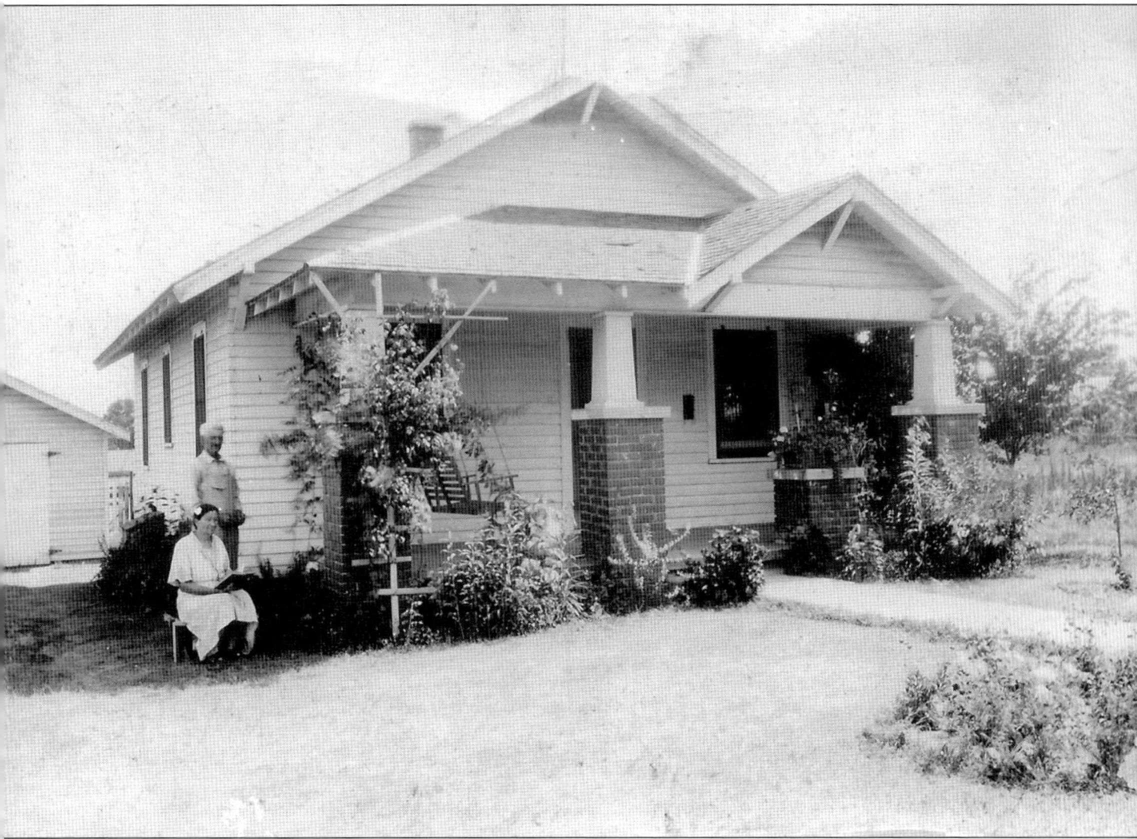

Antoinette and Wesley Yeck, Anna's parents, are shown beside their home on Poplar Street in this c. 1947 photograph. The home is still standing. (Courtesy LaVerne and Victor Benda family.)

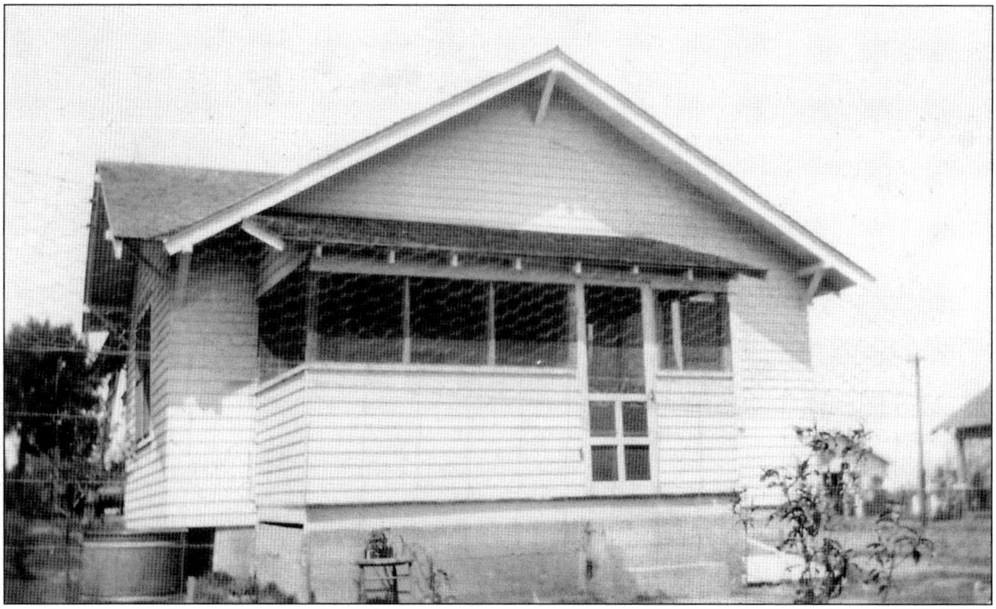

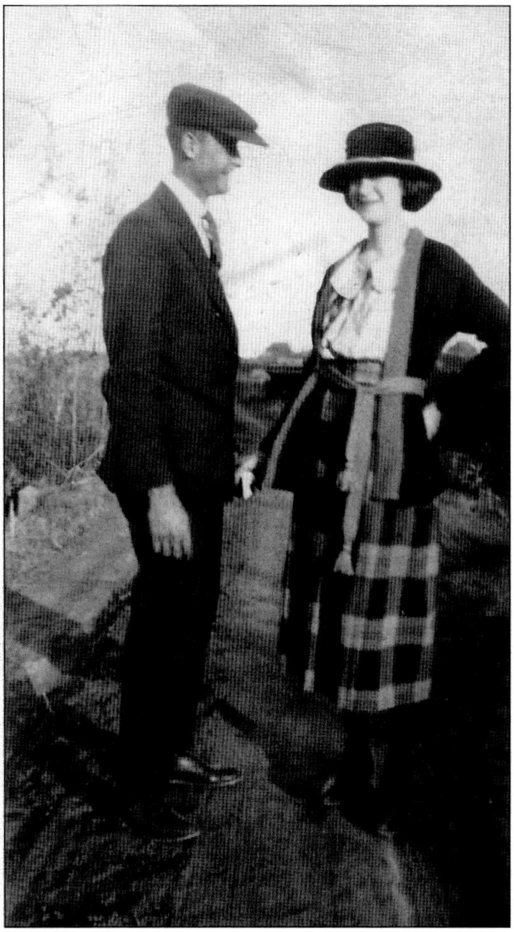

In this c. 1930 photograph, the back of the Yeck family home on Poplar Street can be seen. Czechoslovakian families, who populated the Canadian County and Yukon area, created a close-knit, cohesive, and strong culture. However, they wanted to be Americans while preserving their heritage. (Courtesy LaVerne and Victor Benda family.)

Edward Svejkovsky married Anna Yeck around 1923. Both were of Czechoslovakian ancestry. They are shown together in this 1921 photograph. (Courtesy LaVerne and Victor Benda family.)

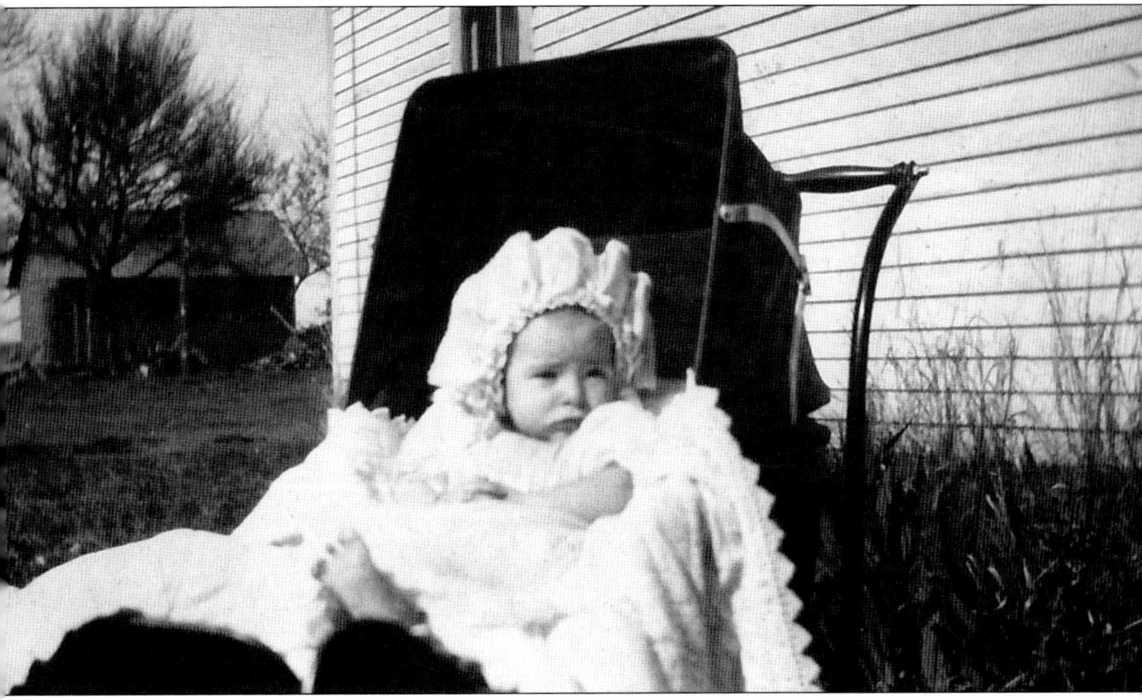

Anna and Edward Svejkovsky's oldest child, Darlene, is in her pram clothed in white. Edward worked as a farmer and roofer. He sold cars at Yukon's Chrysler-Plymouth dealership. He also worked for Douglass Aircraft Corporation and later at Tinker Air Force Base. (Courtesy LaVerne and Victor Benda family.)

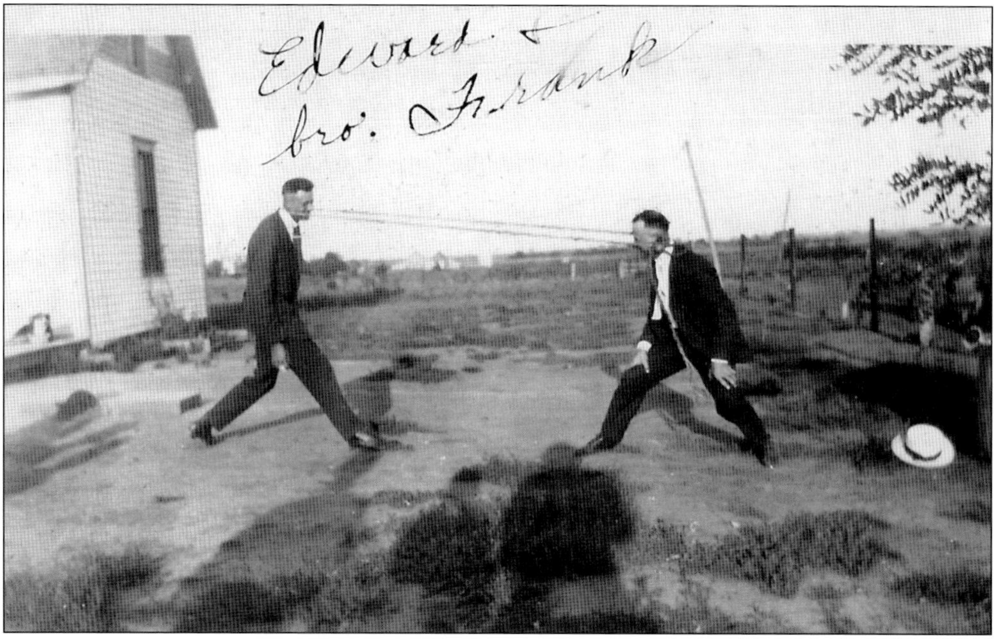

Edward Svejkovsky and his brother Frank are horsing around in this photograph. Frank served abroad in the military during World War I. In 1920, he built Svejkovsky Jewelry Store at 432 West Main Street. He sold jewelry, made violins, and repaired violins and watches. In 1921, he married Allie Swanda. (Courtesy LaVerne and Victor Benda family.)

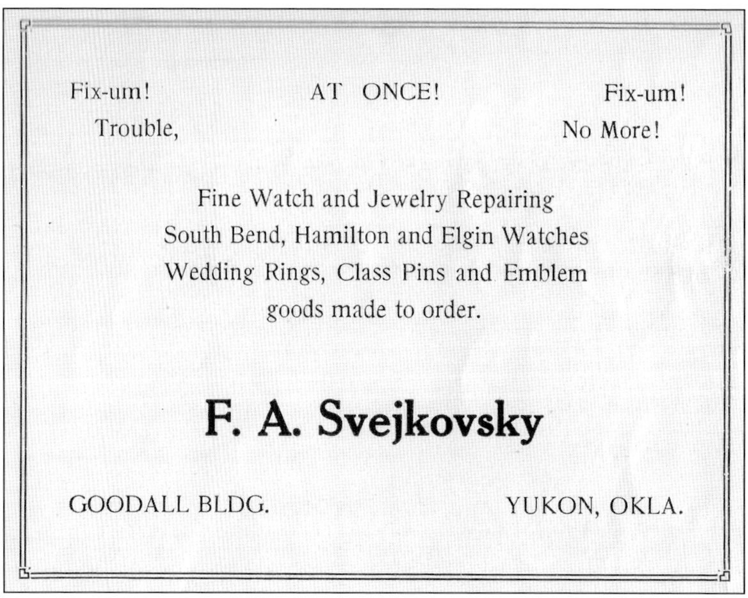

Shown is long-time Yukon businessman Frank Svejkovsky's advertisement in the 1917 Yukon High School yearbook. (Courtesy Phil Carson family.)

Anna and Edward Svejkovsky's older two children were Darlene (left) and LaVerne, shown here around ages seven and five, respectively. Anna and Edward raised their children in a home on Holly Street that still stands in 2021. (Courtesy LaVerne and Victor Benda family.)

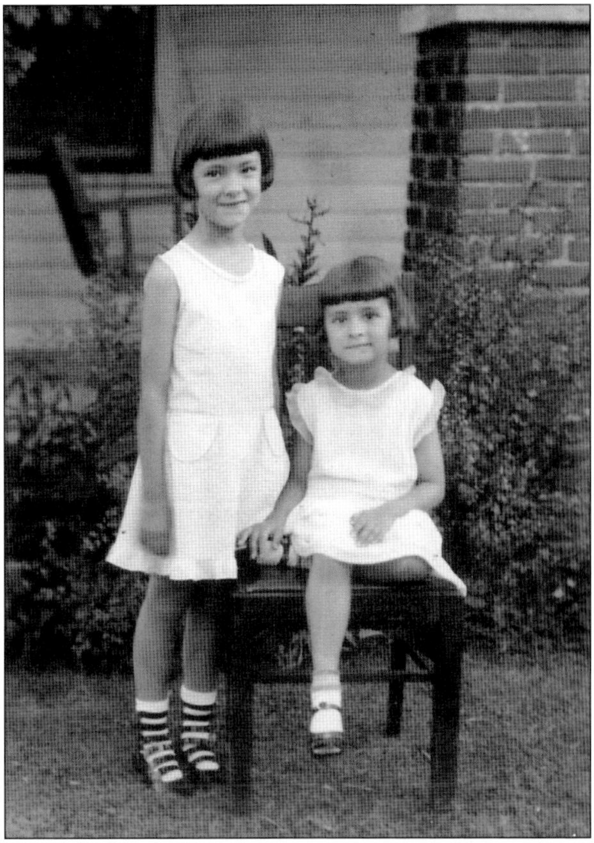

In June 1940, thirteen-year-old LaVerne Svejkovsky received a new bicycle after her May 1940 graduation from eighth grade. On the back of this photograph, she wrote that the bike was red and white and trimmed in blue. LaVerne and her two sisters graduated from Yukon High School. (Courtesy LaVerne and Victor Benda family.)

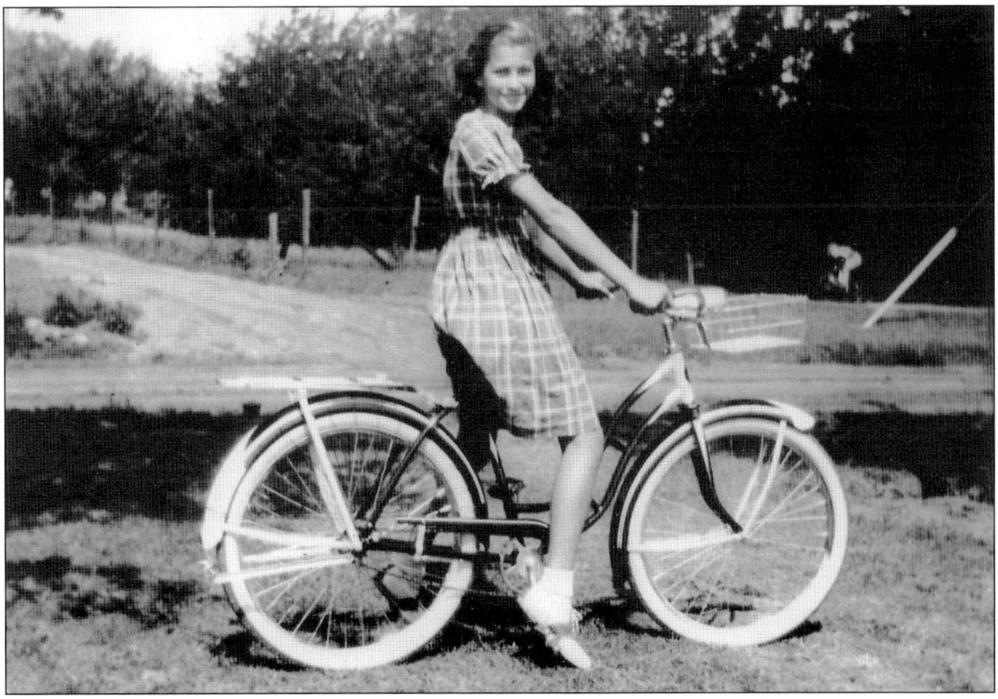

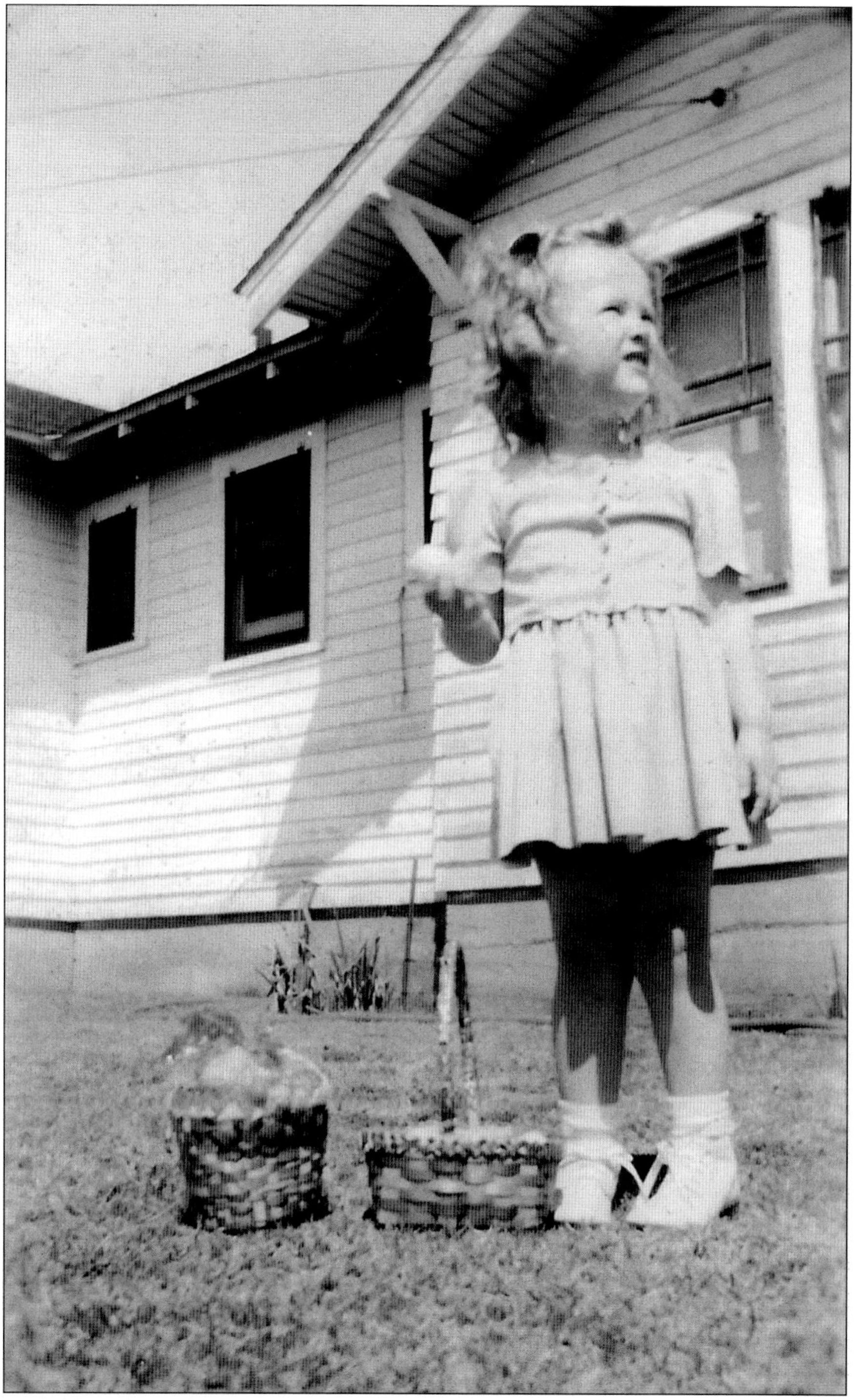

Anna and Edward Svejkovsky's youngest child, Delores, is dressed in her finest for Easter in 1944. She has two Easter baskets beside her. Delores was the youngest of three daughters. In the 21st century, Easter celebrations continue to be major events in Yukon. (Courtesy LaVerne and Victor Benda family.)

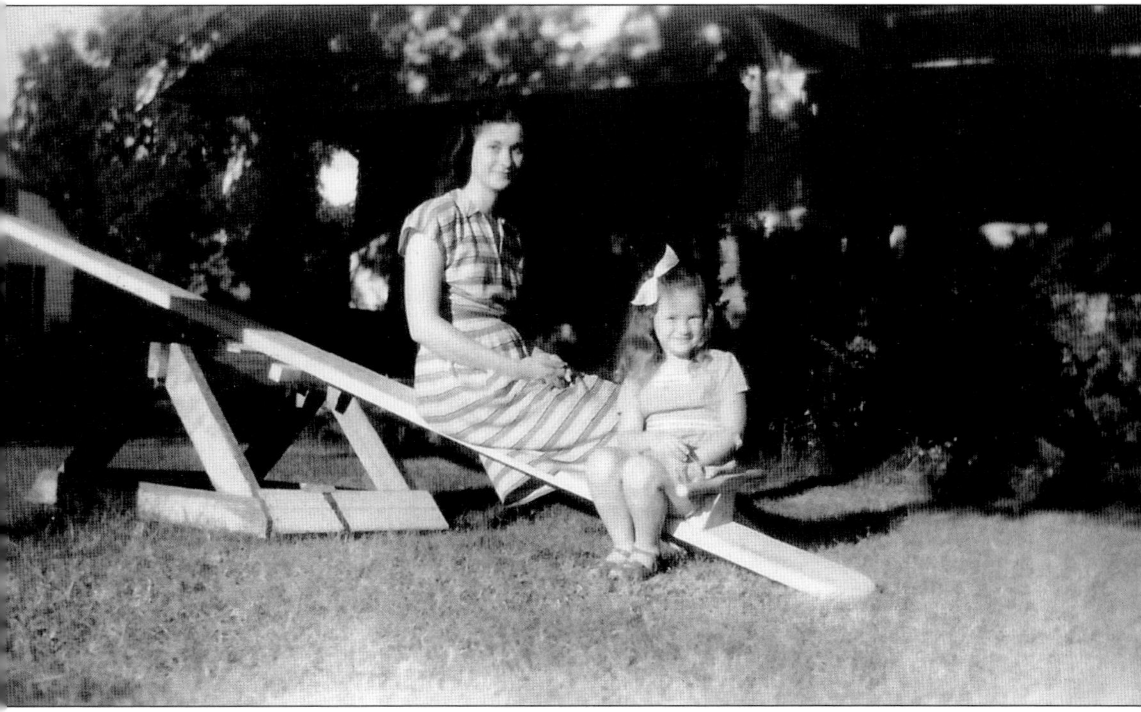

LaVerne Svejkovsky was 14 years older than her sister Delores. This photograph, dated September 2, 1946, shows the two sisters on a teeter-totter at their home on Holly Street. (Courtesy LaVerne and Victor Benda family.)

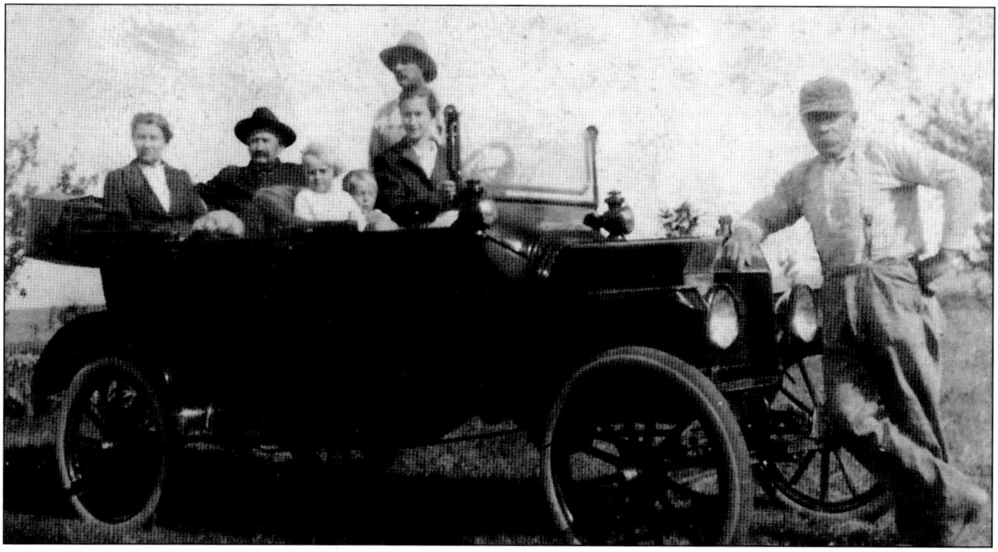

Anna Yeck Svejkovsky is in the driver's seat at the steering wheel, with Grandmother Yeck seated in the backseat. (Courtesy LaVerne and Victor Benda family.)

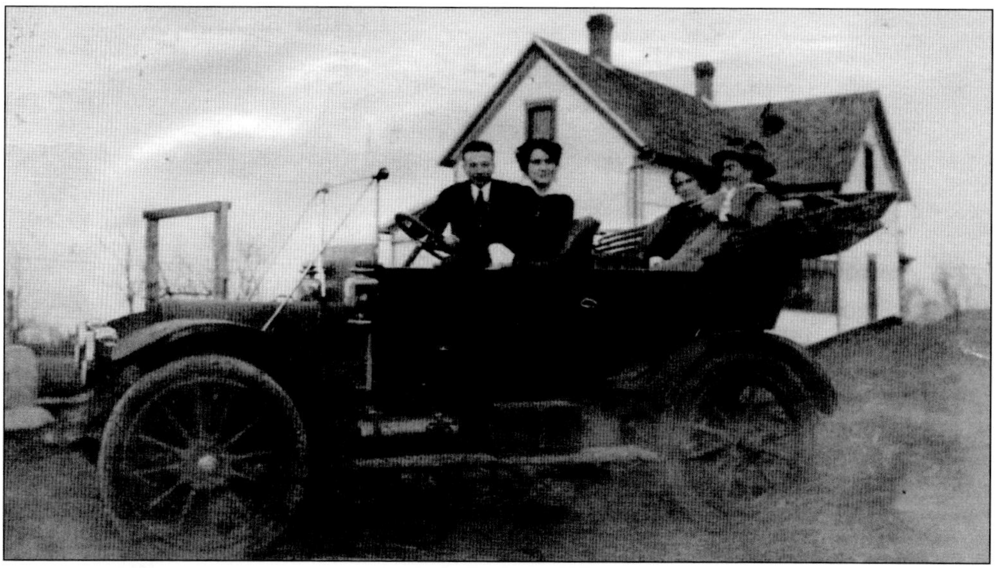

A photographer snapped this picture at Eighth and Poplar Streets, and the names Dan Phillips and May Shehan are written on the back. By around 1915, residents such as Odie Mulvey, Mike Mulvey, John Kroutil, Frank Kroutil, D. Phillips, George Bass, A.F. Dobry, R.M. Fry, I. Cutright, several doctors, and a few others owned cars. (Courtesy Yukon Historical Society.)

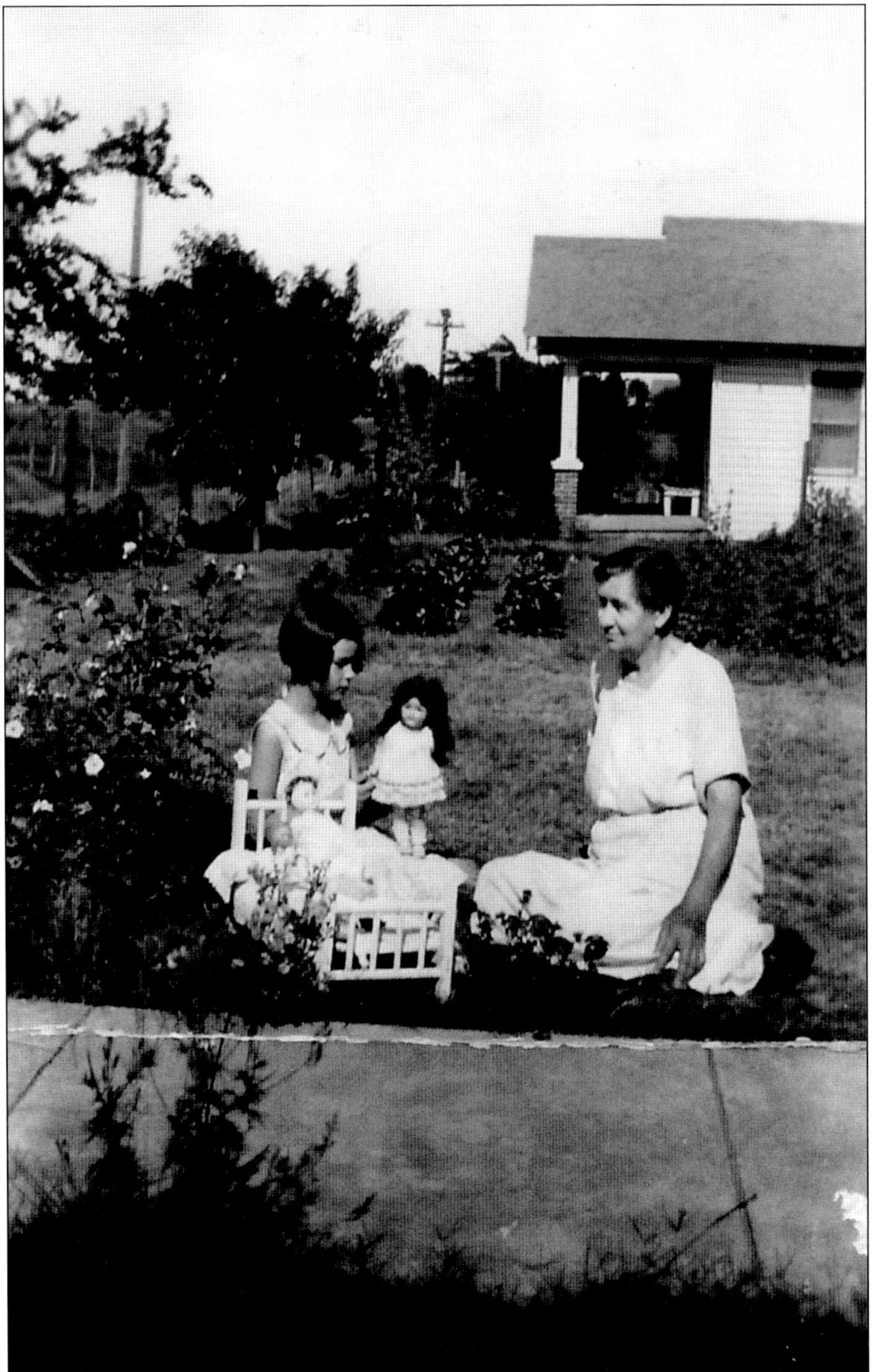

The mother of Anna Yeck Svejkovsky, Antoinette Yeck is shown with one of her granddaughters in the yard at the Yeck home on Poplar Street playing with dolls and doll furniture. (Courtesy LaVerne and Victor Benda family.)

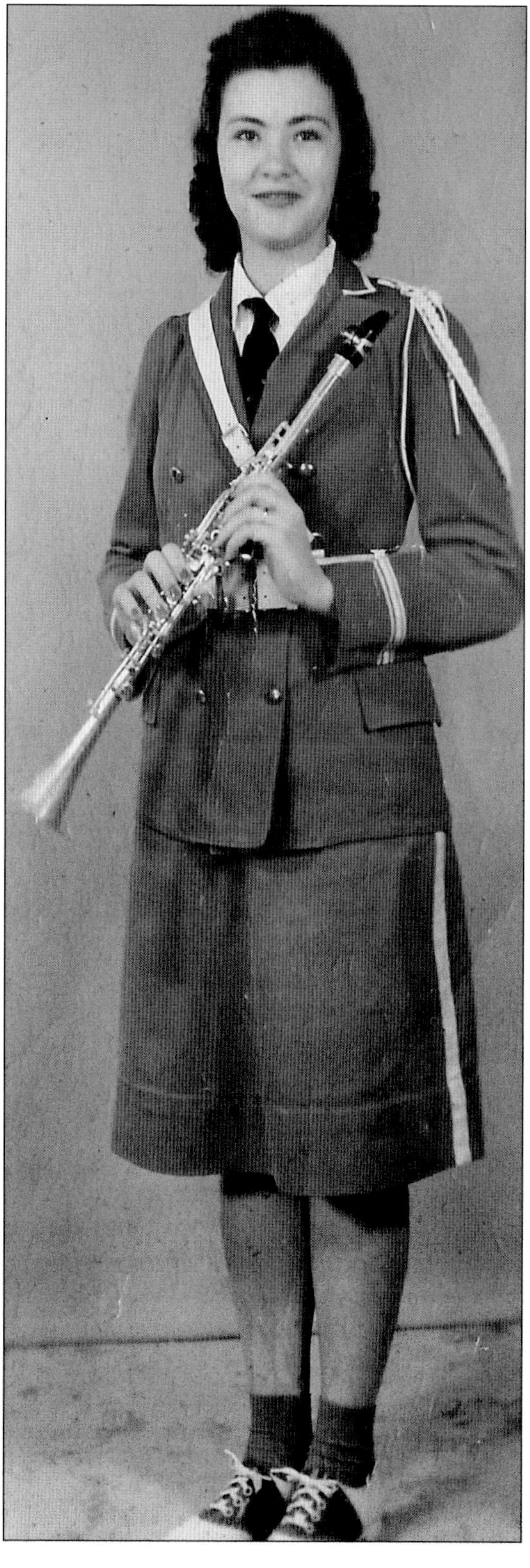

Anna and Edward Svejkovsky's three daughters, Darlene, LaVerne, and Delores, all graduated from Yukon High School. In this photograph, Darlene is shown in her high school band uniform. (Courtesy LaVerne and Victor Benda family.)

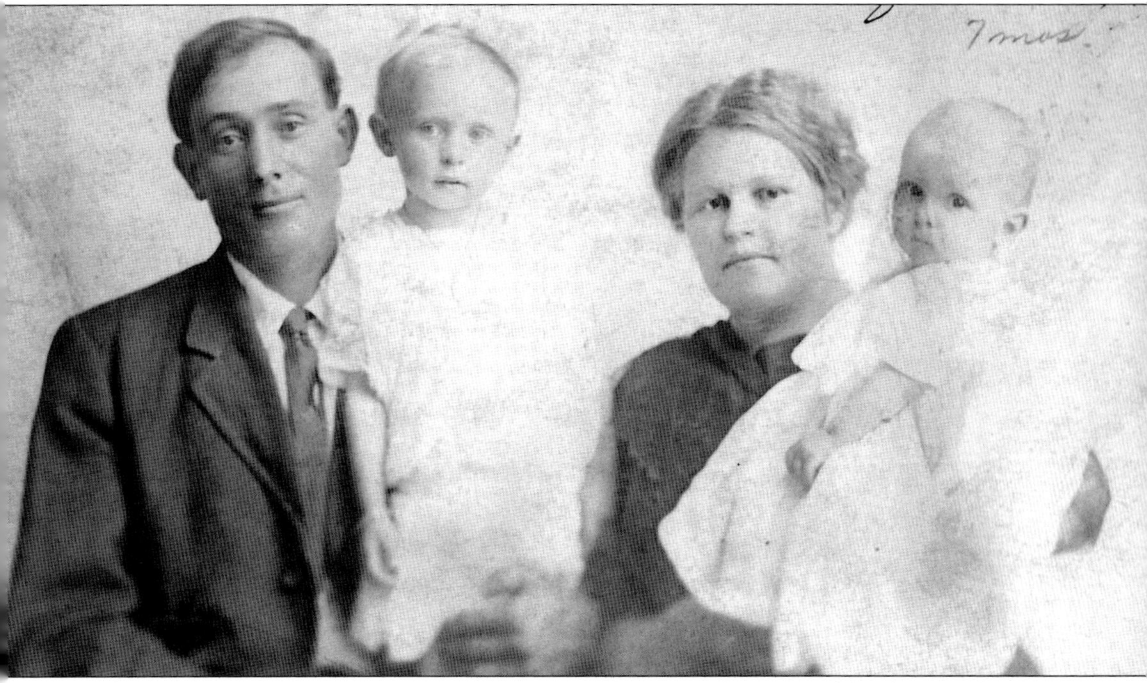

The back of this photograph is simply marked, "Mr. and Mrs. Frank Bingo and family." A Bohemian family, the Bingos were related to Anna Yeck Svejkovsky's mother. As Bohemian families fled persecution in their European homelands, many made their way to the United States. (Courtesy LaVerne and Victor Benda family.)

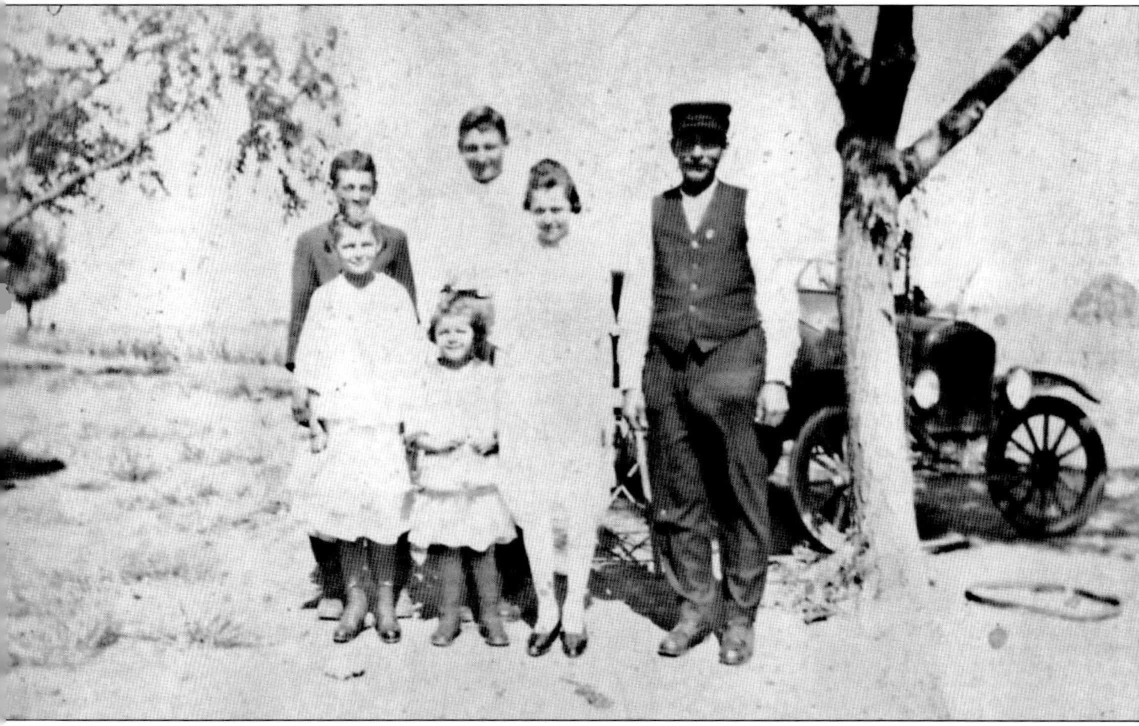

This undated photograph shows the Springler family. Anna Yeck Svejkovsky's mother's maiden name was Springler. The State of Nebraska sent leaflets into the Bohemian homelands, enticing residents to the state, where many ended up living. Some met and married there, but many moved on to other locations such as Yukon. (Courtesy LaVerne and Victor Benda family.)

Three

Growth, Prosperity, and Notoriety

No matter where one steps in Yukon, that spot was once an open prairie where buffalo roamed and native tribes lived. Then came cowboys and thousands of cattle making their way north.

Yukon was bubbling with progress before Oklahoma reached statehood in 1907. As of 2021, it has been 132 years since 89ers claimed their homesteads. It has been 131 years since the founders made Yukon official.

Many who came during the early years, and many who have come since, brought a variety of talents, backgrounds, and ethnicities. And of course, the large Czech community, in Yukon for over 100 years, plays a big role in the area. This makes Yukon a melting pot of ethnic groups and diversity.

Route 66 brings people through Yukon's historic Main Street corridor, which sparkles with nuggets that tell stories of the past. If visitors take the time to sit on Main Street, between Fourth and Fifth Streets, they can imagine the first residents dressed in their late 19th century and early 20th century clothing. Whether farmers or city folks, they were here.

Just as the Spencer brothers did in 1890, celebrities such as Dale Robertson and Bob Funk made their dreams come true by nabbing Yukon's beautiful prairie lands for their enterprises. World War II, the Great Depression, the Yukon Round Up Club, businessmen and businesswomen, and even Grady the Cow have left their mark on Yukon.

The original primitive energy and very old soul live on and will energize and direct the future if Yukon simply opens the past for everyone to experience.

1923 THE JAVELIN 1923

Marguerite Turner
Literary '22.

Gordon Newkirk
Boys' Glee Club.

Sarah Nee Allen
Girls' Glee Club '22, '23; Literary; Class Debate Team.

Leo Whelan
Football '22; Basketball '23; Hi Y '23; Glee Club.

Louise Bartos

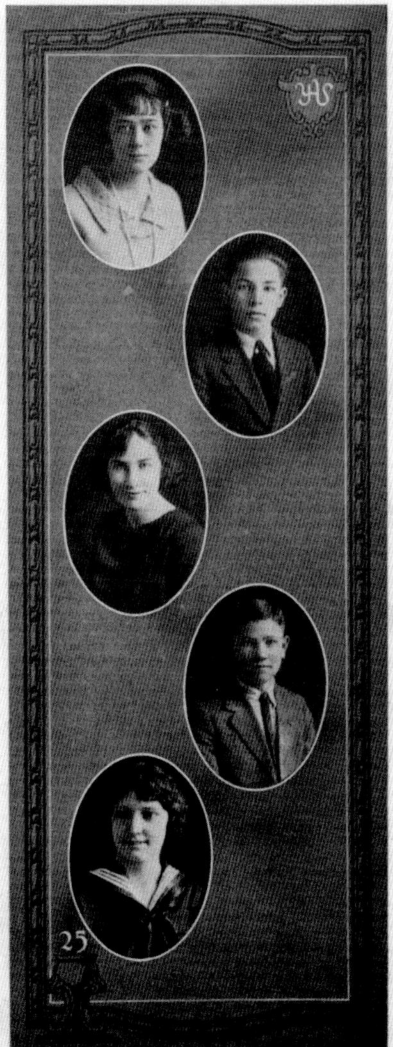

page twenty-three

The future Mrs. Frank Ball, Sara Nee Allen, is third from the top in this 1923 Yukon High School yearbook page. She laboriously and meticulously gathered and documented area history. Her book *Yukon's First Hundred Years* remains a repository of area facts and details. She also contributed greatly to other history publications and endeavors. (Courtesy Phil Carson family.)

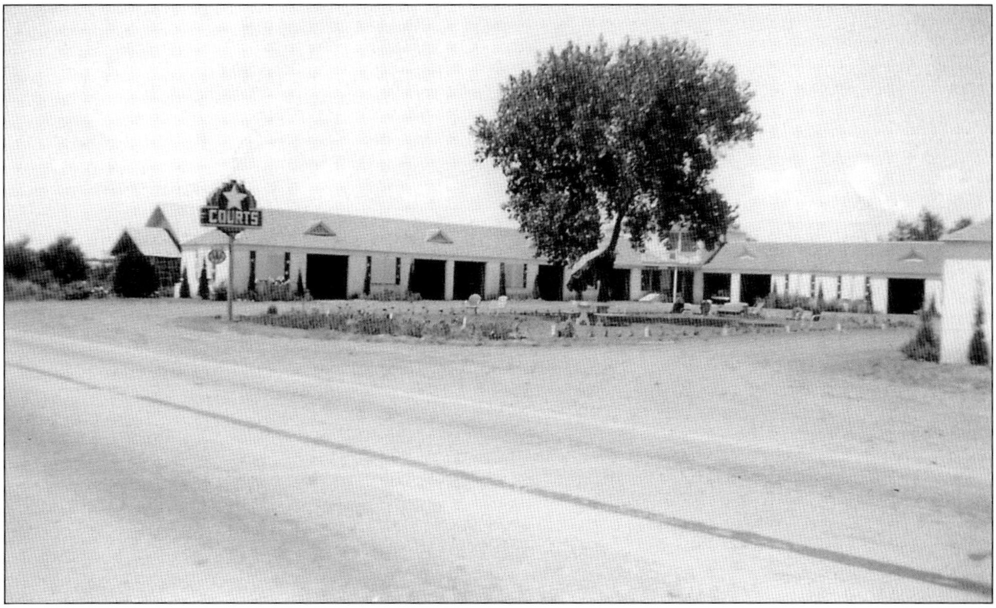

Main Street is also historic Route 66, blazing through Yukon from east to west. All of Yukon's streets were once dirt roads. But in 1925, the process of paving Route 66 began. By 1927, the work was done, giving Yukon its first paved street. This c. 1930s photograph shows Star Courts at 925 West Main Street. Situated right on Route 66, Star Courts was likely Yukon's first motel. (Courtesy Yukon Historical Society.)

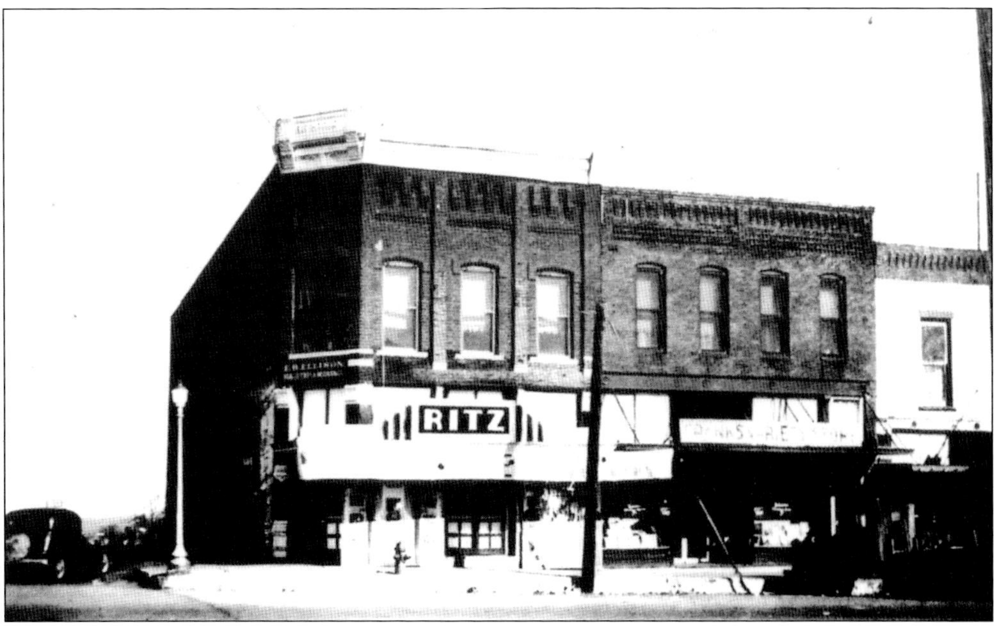

The Ritz movie theater at 459 Main Street was owned by Cecil Davis. It was constructed prior to 1940. (Courtesy Yukon Chamber of Commerce.)

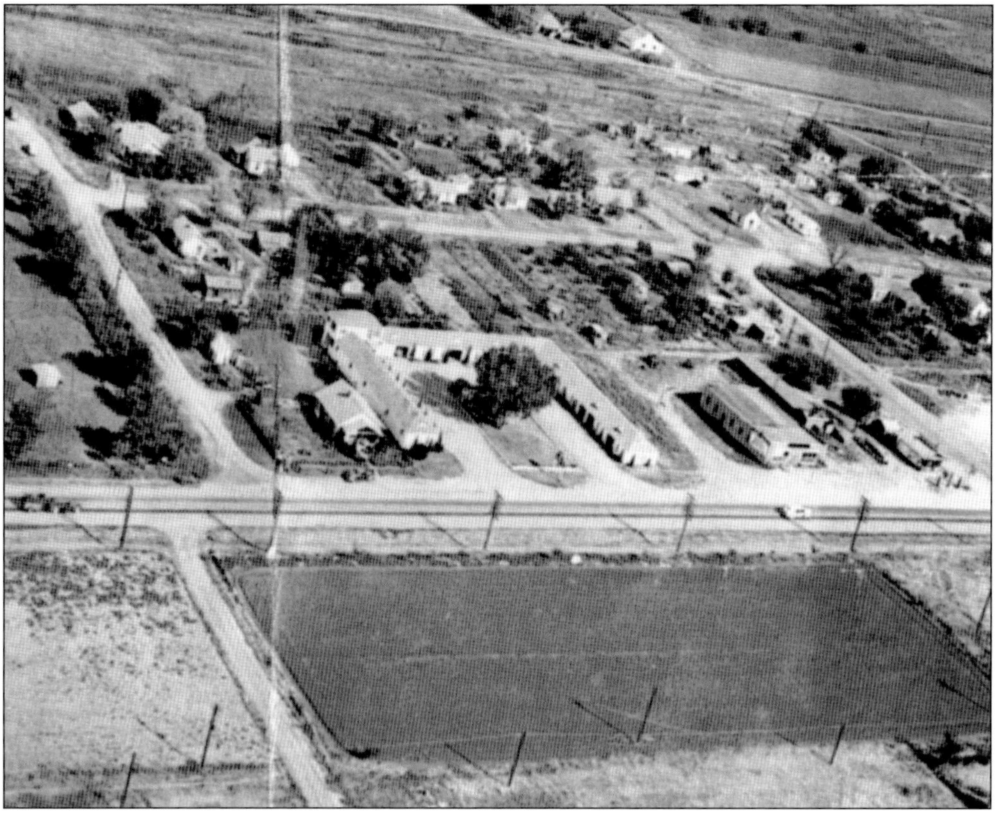

This late-1930s aerial photograph shows Route 66 running left to right. Star Courts motel sits in a prime location at center across from a large field. Flat prairie lands and surrounding farmlands are also visible. (Courtesy Yukon Historical Society.)

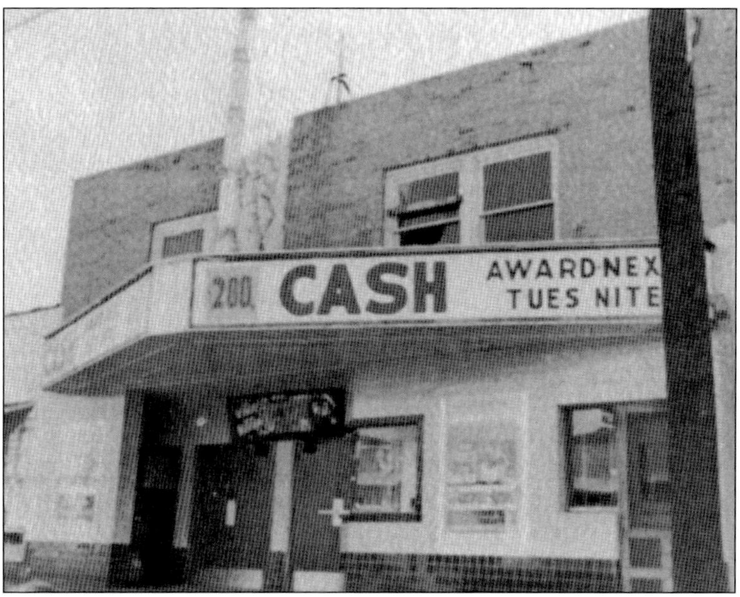

The Larry movie theater was just a few buildings west of the corner of Fifth and Main Streets on the south side of Main. During the 1940s and 1950s, youngsters would see a movie and then safely walk home in the dark. The theater name later changed to the Capri. (Courtesy Phil Carson family.)

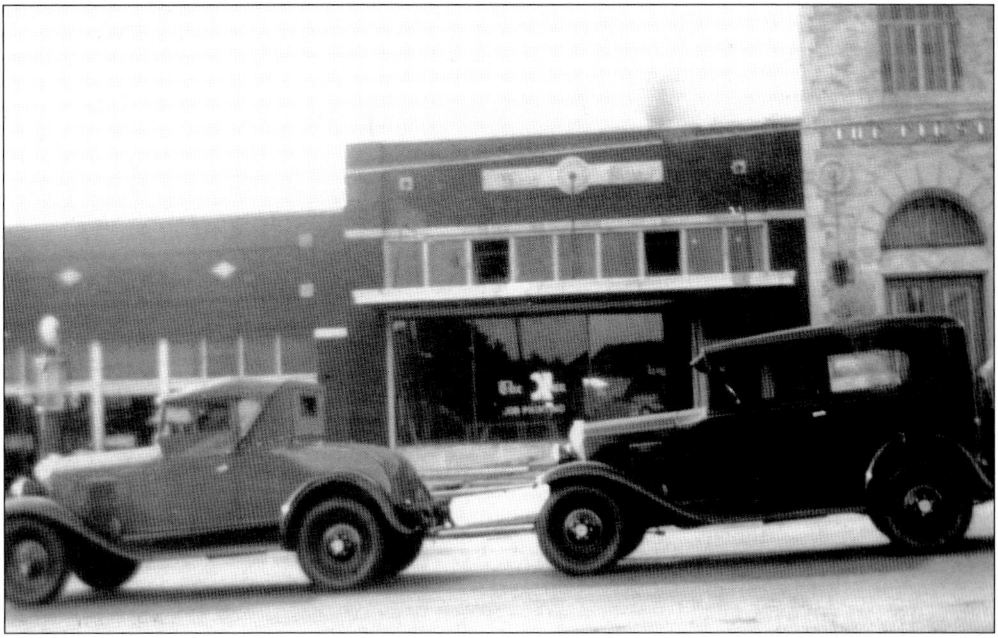

Yukon had newspapers starting in 1891. The *Yukon Sun* was established in 1899, and over time various newspapers were consolidated with various owners. A pioneer newspaper publisher, Poe Vandament came into Oklahoma Territory in 1903. He later bought the *Yukon Sun*. Shown is the *Yukon Sun* building, which remains at Fifth and Main Streets immediately west of the Wheatley Building on the northwest corner. (Courtesy Yukon Historical Society.)

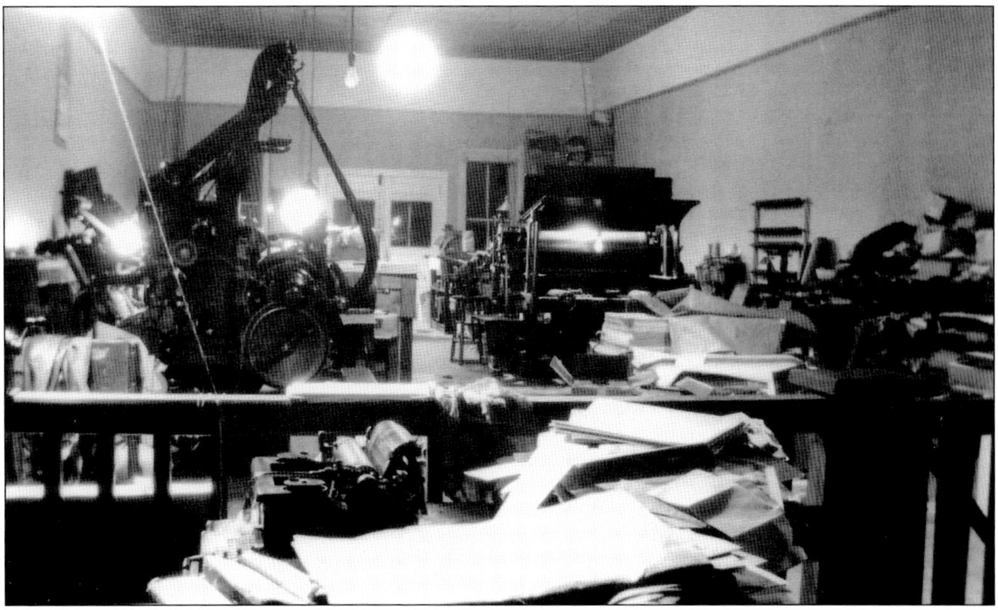

Poe Vandament edited and published the *Yukon Sun* from 1929 to 1948. Vandament was Yukon's mayor for five years, and helped organize Yukon's Lions Club in 1930. He served as president of the Oklahoma Press Association, and was treasurer of the Oklahoma Hall of Fame for 22 years. This undated photograph shows the interior of the *Yukon Sun* with printing presses and a typewriter. (Courtesy Yukon Historical Society)

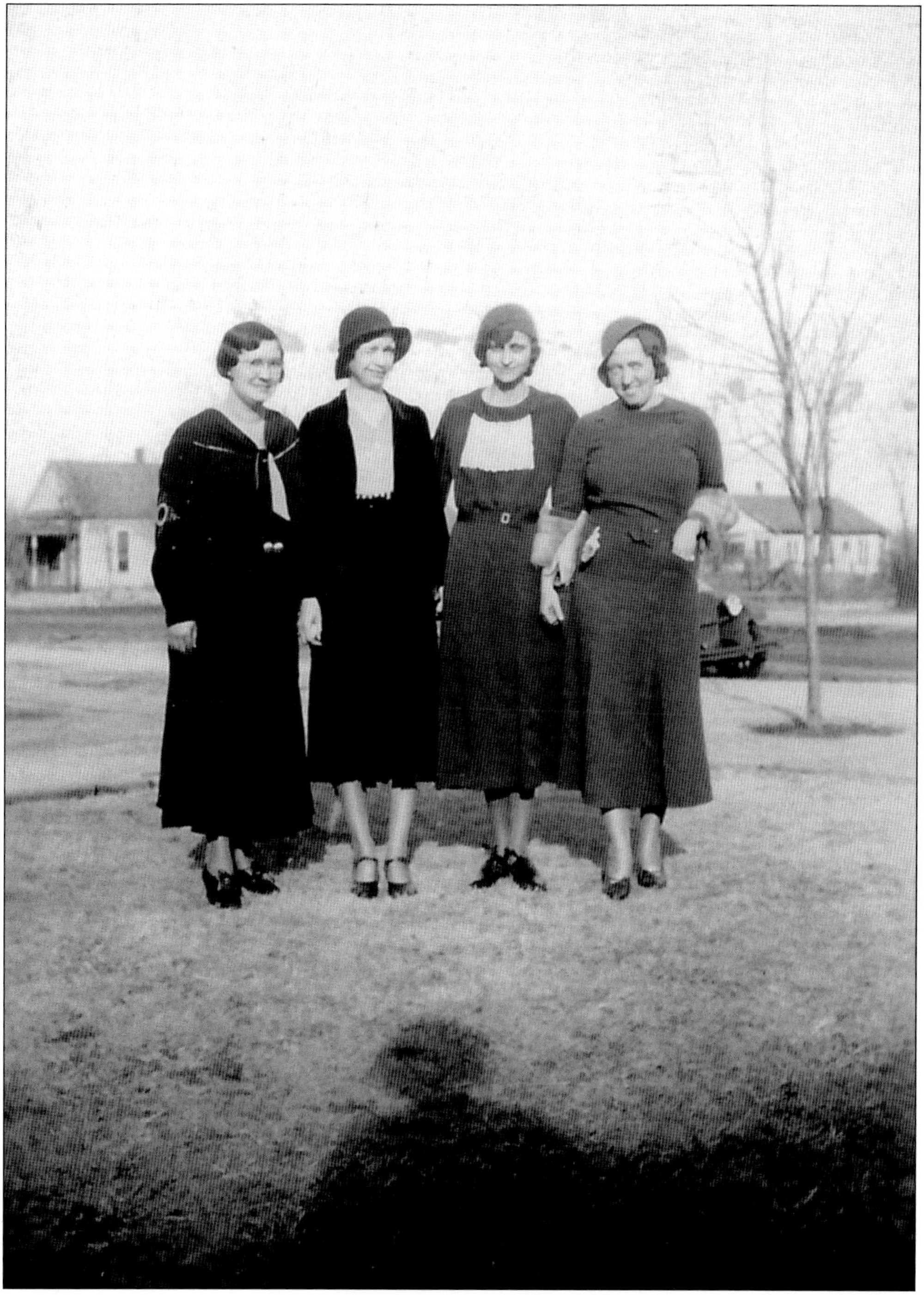

In 1934, Jean Rice Fry (far right) stands with other members of the Music Lovers' Club of Yukon, organized in 1930. Fry, a popular piano teacher, was integral to a hub of women who were intent on bringing culture to Yukon. The club members orchestrated plays and music recitals and participated in state cultural organizations. They held recitals and concerts in churches and halls all over Yukon. (Courtesy Yukon Historical Society.)

STATE OFFICERS

President .... Mrs. E. P. McMahon, Lawton
Vice-President .... Mrs. C. T. Caraker, Duncan
2nd Vice-President .... Mrs. D. H. Roche, Oklahoma City
Corresponding Secretary .... Mrs. H. Ben Turner, Lawton
Recording Secretary .... Mrs. Verne V. Grant, Okla. City
Historian .... Mrs. Orin Ashton, Chickasha
Treasurer .... Miss Marjorie Dwyer, Chickasha
District President .... Mrs. R. L. Fry, Yukon

LOCAL COMMITTEES

REGISTRATION
Mrs. G. Brinkman
Mrs. Porter Wood
Mrs. T. F. Addington

PROGRAM
Mrs. R. L. Fry
Mrs. M. A. Brattin

TRANSPORTATION
Mrs. R. A. Myers
Mrs. C. T. Alexander

ARRANGEMENT
Miss Mable Fry
Mrs. Julius Weber
Mrs. Raymond Kroutil

EXHIBIT
Mrs. Hugh McRee
Miss Emma Ellison

HOSPITALITY
Mrs. M. L. Addington
Mrs. T. A. Kroutil

LUNCHEON
Mrs. O. K. Spindel   Mrs. Chas. Pribyl

USHERS
Mrs. Glen Swope   Mrs. Paul Davis
Mrs. W. C. Bryan   Miss Merl Miller

PAGES
Altena Denning   Margie Little
Violet Cassel

———0———

THE CLUB COLLECT

We praise and thank Thee, Father, for the gift of music. Through us as channels of Thy Grace, may this blessed legacy be shared with all mankind. Grant that we may exemplify in our own lives the harmony of Thy great purpose for us. Give us magnitude of soul and such understanding hearts that we who make music may be as players upon rightly tuned instruments responding to Thy leading. Let us with renewed consecration dedicate ourselves to the purpose of our Federation to bring the spiritualizing force of music to the inner life of our nation.
Open our minds that Divine knowledge and wisdom may teach us how best to execute our pledge.

FIRST ANNUAL CONVENTION

Of The

FOURTH DISTRICT

OKLAHOMA FEDERATED MUSIC CLUBS

CHRISTIAN CHURCH

6th Street and Maple Ave.

YUKON, OKLAHOMA

NOVEMBER 9, 1931

HOSTESS CLUB

MUSIC LOVERS' CLUB, YUKON

Hosted by the Yukon Music Lovers' Club at the Christian Church in Yukon, this 1931 program for the first annual convention of the Fourth District of the Oklahoma Federated Music Clubs includes Jean Rice Fry's name, and the surnames of others who were part of Yukon's original, entrepreneurial families. (Courtesy Yukon Historical Society.)

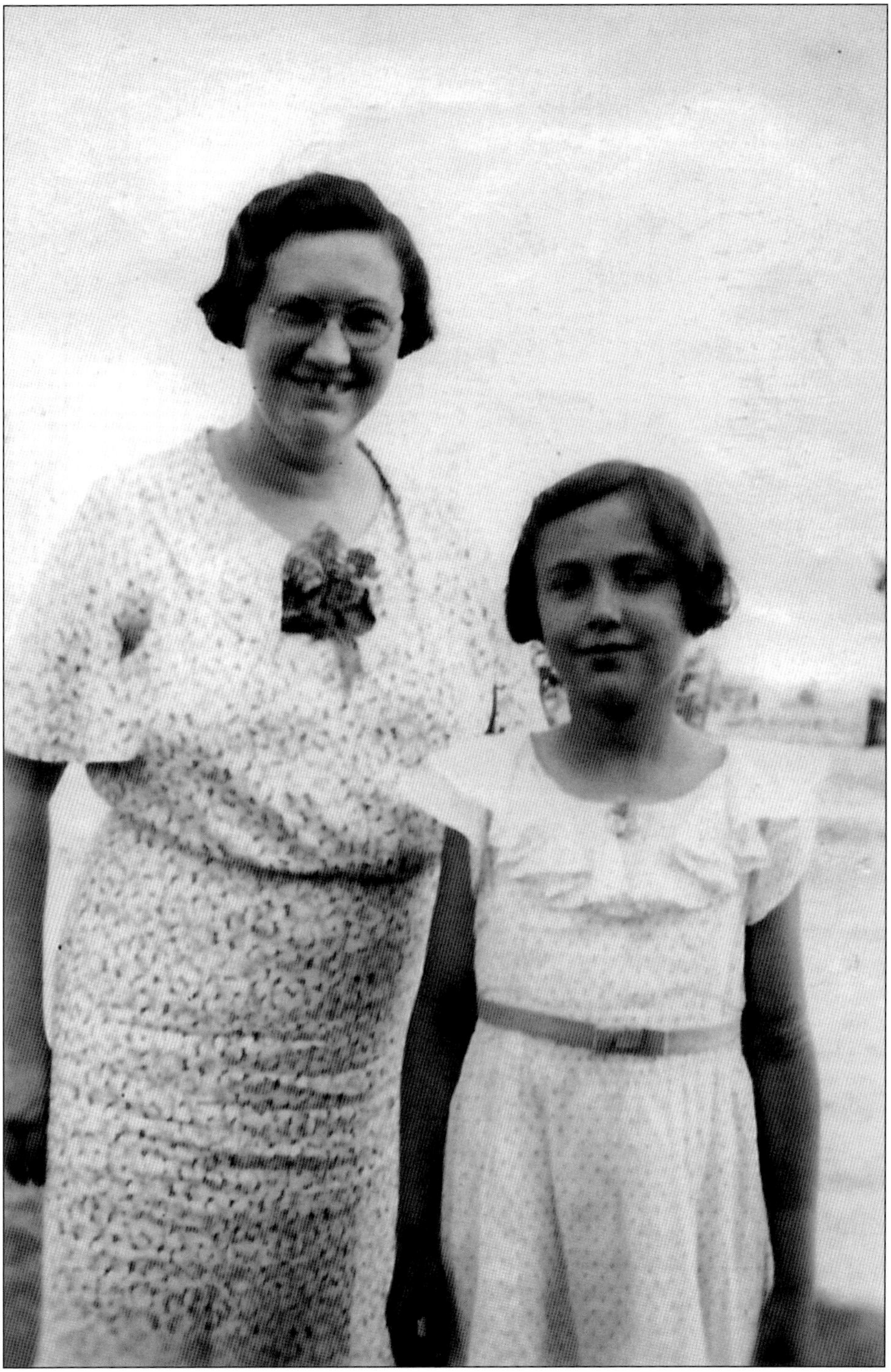

Jean Rice married Robert Fry, Mabel Fry's brother. Jean was an active member of the National Guild of Piano Teachers USA. A musician in her own right, she organized a youth choir and numerous other cultural events. In this 1937 photograph, she is with her daughter Jean Claire Fry. (Courtesy Yukon Historical Society.)

A family scrapbook highlights Jean Rice Fry's life, including programs from recitals, plays, and other events, along with pictures of her students, including this undated photograph of Lula Mae Rowland. Many of her students had the surnames of the original families who helped build Yukon. (Courtesy Yukon Historical Society.)

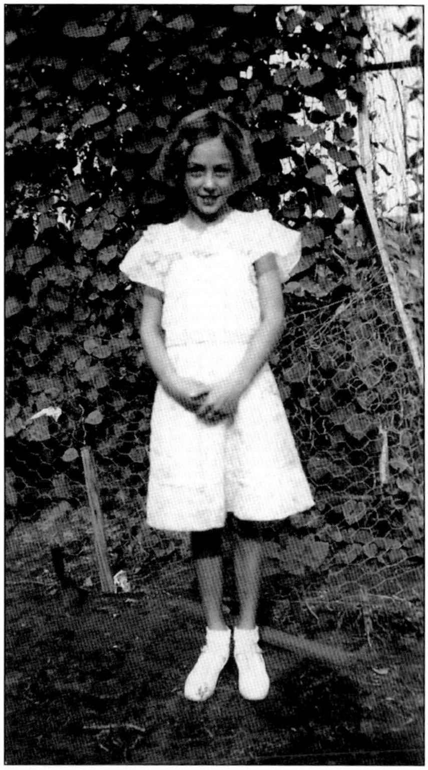

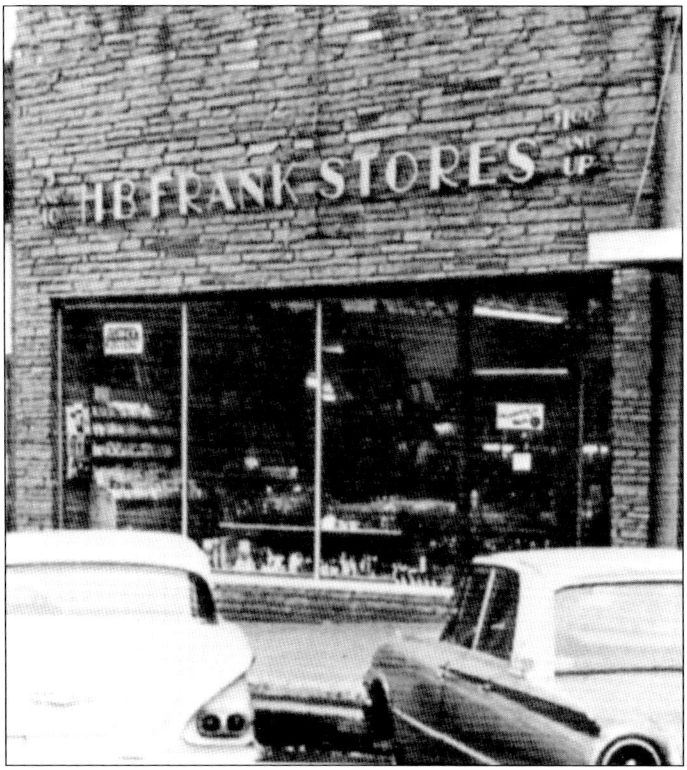

Myrel and Howard Boone "H.B." Frank Sr. arrived in 1935. Their H.B. Frank Store at 454 West Main Street was previously Stafford's Saloon in 1904, then Jeffers Sanitary Confectionery, then a café. The Franks were in the variety store business for 55 years. The Yukon Chamber of Commerce Citizen of the Year Award is named after H.B. Frank. (Courtesy Donna Anderson Mills.)

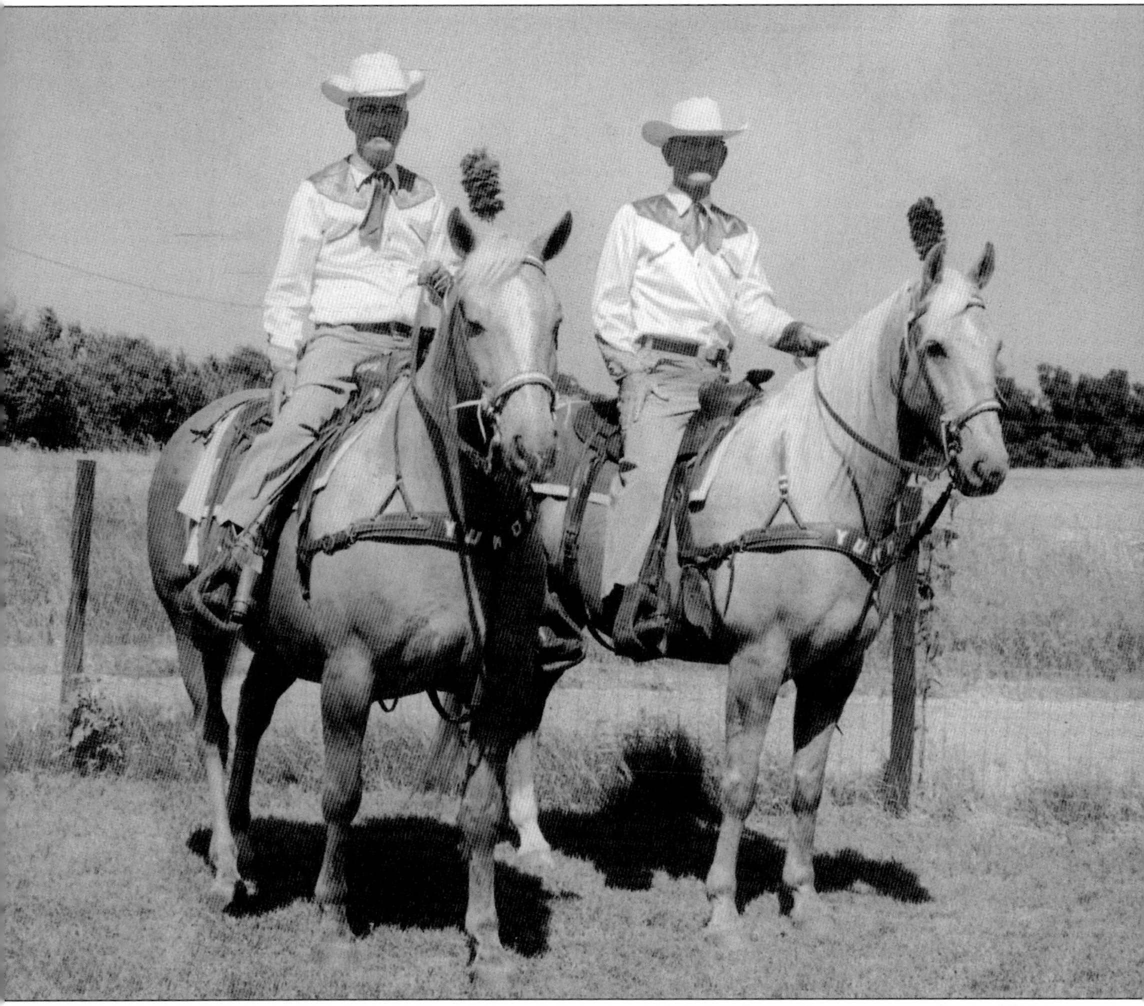

A founder of the Yukon Round Up Club, Glen Cornwell, is on the right. He arrived in Oklahoma Territory in 1898, settling in Frisco, then relocating to Yukon in 1910. He was Yukon's Chevrolet dealer from 1927 to 1935. Partnering with Walter Neal in 1937, Cornwell started the Yukon Livestock Auction, also known as the Yukon Sale Barn. (Courtesy Shirley Davis.)

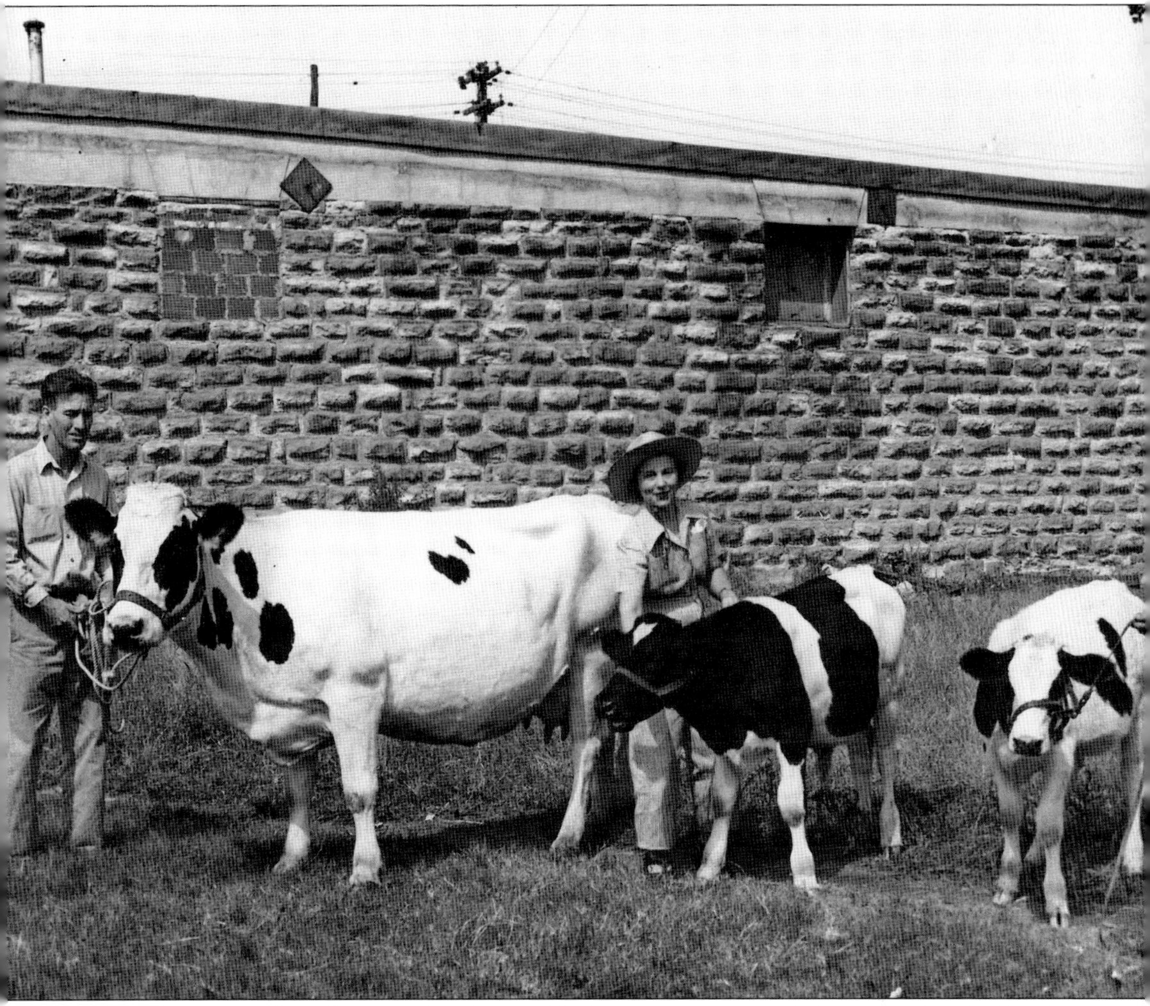

Mary Jane Cornwell Ochsner, Glen Cornwell's daughter, is pictured here with her husband, Ferol Ochsner, who eventually became Cornwell's partner when Walter Neal died. Farmers from miles around arrived in Yukon to attend the weekly cattle auctions, which sometimes included horses. Cornwell once had 200 dairy calves flown in from California. The plane was late, and the sale did not start until 11:00 p.m., making the news from Oklahoma to Los Angeles. (Courtesy Shirley Davis.)

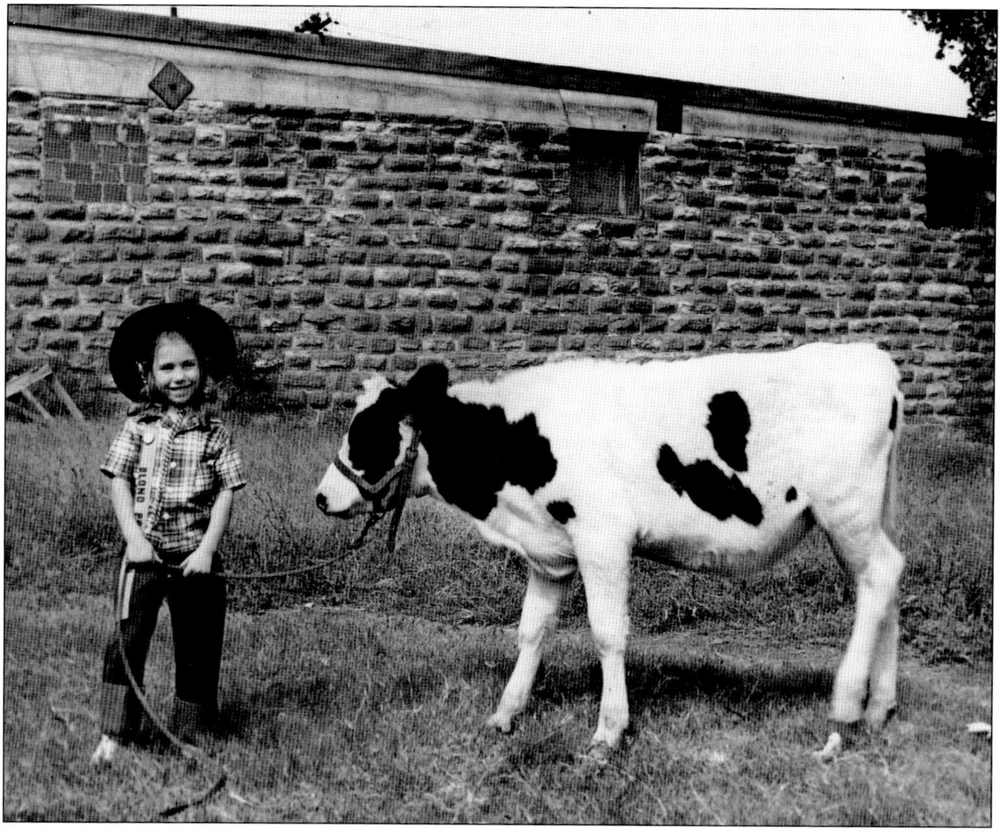

Glen Cornwell's granddaughter Glenda Ochsner is standing with a cow. Known for saying "By jing," Cornwell was the auctioneer at the Yukon Sale Barn he owned and operated until retiring in 1972. The barn was also used for social events including square dances. (Courtesy Shirley Davis.)

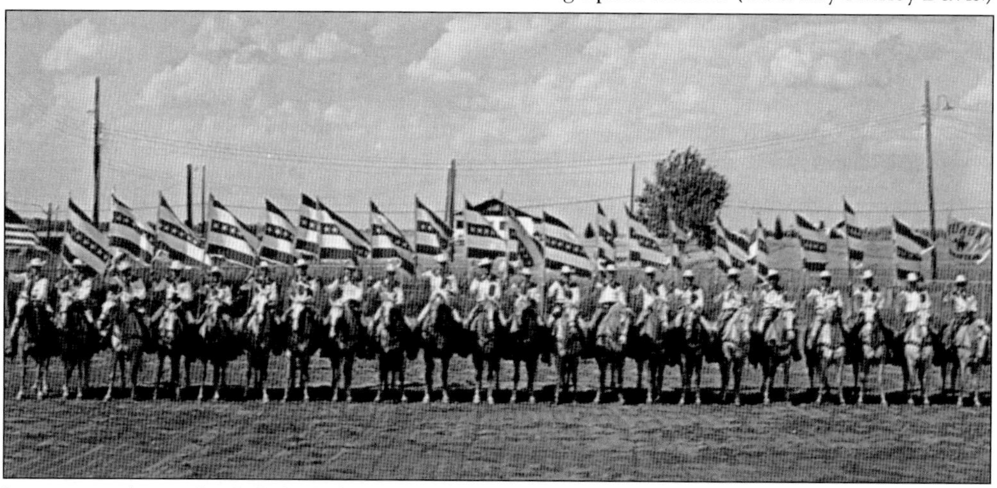

Incorporated in early 1947, the Yukon Round Up Club initially required members to ride palomino horses. The club's precision drill team members wore red and white, performed around the state, and rode in parades. The club hosted rodeos and other events. In 2013, the club donated its rodeo arena and property to the Canadian County Cowboy Church, 550 East Main Street. (Courtesy Canadian County Cowboy Church, Yukon Round Up Club.)

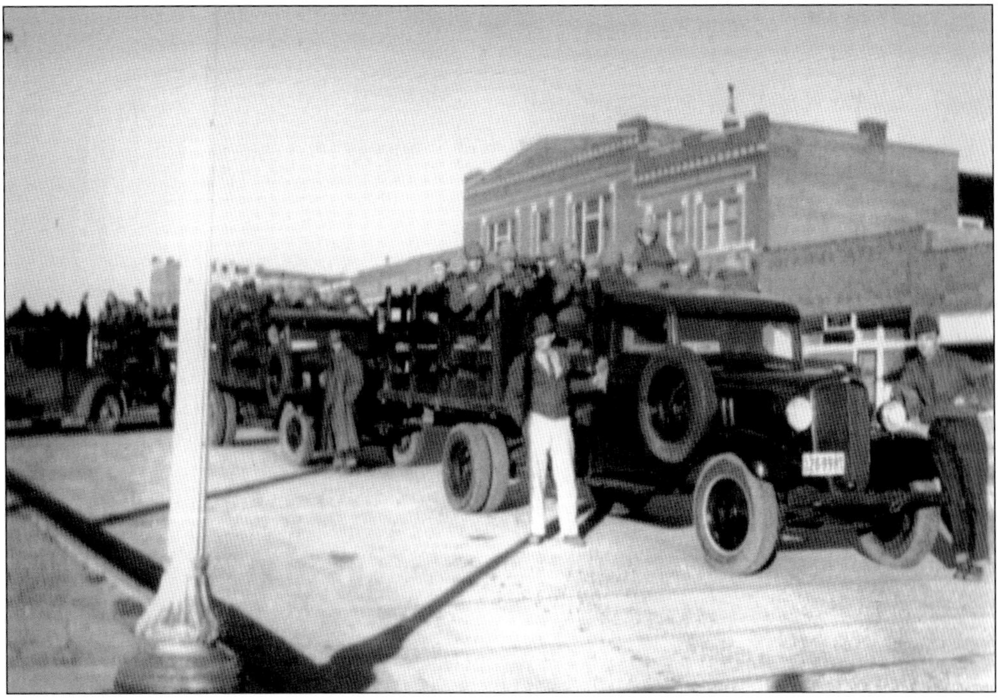

During the bleakest years of the Great Depression, the federal Works Progress Administration created jobs for Americans. In Yukon, the WPA improved the water system and fire hydrants and also built a municipal building to house city hall, a city jail, and fire equipment, along with other projects. This photograph shows WPA workers in Yukon on December 5, 1935, in front of the Mulvey Mercantile building. (Courtesy Genie Vinson.)

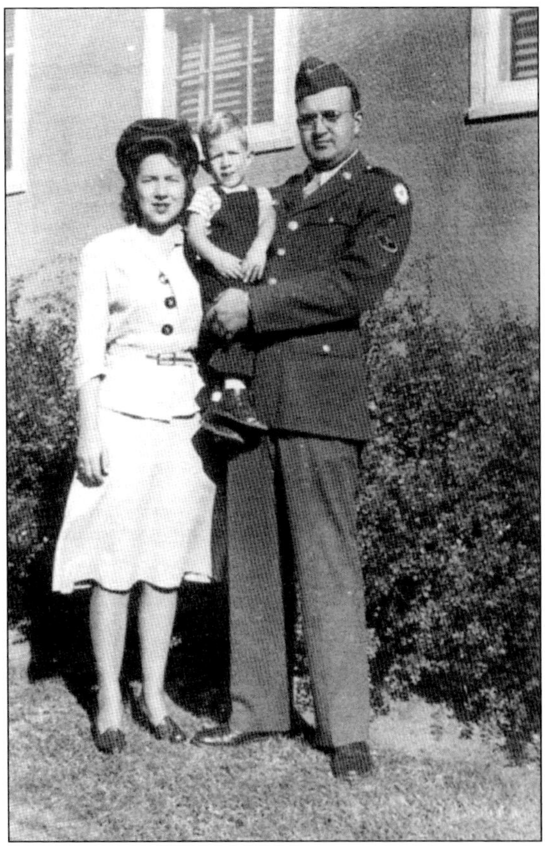

Standing beside his wife, Jane, in 1945, Milton Shedeck holds their son Milo. Milton served in the US Army during World War II. Interstate 40 cut through the farm that Milton inherited, so he and Jane donated land for Shedeck Elementary School. They were both Yukon educators. (Courtesy Betty Sackett.)

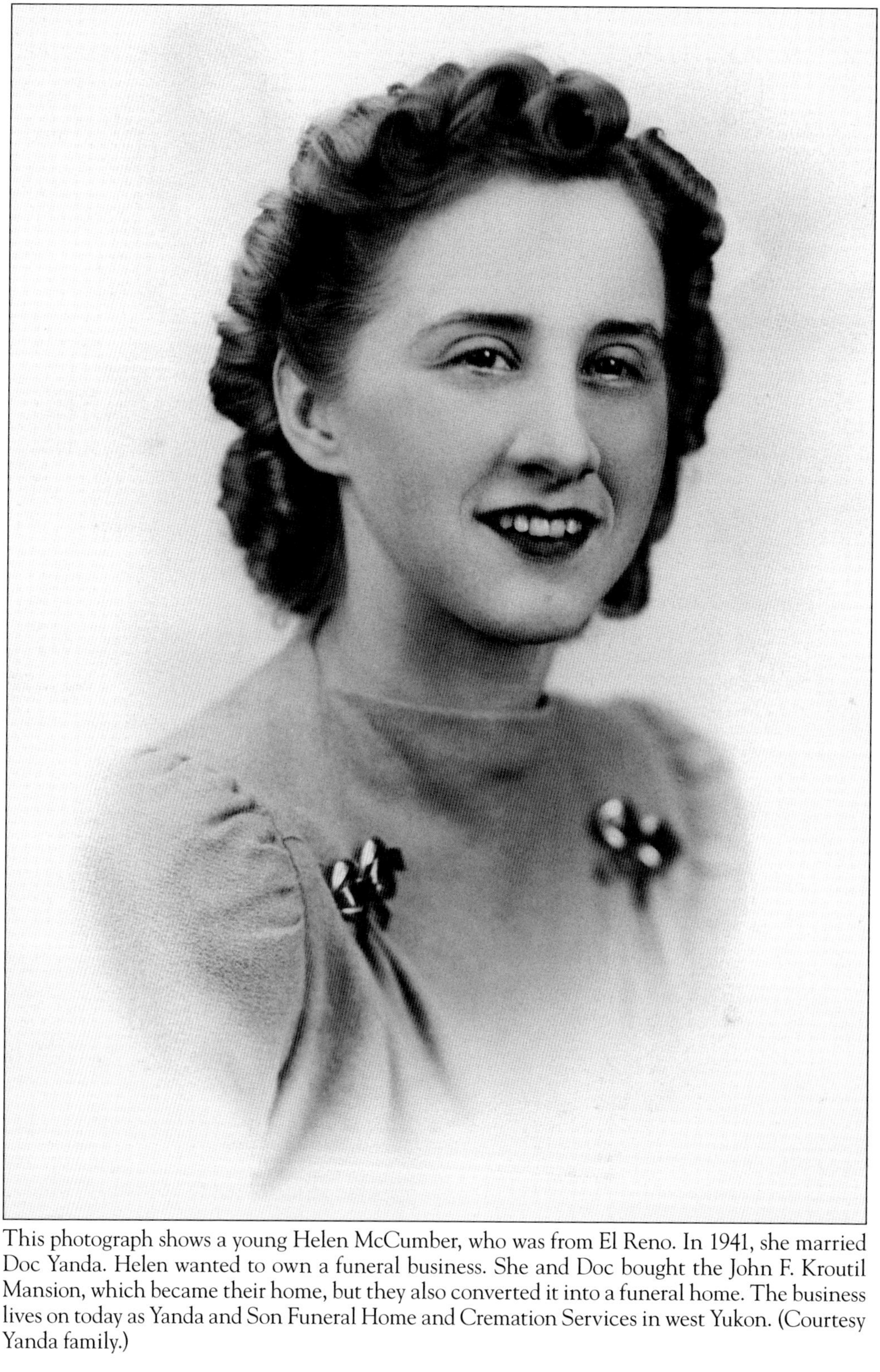

This photograph shows a young Helen McCumber, who was from El Reno. In 1941, she married Doc Yanda. Helen wanted to own a funeral business. She and Doc bought the John F. Kroutil Mansion, which became their home, but they also converted it into a funeral home. The business lives on today as Yanda and Son Funeral Home and Cremation Services in west Yukon. (Courtesy Yanda family.)

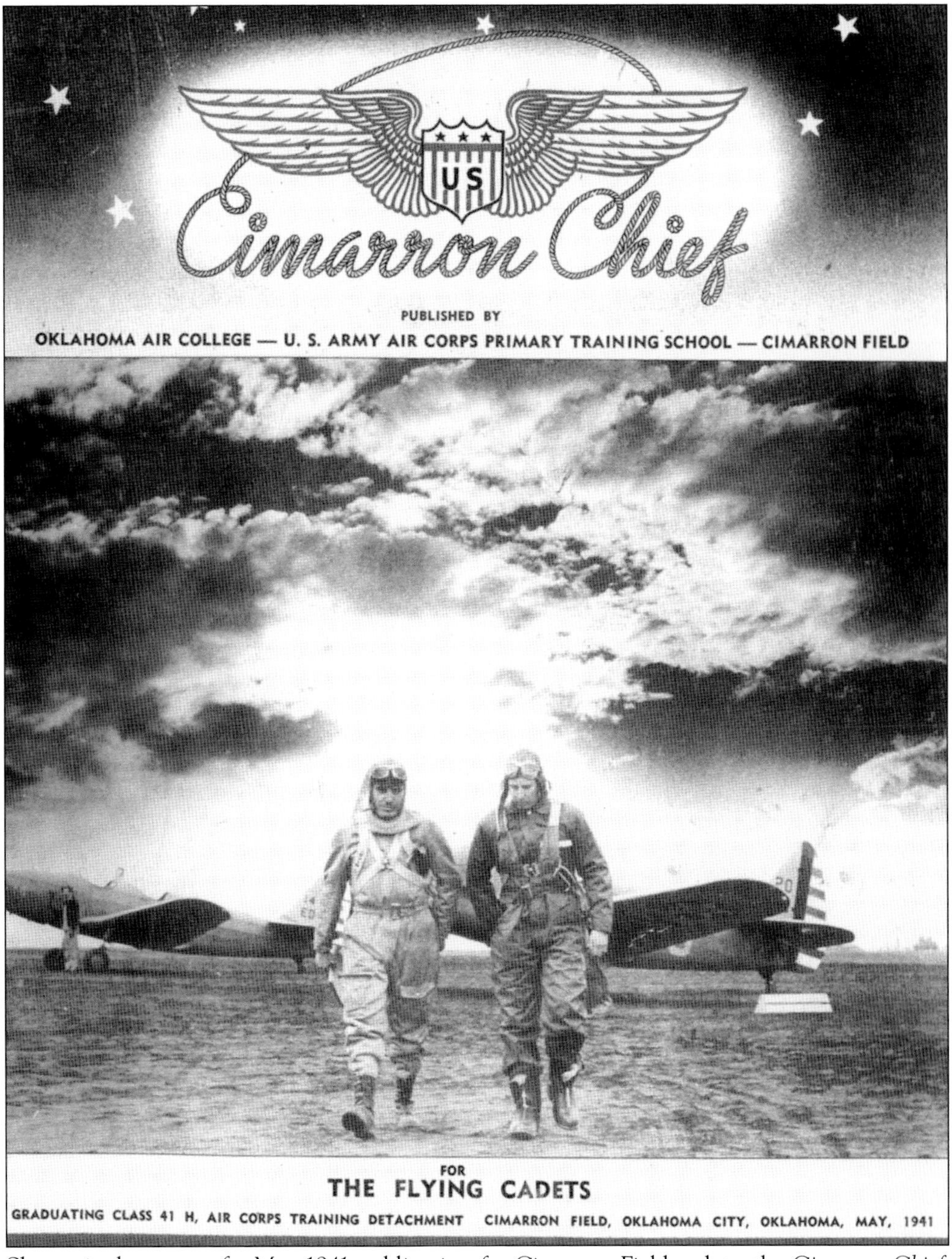

Shown is the cover of a May 1941 publication for Cimarron Field cadets, the *Cimarron Chief*. During World War II, the Oklahoma Air College, a contract school, opened at Canadian County's Cimarron Field at 2300 North Cimarron Road. Administered under the US Army Air Corps 2nd Air Force, it involved a partnership with Clarence Page, John Burke, Jess Sass, and Ted Colbert. (Courtesy Carnegie Library, El Reno.)

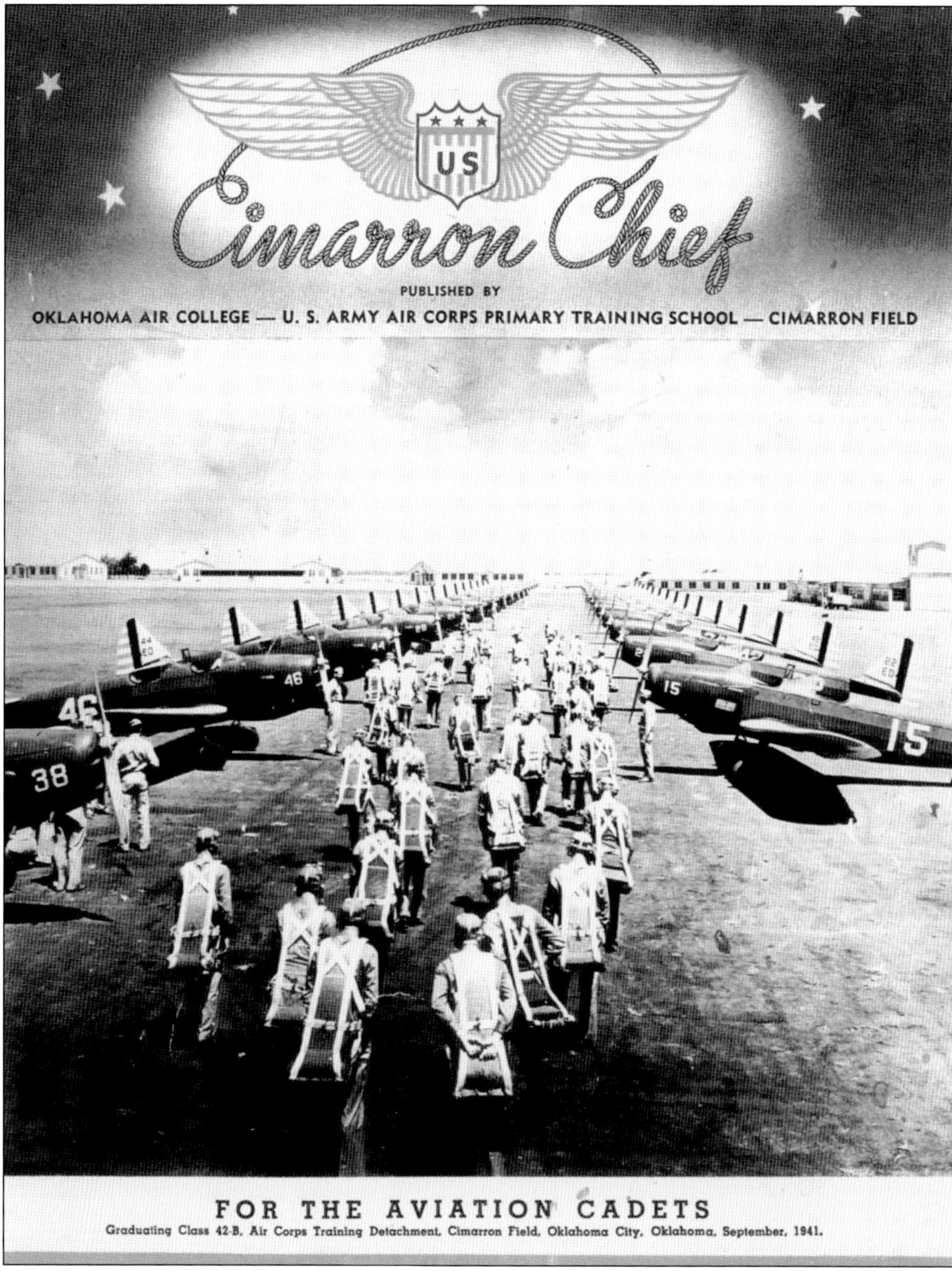

This September 1941 *Cimarron Chief* cover shows airplanes on the airstrip. Five sod airstrips, barracks for cadets, a dining hall, and an administration building were erected. Construction required filling in old buffalo wallows. More than 4,000 cadets were trained here between 1941 and 1944 as fighters, bombers, and for ground attack. Some Yukon soldiers were stationed at Cimarron Field. (Courtesy Carnegie Library, El Reno.)

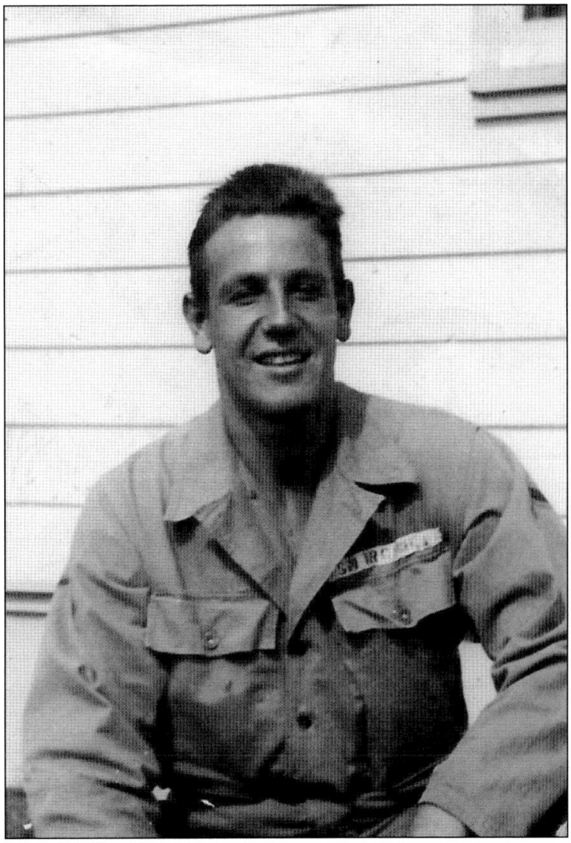

Yukon residents were aware of the Cimarron Field soldiers, and Yukon Czech Hall allowed free admission for anyone in a military uniform to Saturday night dances. One of the Czechoslovakian girls who danced with soldiers on Saturday nights received this picture in the mail from England. The back reads, "Best of luck, Peter." (Courtesy LaVerne and Victor Benda family.)

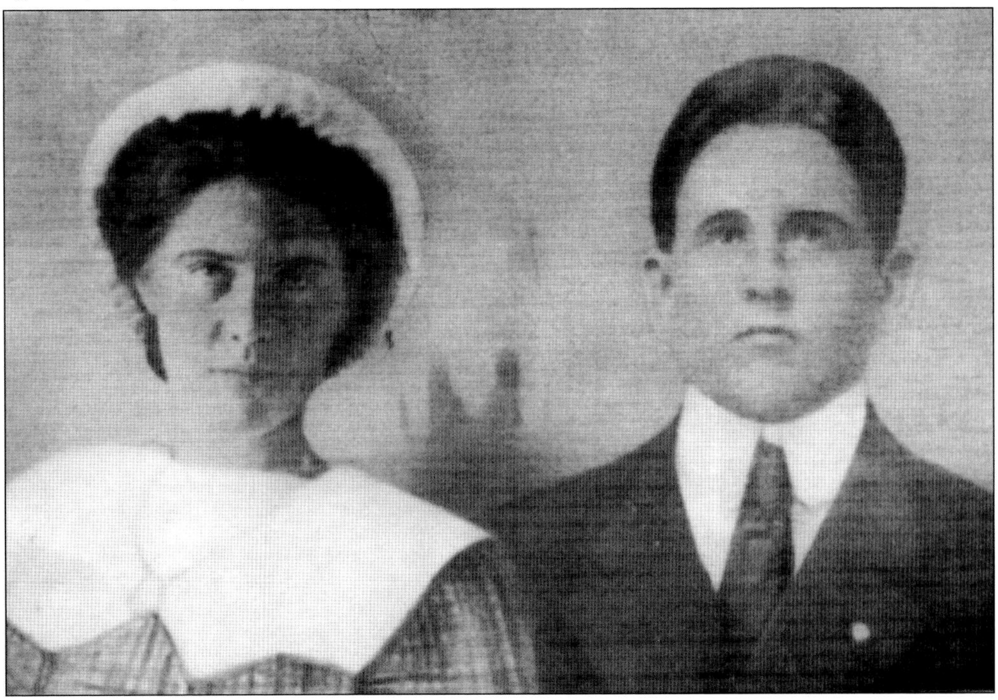

Three of Stella and Hezekiah Bryan's sons served in the armed forces during World War II. Both Pershing and Alton Bryan were captured, and survived by eating worm soup as prisoners of war. Joulin, known as "J.C.," was injured and awarded the Purple Heart. Along with nine others, J.C. returned to Yukon High School, graduating at age 25. (Courtesy Betty Sackett.)

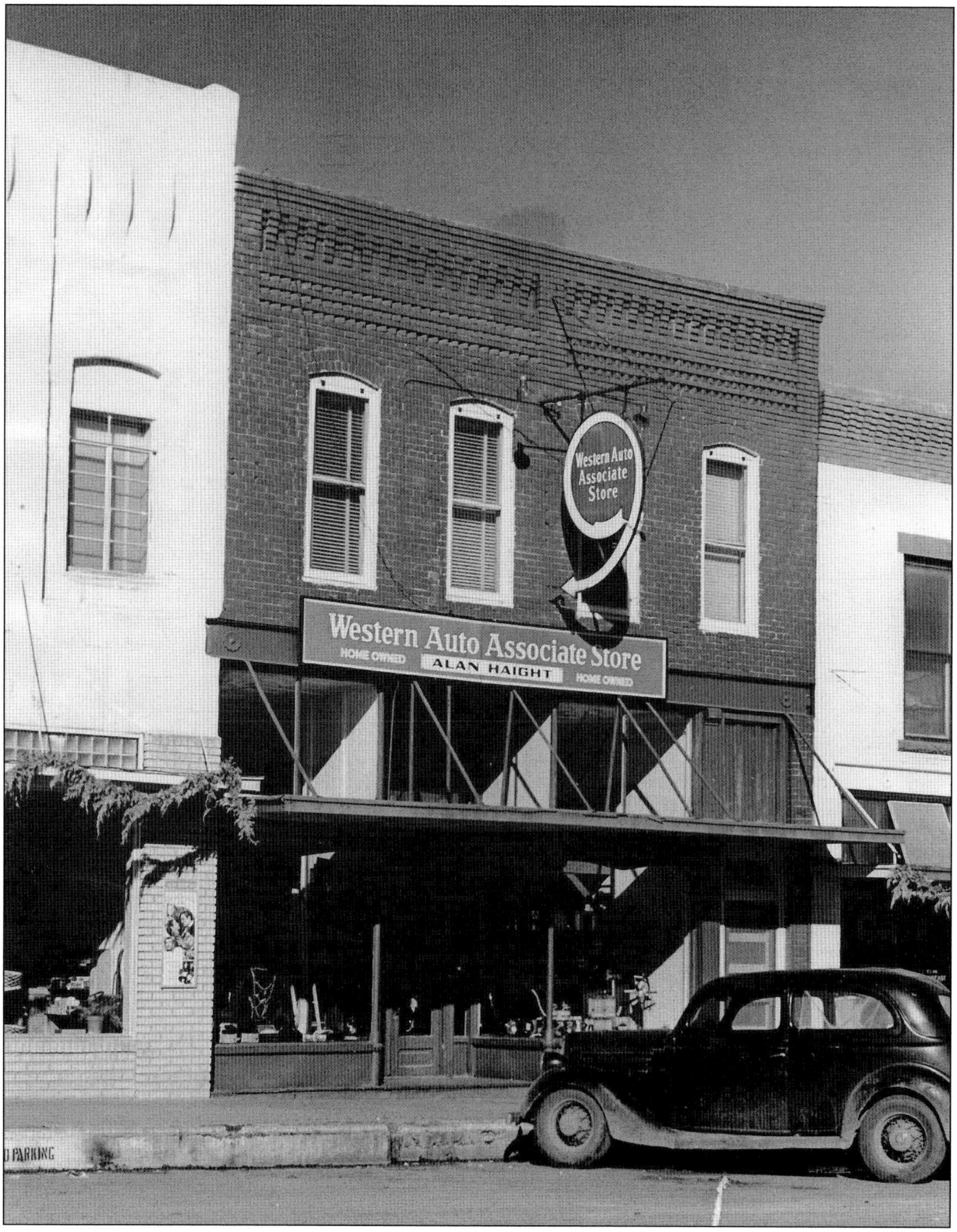

This 1944 photograph shows a retailer at 455 West Main Street. Signs read "Alan Haight," "Home Owned," and "Western Auto Associate Store." On the north side of Main Street between Fourth and Fifth Streets, this building is occupied today by another retailer. (Courtesy Yukon Historical Society.)

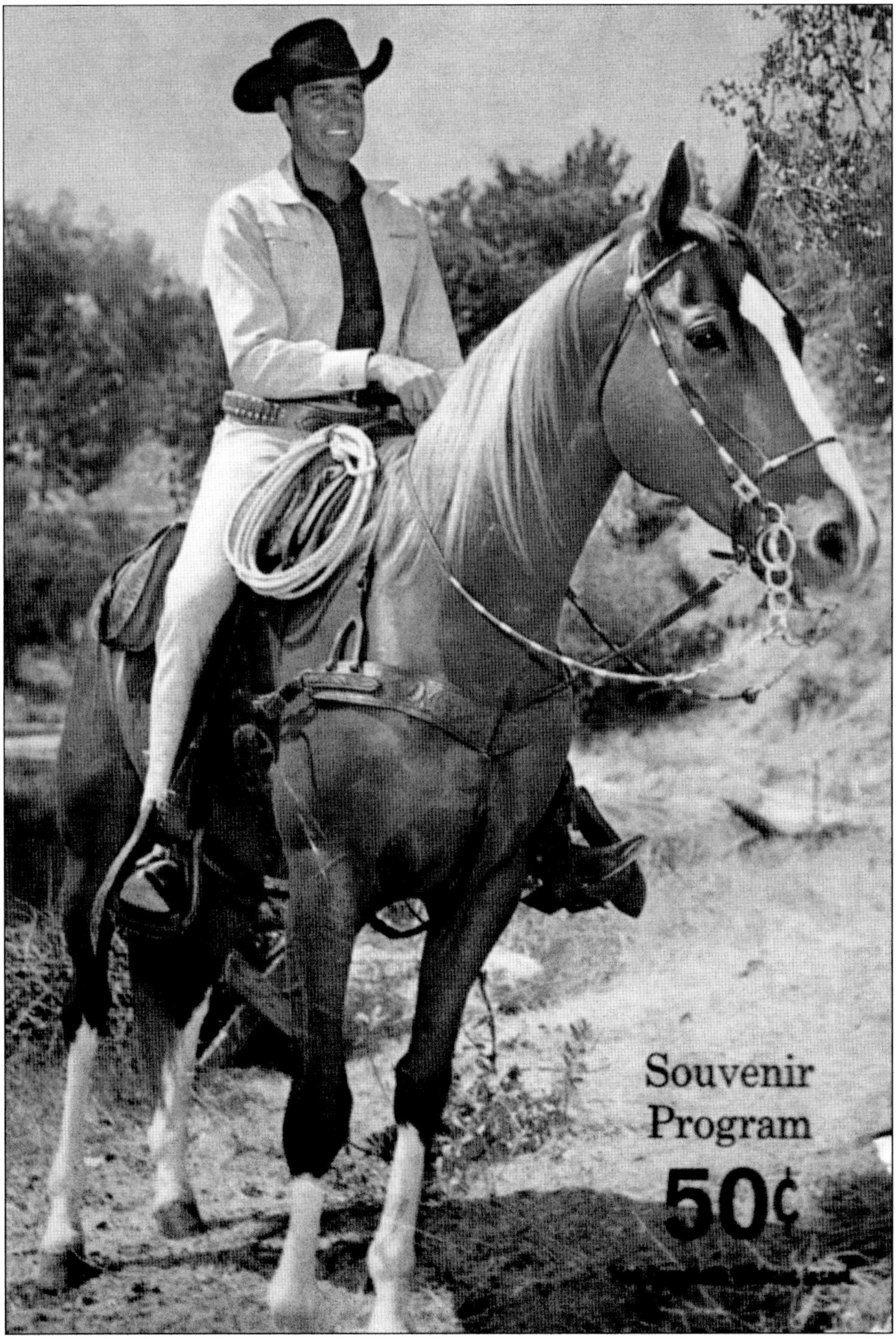

Seen here on a rodeo program cover, Oklahoman Dale Robertson began his acting career in 1946. Known in Western movies and television, Robertson made his home in Yukon, where he raised thoroughbred horses and planned to establish a horse racing track. But he sold his Haymaker Farm, which is now part of a privately owned Yukon cattle ranch operation. (Courtesy Yukon Historical Society.)

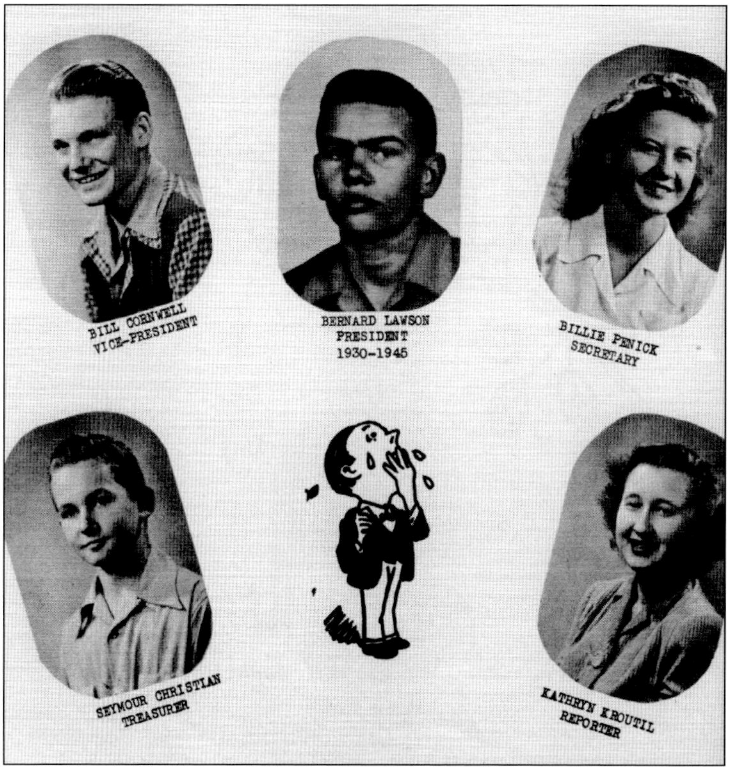

Kathryn Kroutil is shown at bottom right on this 1946 Yukon High School yearbook page. Her grandfather Frank Kroutil was one of the Yukon Mill and Grain Company's founders. She married Clarence Wright. In 1992, Kathryn and Clarence donated 50 acres that became Chisholm Trail Park. The south half was once Mulvey Dairy Farm, and the north half was once McClure's Dairy Farm. (Courtesy Yukon Historical Society.)

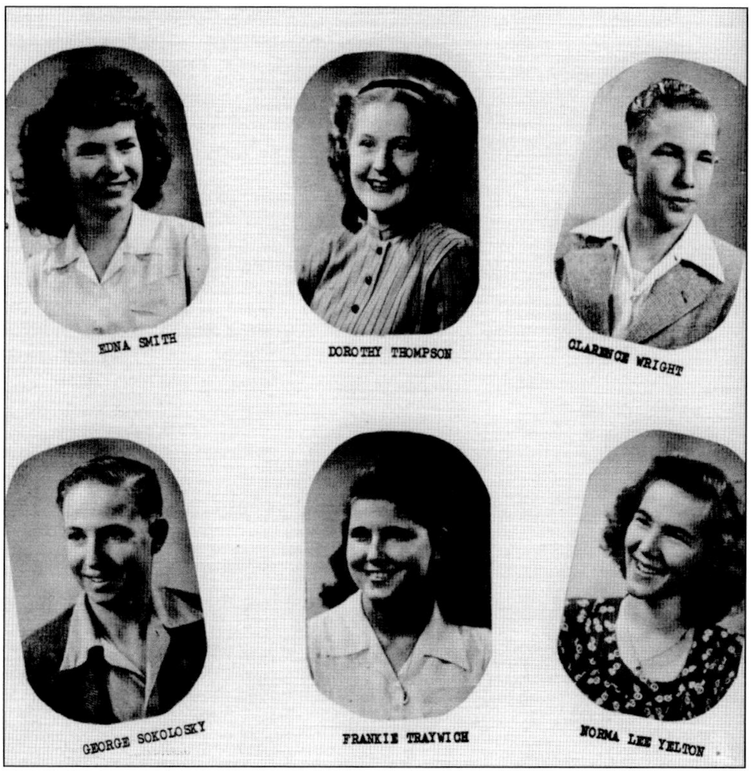

This 1946 Yukon High School yearbook image shows Clarence Wright at top right. In 1962, the entrepreneurial Wright became controlling owner of Yukon National Bank; later, his three children took ownership through a trust. (Courtesy Yukon Historical Society.)

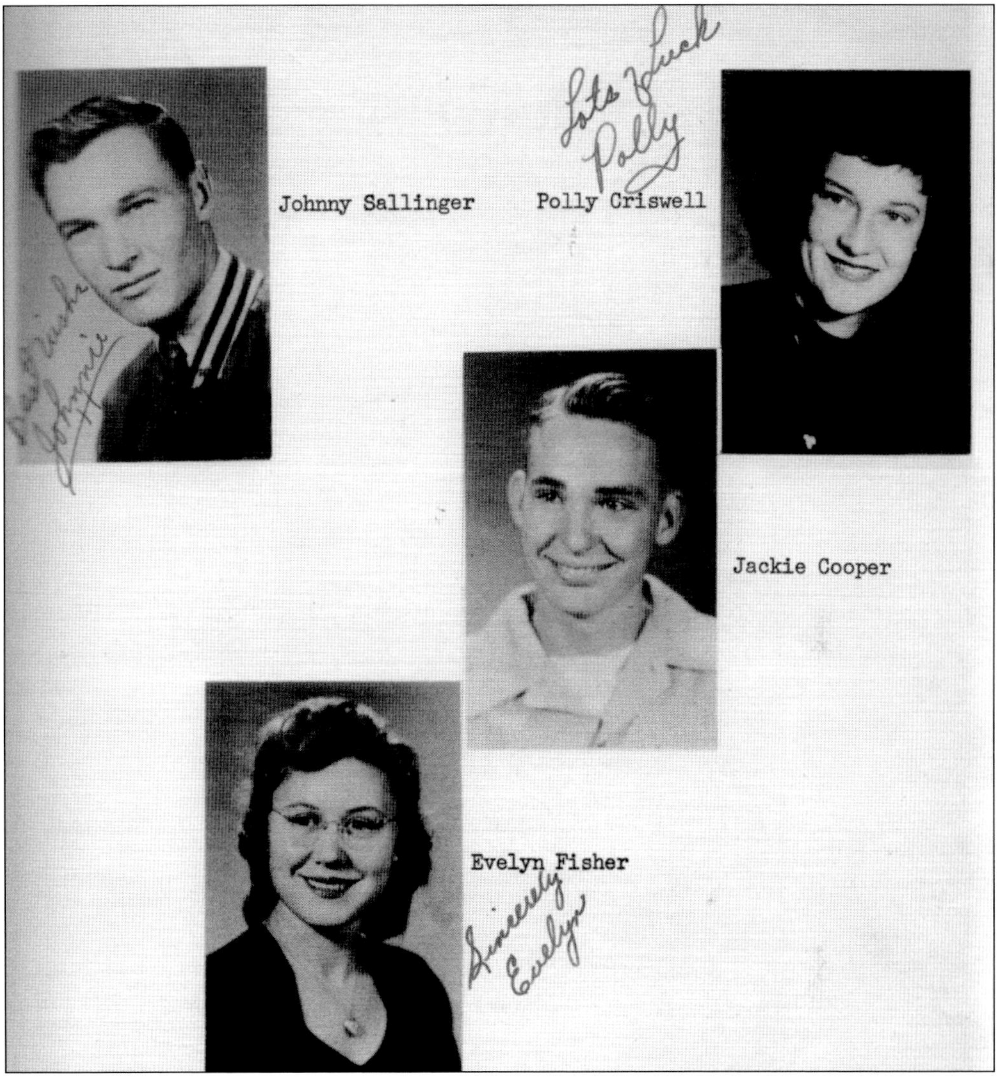

Born in Yukon in 1932, Jackie Cooper is shown in the 1949 Yukon High School yearbook. Taking over his father's Yukon Oldsmobile dealership at age 21, Cooper became the youngest General Motors dealer in the country. With his showroom on Route 66, his dealership became one of the largest Oldsmobile dealerships in the nation. Cooper was a philanthropist who founded the Oklahoma AIDS Care Fund. (Courtesy Yukon Historical Society.)

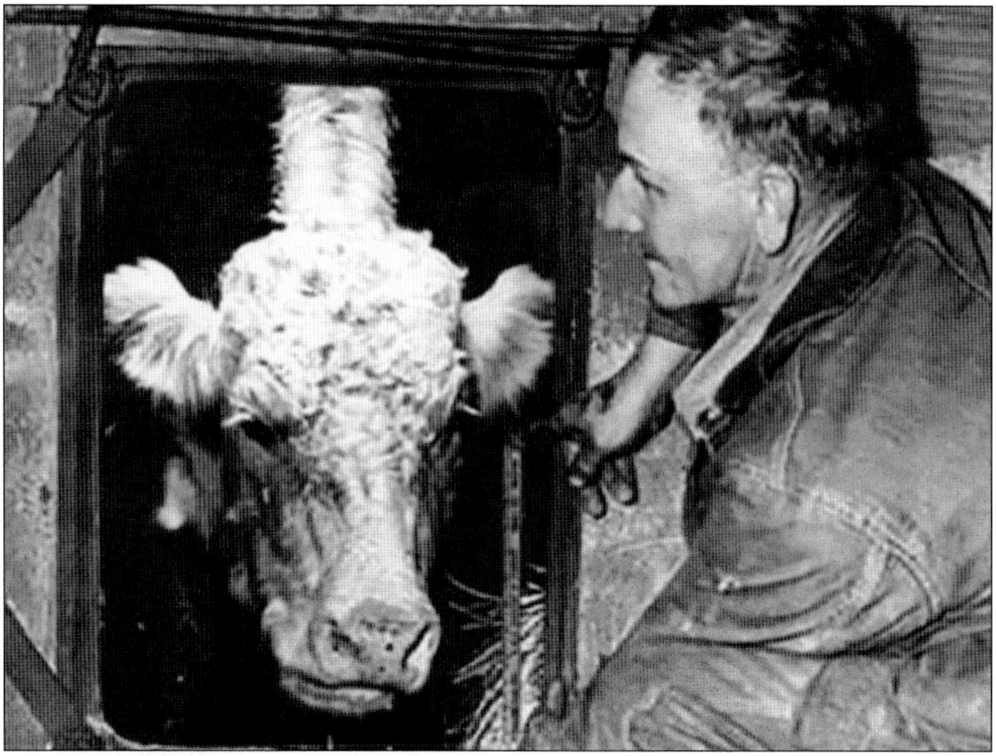

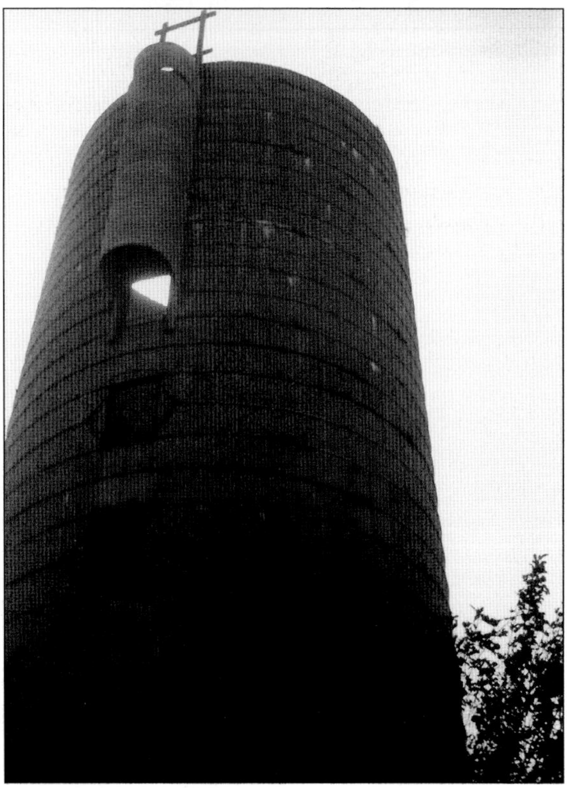

In February 1949, Bill Mach's 1,200-pound heifer Grady was having trouble calving. She bolted and somehow squeezed through an opening in the silo on Mach's 160-acre farm. The steel-encased opening was much smaller than Grady. Mach put out a plea, asking for help to get Grady out of the silo. His plea went viral, and ideas came in from around the world. (Courtesy the Yukon Historical Society.)

After receiving sedative shots, Grady was heavily greased with axle grease. Men pushed her through the opening of the silo, shown here. Grady made Yukon globally famous, and children's books have been written about her. The Machs sold the farm, and in 1997, the silo was destroyed. In 2021, INTEGRIS Medical Center sits at the site of the farm and silo. (Courtesy Yukon Historical Society.)

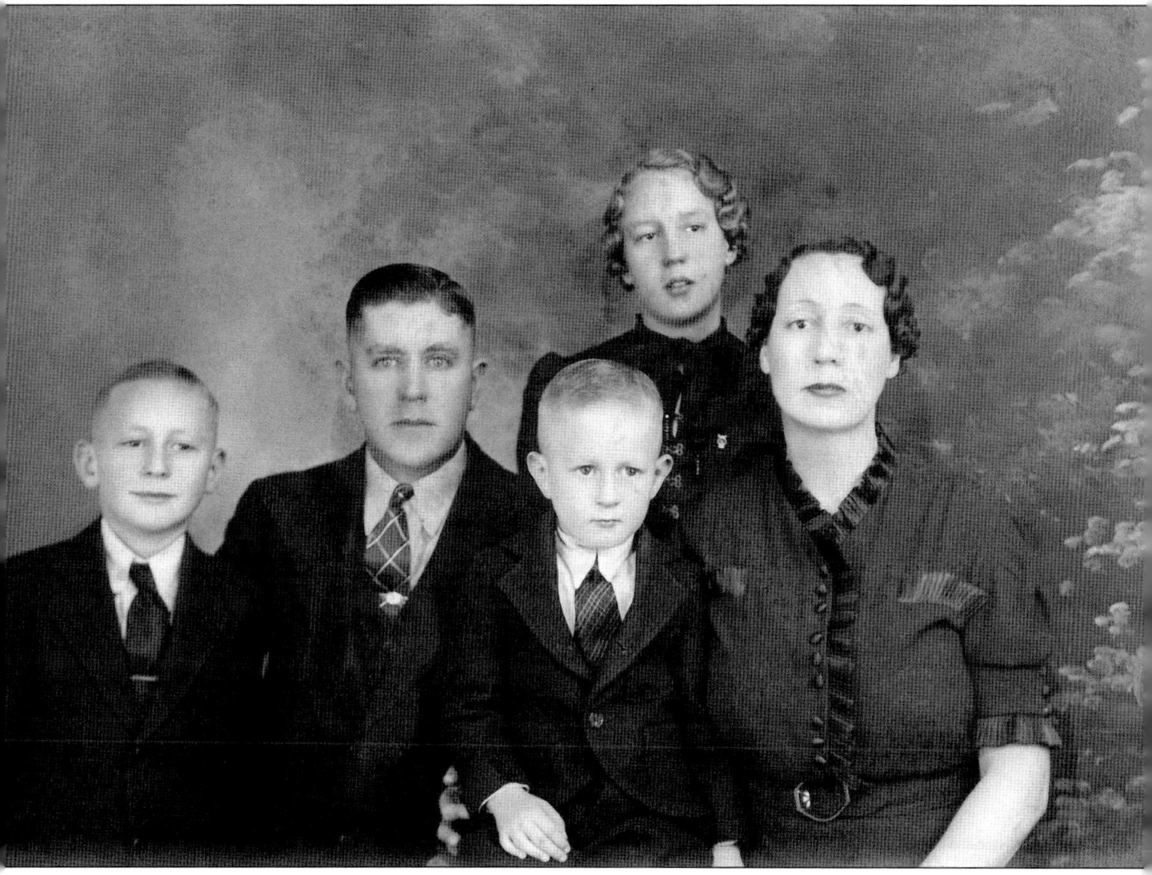

Opal and L.B. Anderson are shown in this c. 1937 photograph with their children, from left to right, Don, Ralph, and Nelda. The Andersons owned large tracts of farmlands. The largest 900 acres of their farm reached from Highway 4 west to Cemetery Road and from Wilshire Boulevard going south. Their farm home, barns, and other structures were on this land. Opal was the astute head of farm business operations. (Courtesy Donna Anderson Mills.)

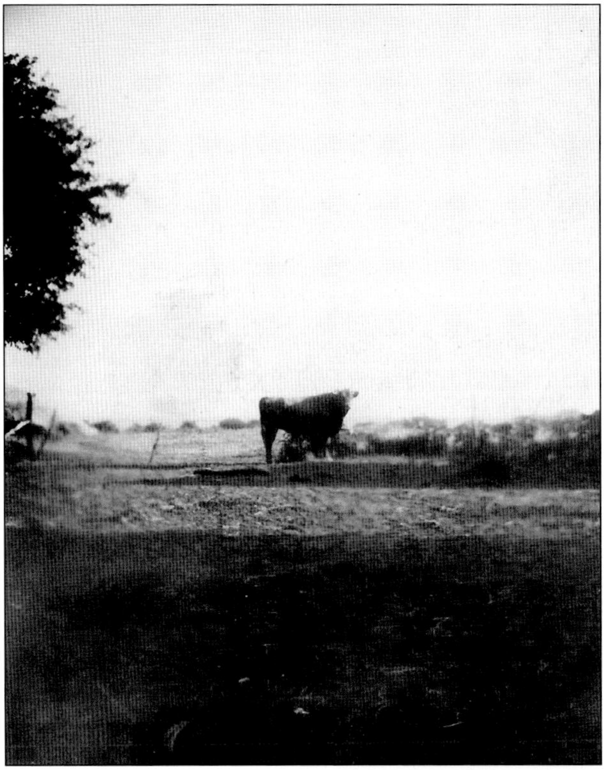

The Anderson farmlands produced cattle, wheat, cotton, hay, corn, chickens, hogs, sheep, and horses. Four generations of the Andersons lived on the 900-acre part of their Yukon farm. Those 900 acres now belong to entrepreneur and philanthropist Robert "Bob" Funk. The owner of Express Employment Professionals, Funk owns massive tracts of land in Oklahoma and other states. (Courtesy Betty Sackett and the Trch family archives.)

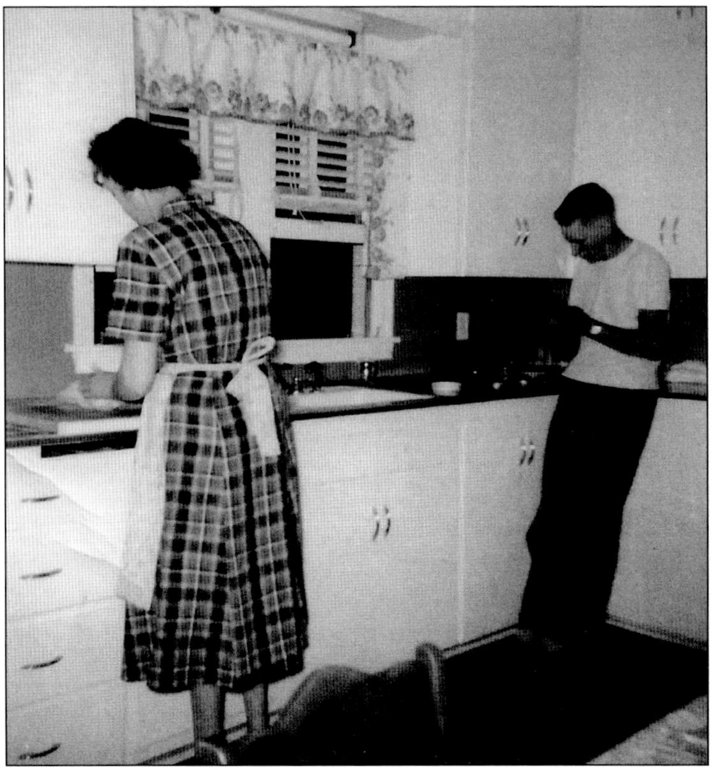

In this 1947 photograph, teenager Don Anderson, son of Opal and L.B. Anderson, is with his mother in their Yukon farmhouse kitchen. As an adult, Don owned Anderson's Dari-D-Lite at 934 West Main Street and Anderson's Skelly Station at 1000 West Main. He was also a member of the Yukon Round Up Club. (Courtesy Donna Anderson Mills.)

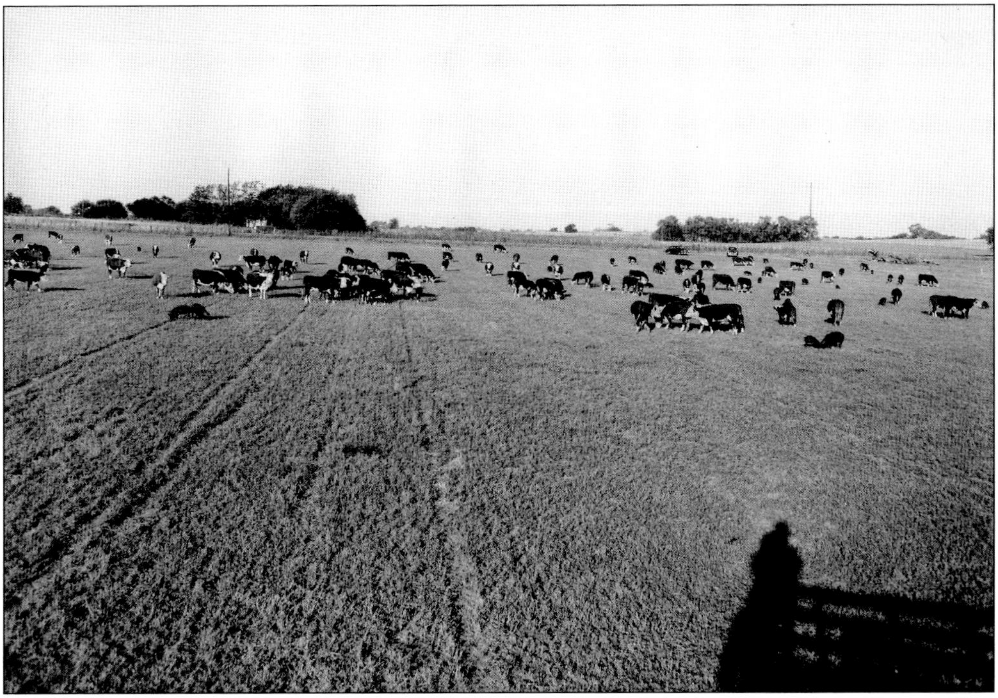

Opal and L.B. Anderson also owned smaller tracts of land in the area, including this one they called "the 80," where their cattle are seen grazing. Bob Funk purchased this land and other farmlands and created Express Ranches, headquartered in Yukon. Funk is part of every phase of the beef production process. In 1997, he fully restored a 1936 barn, which is now a local attraction. (Courtesy Donna Anderson Mills.)

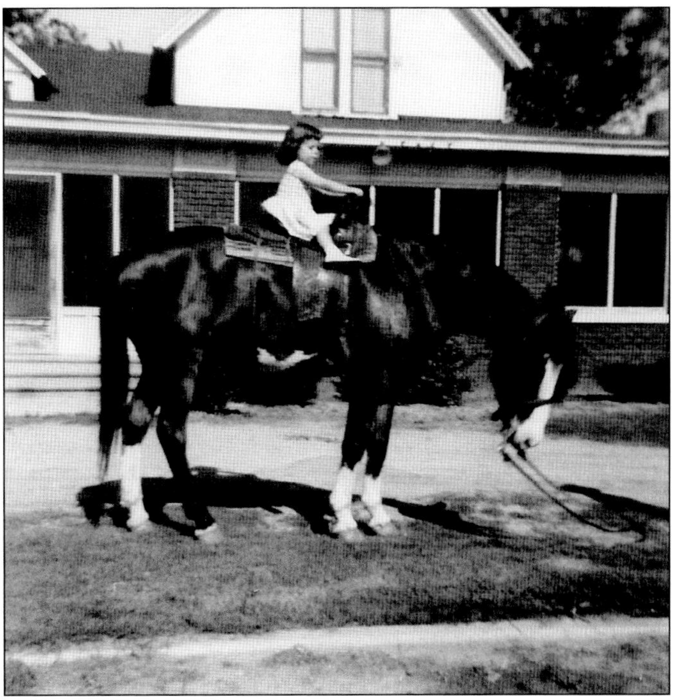

One of Opal and L.B. Anderson's grandchildren rides a horse in front of the Anderson farmhouse. An internationally known businessman, Bob Funk owns draft horses, including Percherons and world-champion Clydesdales. He takes his horse teams to competitions, parades, and other events across North America. His Yukon ranch, barn, cattle, and horses are an attraction enjoyed by locals and tourists. (Courtesy Donna Anderson Mills.)

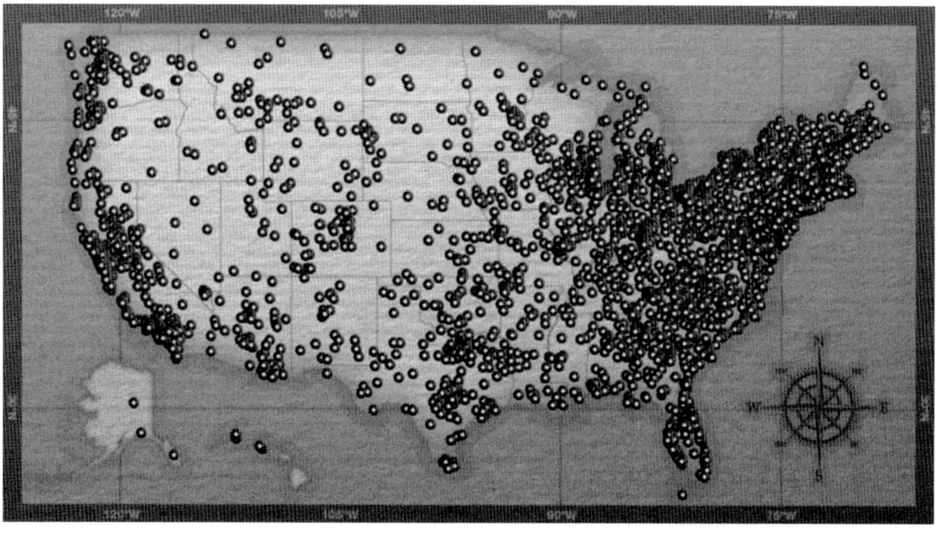